The 40 Laws of Nonprofit Impact

D. T. TIMMERMAN

Copyright © 2021 by D. T. Timmerman, Sparrow Nonprofit Solutions

In accordance with the U.S. Copyright Act of 1976, the scanning, uploading, and electronic sharing of any part of this book without the permission of the publisher is unlawful piracy and theft of the author's intellectual property. If you would like to use material from the book (other than for review purposes), prior written permission must be obtained by contacting the publisher at derik@sparrowns.com. Thank you for your support of the author's rights. This publication is sold with the understanding that neither the author nor the publisher is engaged in rendering legal, accounting, or any other professional service. If legal advice or other expert assistance is required, the services of a competent professional person should be sought.

ISBN paperback: 9798495388437

Visit the Author's website: Sparrow Nonprofit Solutions, sparrowns.com

Book Cover: Content Hacker Writing & Design contenthacker.com

*For Matt, Nate, Wes,
and all other sons and daughters
who deserve a better world.*

Table of Contents

Introduction 7

LAWS OF IDENTITY 11
    Law 1:   Know why you exist. 12
    Law 2:   Define the win. 20
    Law 3:   Know who you are when you're winning. 27
    Law 4:   Plan a strategy to win. 34

LAWS OF COMMUNITY 41
    Law 5:   Your network is everything. 42
    Law 6:   Give to gain. 49
    Law 7:   Assemble your dream team. 56
    Law 8:   Run with achievers of character. 63

LAWS OF CAPABILITY 69
    Law 9:   Unleash your unique strengths. 70
    Law 10: Mitigate your limiting weaknesses. 77
    Law 11: Hire with ruthless selectivity. 84
    Law 12: Cultivate super-volunteers. 90
    Law 13: Act quickly when it's not working. 98
    Law 14: Win while you're sleeping. 105

LAWS OF DIVERSITY 113
    Law 15: Look like your beneficiaries. 114
    Law 16: You get more of what you platform. 121
    Law 17: Acknowledge past trauma in staff and volunteers. 128
    Law 18: Celebrate and elevate. 135

LAWS OF LEADERSHIP 141
    Law 19: Eat last and get dirty. 142
    Law 20: Embody the nonprofit's values. 149
    Law 21: Know your people. 156
    Law 22: Have a grand narrative. 164
    Law 23: Be interested and interesting. 172
    Law 24: Shine in moments of truth. 179

LAWS OF FINANCE 187
    Law 25: Be frugal. 188
    Law 26: Don't spend—invest. 195
    Law 27: Activate one donor per day. 203
    Law 28: Sell things. 210
    Law 29: Keep it legal. 217
    Law 30: Dream bigger. 224

LAWS OF ENGAGEMENT 231
    Law 31: Start and learn. 232
    Law 32: Aim small. 239
    Law 33: Use email to inform. 246
    Law 34: Use in-person visits to influence. 254
    Law 35: Be social on social media. 261
    Law 36: They are the heroes. 268

LAWS OF OPERATING 275
    Law 37: Map your value streams. 276
    Law 38: Establish improve-and-lock systems. 284
    Law 39: Measure what matters. 291
    Law 40: Your board sets the pace. 298

Introduction

> *A passionate commitment to social justice is no substitute for knowing what the hell you're talking about.*
>
> *Thomas Sowell (1930–)*

The secret doesn't disappear all at once.

Almost every nonprofit leader starts out seeing it clearly—the secret to nonprofit impact which has been responsible for nearly every major advance in social change since the late nineteenth century. For a while, perhaps even years, the nonprofit leader works faithfully and productively. The secret breathes life into everything they do. Lives, even generations, are forever changed as a result of their work. Setbacks are barely noticed, resistance hardly registered, patience inexhaustible.

But something happens along the way. Out of the blue one Sunday afternoon, the nonprofit leader detects an unfamiliar feeling: a looming dread of the week to come. A mind once brimming with enthusiasm is filled with disquiet about the budget, anxiety over fundraising, or resentment toward the board. It becomes increasingly difficult to recall the sunlit days and zealous nights of dream-chasing that had come so easily before.

This book offers the chance to discover (or *re*discover) the secret that has fueled the world-changing lives of thousands of nonprofit leaders. The secret was with Dr. King as he sat drenched in sweat in Birmingham Jail in 1963. It was with Clarence and Florence Jordan in 1942 when they spent their life savings to purchase the Georgia farm that would lead to Habitat for Humanity. The secret gave Wendy Kopp of Teach for America the courage she needed to persist in the face of withering criticism from many in the education establishment. It united Harriet Shetler and Beverly Young as they struggled to raise children with mental illness and founded the National Alliance for the Mentally Ill. It energized farmers' children in 1910 to use 4-H clubs to take new agricultural developments to their reluctant parents. It fueled President Franklin Delano Roosevelt to mobilize millions of tiny donations, a "march of dimes," to eradicate polio, the disease that had crippled him. It inspired Eunice Kennedy Shriver in 1960 to run a camp for physically disabled children in her backyard that would become the Special Olympics. It outraged John and Revé Walsh following the tragic abduction and murder of their son, ultimately leading to the formation of the National Center for Missing and Exploited Children. It motivated Yale graduate and Bronx high school teacher Charles Best to found DonorsChoose to match thousands of teachers' needs with generous donors. And it whispered gently to Mother Theresa to trade her teaching position at a respectable school for a life spent caring for the poorest of God's children.

The secret was brought to my attention a quarter of a century ago in my hometown of Charlotte, North Carolina. My parents, dismayed by the excesses of a school-run senior-year ski trip to a luxurious mountain village in Colorado, insisted instead that I spend my spring break volunteering with a local nonprofit. Annoyed as I was at missing a week of fun in the snow, I begrudgingly reached out to a local nonprofit called Lifespan. Then, as now, it provided services to people with disabilities, from young infants to senior adults. The cheerful volunteer coordinator assigned the mildly enthusiastic seventeen-year-old before her to spend the week in a public-school classroom, assisting teachers as they served fifteen or so students with disabilities.

That's where I met Peter. The teacher who introduced me to Peter told me he was twenty years old, but he looked no older than ten. Thin, frail, and contorted, he sat in a wheelchair. There he would remain as countless seniors that week were hitting slopes and beaches across the United

States. I spent a lot of time with Peter during that week. As I soon learned, he had a thing for hands. His cramped and twisted hands would grab one of mine and hold it an inch from his eyes. He'd examine every inch of my palm, thumb, and fingers, sometimes switching hands, turning each one over again and again.

Peter was unable to tell me the reason for his examinations. But I remember imagining then—and recalling with tears countless times since—that Peter was delighting in the beauty of the world. Here, he may have thought, was a thing far different from his own painful, gnarled extremities, a thing worth close attention, worth celebrating.

For my part, I'll be forever grateful to Peter. It was *he* that inspired *my* delight over the world's beauty. *He* was worth close attention, worth celebrating. *He* shared with me a secret I could never have discovered on a Colorado ski trail.

This secret appears no fewer than two hundred times throughout this book. I have not directly named it, because its magic seems more potent when it is uncovered and left in the open to cast its spell on those who are ready. Peter didn't need to name it, nor have the millions of other teachers-of-the-secret, those who are served by nonprofits around the world. If you are ready to put it to use, you will recognize the secret in every one of the 40 Laws presented here. I wish I could say precisely how you might know whether you are ready, but any attempt to do so would rob you of the joy of experiencing the magic in your own way.

For many years prior to writing this book, I have been coaching nonprofit leaders across a wide range of causes. They are fighting human trafficking, addressing food insecurity, supporting foster families, providing clothes and skills for job seekers, connecting local businesses with social causes, growing community volunteerism, helping children and families heal from bullying, assisting low-income students to access higher education, and, like Lifespan, caring for adults and children with disabilities. In many cases, my work with these leaders has helped them to rediscover the secret they had forgotten and use it so effectively that they approach each week with a zeal and joy they didn't think was possible.

For each of the 40 Laws, I share a story of a nonprofit leader, past or present, who applied the secret to their world-changing work. When you read their stories, perhaps you'll dismiss any feeling of doubt about the secret's existence or the promises of its availability to you now. And if, as with most nonprofit leaders at some point in their journey, you find yourself discouraged or hopeless, perhaps these true stories of nonprofit leaders will provide the renewal for which you've been searching.

In addition to these true stories, each of the 40 Laws provides practical actions that nonprofit leaders can take to maximize their world-changing impact. American economist Thomas Sowell is often (unverifiably) credited with saying, "A passionate commitment to social justice is no substitute for knowing what the hell you're talking about." A slight revision of this quote makes as good a thesis statement for this book as any: *A passionate commitment to nonprofit impact is no substitute for knowing what the hell you're doing.*

The causes and missions of today's nonprofits deserve our very best—our best effort, our best talent, our best ideas, and our best execution. The age of the well-intended, big-hearted, and fully funded nonprofit leader is over (if it had ever existed). Ours is the age of the just-as-big-hearted, impact-driven, continuously improving, talent-obsessed nonprofit leader.

As you read the stories and practical actions presented in the 40 Laws, the secret will, if you are ready for it, leap from the page and stand boldly before you. Whether this happens in the first or last of the 40 Laws, pause for a moment when the secret presents itself and celebrate—for that occasion will mark the most important turning point in your nonprofit leadership.

We begin with the first of the 40 Laws of Nonprofit Impact, the Law on which all other Laws depend: *know why you exist.*

*LAWS OF
IDENTITY*

LAW 1:

Know why you exist.

> *Human progress never rolls in on wheels of inevitability; it comes through the tireless efforts of men willing to be coworkers with God, and without this hard work, time itself becomes an ally of the forces of social stagnation.*
>
> **Martin Luther King Jr. (1929–68)**
> Letter from Birmingham Jail (1963)

In April 1963, African American civil rights leader Martin Luther King Jr. was in crisis.

King and other marchers had been arrested on April 12 for violating a circuit court judge's blanket injunction, made two days prior, against "parading, demonstrating, boycotting, trespassing, and picketing."[1] King was detained in Birmingham City Jail. During his incarceration, resistance against him grew from an unexpected quarter—a groundswell of clergymen from various faiths were speaking up against the "unwise and untimely" nonviolent demonstrations for which King had been arrested. News of this growing disquiet had reached him in Birmingham City Jail. The threat was serious. Opposition from within the faith community could jeopardize his work in ways even more detrimental than resistance from the Ku Klux Klan. The civil rights project was in peril and its leader behind bars.[2]

King's written response to his critics (a rare occurrence, as he mentions in the letter) will live forever as one of mankind's greatest examples of a leader combining the transcendently philosophical with the imminently practical. King could scarcely have guessed that four short months after penning "so long a letter" on April 16, 1963, he would stand on the steps of the Lincoln Memorial to deliver his famous "I Have a Dream" speech, heard by 250,000 contemporaries, and by countless millions since.

What gave King's *Letter from Birmingham Jail* such world-changing power?

Certainly, the brilliance of its content contributed to its exceptional strength. King supported his argument with appeals to great thought leaders ranging from the Apostle Paul to Paul Tillich.[3] With remarkable accuracy, King not only described the political activities of various local leaders by name, but thoughtfully considered each of their objections before offering counterarguments using the very beliefs the clergymen themselves held dear.[4] On these merits alone the letter deserves every bit of its fame.

But I'm convinced that the letter's uncommon power springs from something beyond the quality of its content. Something that was rare then and is even rarer now.

Clarity.

Clarity and Identity

The letter evidences both a *foundational clarity* about the world and a *situational clarity* about King's position within it. The following implicit and explicit beliefs from the letter comprise King's foundational clarity:

- *God exists and is the source of all things.*
- *By virtue of God's existence, there exists God's moral, universal, "natural" law.*
- *All manmade laws are either just or unjust.*
- *Just laws "square with" God's law; unjust laws are "out of harmony" with God's law.*

- "Injustice anywhere is a threat to justice everywhere."
- "Freedom is never voluntarily given by the oppressor."
- People should be coworkers with God to bring about justice.
- Nonviolent campaigns to bring about justice require observation, negotiation, self-purification, and direct action.
- Nonviolent direct action creates the necessary tension to compel obstinate power-holders to enter into negotiations with the oppressed.

These touchstone beliefs were fundamental to King's view of the world. We might refer to the totality of these beliefs as the *world-story* according to Martin Luther King Jr. A world-story is one person's attempt to explain The Whole Thing—existence, value, life, meaning, etc.—to themselves.[5]

We all tell ourselves a world-story. Maybe your story shares many similarities with King's, or maybe the commonalities are few and far between. Either way, like King's world-story, yours is beholden to the truth—it is either wholly correct, partially correct, or wholly incorrect.[6] Moreover, contrary to what some would have you believe about "finding your why," we don't get to choose what The World-Story actually *is*.[7]

What we do get to choose is which world-story we tell ourselves. Which one we *believe*.

Convincing you of King's or my or anyone else's world-story (if such a thing were even possible) is beyond the scope of this book. Rather than endorsing a particular world-story, instead I suggest embracing the tremendous value of *clarity* about what we believe The World-Story to be. It takes hard work—and, as King found, perhaps even a jail cell—to hammer your world-story into words. But this work is essential if we are to follow Law 1 and *know why we exist*.

Clarity and Impact

Foundational clarity is imperative to approach our lives, our relationships, and our decisions with *situational clarity* about our position within the world. The implicit and explicit beliefs found in King's letter vividly demonstrate what it looks like to have situational clarity:

- *The Southern Christian Leadership Conference (SCLC), of which King is president, should work with God to bring about justice.*
- *The SCLC's affiliation with other justice-seeking organizations across the South is essential to bring about justice.*
- *When an affiliate calls for aid, the SCLC should provide it if it can.*
- *The Birmingham affiliate has called for aid.*
- *Nonviolent direct action to create community tension has been an appropriate response to the intransigence of Birmingham's political and economic power-holders, even if it has resulted in King's and others' imprisonment.*
- *Church leaders who are critical of the SCLC's actions in Birmingham represent a contemporary church guilty of a "weak, ineffectual voice with an uncertain sound."*
- *The power of the written word may help to silence the critics, embolden cautious ones who have yet to join the struggle, and encourage weary souls who may be wavering.*

All of these beliefs appear in one way or another throughout King's letter. As before, in the case of foundational beliefs, these situational beliefs may be correct or incorrect. But, regardless of their accuracy, King is undeniably *clear* about *his* belief in their correctness.

It's only on the basis of clear foundational and situational beliefs, whether they be these or others, that one can begin to think and speak intelligibly of *impact*. The very idea of impact only begins to make sense when situated in a specific context (situational beliefs) within a broader world-story (foundational beliefs).

> Impact: An individual or group's accomplishment of situational aims that they deem valuable within a particular world-story.

This definition is easily adapted to any specific kind of impact, including what has variously been called social impact, humanitarian impact, or *nonprofit impact*.

> Nonprofit Impact: A nonprofit organization's accomplishment of situational aims that it deems valuable within a particular world-story.

In other words, a nonprofit's impact is equivalent to the achievement of outcomes that it deems valuable within a given world-story. Accordingly, as long as disagreements persist about which world-story is *The* World-Story, people will disagree about what constitutes nonprofit impact.[8] For example, people whose world-story affirms the equal value of all living things will take a favorable view of the nonprofit impact of animal-rights organizations. People who prefer a world-story that disvalues human suffering will take a favorable view of the nonprofit impact of hospitals. People whose world-story holds Jesus of Nazareth to be the Son of God will take a favorable view of the nonprofit impact of Christian churches.

The good news for nonprofit leaders is that world-story disagreements need not detain us from rolling up our sleeves and getting to work. That's what a *mission statement* is all about: broadcasting to the world a clear definition of how the organization itself views nonprofit impact. Someone disagrees? More's the pity! On we go with our merry work.

Clarity and Mission

Of course, not all mission statements are created equal—some are more effective than others at communicating a definition of nonprofit impact.

So, what makes an effective mission statement?

An effective mission statement should fully answer the question "Why do we exist?" in as few words as possible and in a way that clarifies a definition of nonprofit impact. Consider the following examples.

TED: Spreading ideas.

The Humane Society of the United States: Celebrating animals, confronting cruelty.

The Smithsonian Institution: The increase and diffusion of knowledge.

Wounded Warrior Project: To honor and empower wounded warriors.

Kiva: To connect people through lending to alleviate poverty.

Livestrong: To inspire and empower people affected by cancer.

Environmental Defense Fund: To preserve the natural systems on which all life depends.

Using no more than ten (and as few as two) words, these organizations have done themselves a powerful service: *they've clarified for themselves and for the outside world what constitutes nonprofit impact for their organization.*

The anatomy of an effective mission statement adheres to a simple formula.

Mission Statement = [Core Action] + [Core Object] + [Differentiator]

Examples:

[to conserve] + [the lands and waters] + [on which all life depends]

[to serve] + [individuals and families] + [in the poorest communities in the world]

[to inspire and empower] + [people] + [affected by cancer]

Does your nonprofit's mission statement align with this formula? If not, how would you restate your nonprofit's mission to be as clear and concise as possible?

Summary

Dr. Martin Luther King Jr. is an exemplar for today's nonprofit leader in countless ways. His *Letter from Birmingham Jail* provides a timeless example of a leader grounded in foundational and situational clarity. Today's nonprofit leaders can aspire to the same in their own lives by doing the necessary work to gain foundational and situational clarity. Only after having done this work can they define impact, for themselves and their organizations. Mission statements are an essential tool to articulate and broadcast this perspective on nonprofit impact. An effective mission statement combines a core action, a core object, and a differentiator.

The key to the first law of nonprofit impact—*know why you exist*—is clarity on your nonprofit's mission.

Recommended Further Reading

BASS, S. JONATHAN. *Blessed Are the Peacemakers: Martin Luther King Jr., Eight Religious Leaders, the Media, and the Letter from Birmingham Jail*. Updated ed. Baton Rouge, LA: Louisiana State University Press, 2021.

KING JR., Martin Luther, and James Melvin Washington. *A Testament of Hope: The Essential Writings and Speeches of Martin Luther King, Jr.* New York: HarperOne, 2006.

NAUGLE, DAVID K. *Worldview: The History of a Concept*. Grand Rapids, MI: Eerdmans, 2005.

---

1 *Walker v. City of Birmingham*, 388 US 307 (1967).

2 Martin Luther King Jr. and James Melvin Washington, *A Testament of Hope: The Essential Writings and Speeches of Martin Luther King, Jr.* (New York: HarperOne, 2006), 28; Malinda Snow, "Martin Luther King's 'Letter from Birmingham Jail' as Pauline Epistle," *Quarterly Journal of Speech* 71, no. 3 (1985): 318–34.

3 King was fond of using Tillich's "sin is separation" quote in his writings and speeches. For more on Tillich, see F. Forrester Church and Paul Tillich, *The Essential Tillich: An Anthology of the Writings of Paul Tillich* (Chicago: University of Chicago Press, 1999).

4 S. Jonathan Bass, *Blessed Are the Peacemakers: Martin Luther King Jr., Eight Religious Leaders, the Media, and the Letter from Birmingham Jail*, updated ed. (Baton Rouge, LA: Louisiana State University Press, 2021), 2.

5 Simon Sinek, David Mead, and Peter Docker, *Find Your Why: A Practical Guide for Discovering Purpose for You and Your Team* (United Kingdom: Portfolio Penguin, 2017).

6 For a good introduction to world-stories or what are more commonly called "worldviews," see Clement Vidal, "What is a Worldview?" in *Nieuwheid Denken. De Wetenschappen en het Creatieve Aspect van de Werkelijkheid*, ed. H. Van Belle and J. Van der Veken (Brussels: Free University of Brussels Press, 2008), 3.

7 Simon Sinek, David Mead, and Peter Docker, *Find Your Why: A Practical Guide for Discovering Purpose for You and Your Team* (United Kingdom: Portfolio Penguin, 2017).

8 Kathryn A. Johnson, Eric D. Hill, and Adam B. Cohen, "Integrating the Study of Culture and Religion: Toward a Psychology of Worldview," *Social and Personality Psychology Compass* 5, no. 3 (2011).

LAW 2:
Define the win.

> *Before we can do anything, we have to be something. Our actions have to spring from our inner character.*
>
> **Clarence Jordan (1912–69)**

As a young boy growing up in the Deep South in the 1920s, Clarence Jordan was troubled by what he saw.

Severe economic and racial injustices plagued his small-town community of Talbotton, Georgia. Jordan saw them every day and, unlike many of his contemporaries living in the South, this bothered Jordan deeply. Even at a young age, he sensed that education was a critical part of the solution to these inequities.

As Jordan grew into young adulthood, he enrolled at Southern Baptist Seminary to pursue a degree in agriculture, in hopes of helping oppressed sharecroppers by teaching them sophisticated farming techniques. During his studies, Jordan came to believe that poverty was not only the result of economics, but derived from spiritual problems as well. He grew convinced that his aspirations to help the working poor would not be achieved without divine assistance. Jordan emerged from his school years in 1938 at the age of twenty-six, doctorate in hand, as an ordained Southern Baptist minister.

Soon after, in 1942, he and his wife Florence purchased 440 acres of land in Sumter County, Georgia. Together, they developed an interracial Christian community they called Koinonia Farm—a reference to a Greek

New Testament term (κοινωνία) used by biblical authors to describe the early Christian Church, a community of deeply knit fellowship.[1]

Jordan's goal for this community was to promote equality, nonviolence, environmental stewardship, and common ownership of material goods. Even though his beloved Florence recalled hard days "of cooking on a wood stove, washing in the old iron pot, and carrying water... [with] sagging barns, outbuildings, and sheds, one large, unpainted house, and two rundown tenant houses," Jordan's vision came to life.[2] The community grew; by 1950, a multiracial and multigenerational group of nearly two dozen adults made Koinonia Farm their home.

But before long, local backlash against the national civil rights movement made it dangerous to be a part of Jordan's community. As racial tensions rose in the South, the area's white citizens responded by viewing Koinonia Farm as a threat. In the 1950s and 60s, Koinonia experienced a crippling economic boycott, hostility from neighbors, and numerous acts of violence. On one night in 1956, nearly 300 fruit trees were cut to the ground. Florence recalled, "sometimes there was shooting two and three times a week, and we knew there was a chance that somebody might be killed...But we said, 'Well, that's okay too. We're not the first Christians who will have died for what we believe, and we won't be the last.'"[3]

In spite of extreme difficulty, Koinonia prevailed. The farm's story spread, and many were inspired by Jordan's efforts and the community's success. Those who followed the community's example included self-made millionaires Millard and Linda Fuller, who sold their belongings and came to live at Koinonia, eventually becoming partners with Jordan and working to develop a bigger, bolder direction for the group.

Among the Fullers' ideas was "Partnership Housing," a plan to develop and sell affordable, quality houses to low-income local families at cost with zero-interest mortgages. After several years working and living in the Georgia community, the Fullers went on to test an international version of Partnership Housing in Zaire (now the Democratic Republic of Congo) and built homes there for three years. The model spread rapidly to other areas, and in 1976 Partnership Housing became Habitat for Humanity. Since then, the organization has helped more than four million people break the cycle of poverty by providing affordable homes in which they can thrive.

What gave Koinonia Farm—and later, Habitat for Humanity—such world-changing power?

A clear *fundamental unit of impact* and a *vision* for multiplying that key unit.

Your Fundamental Unit of Impact

As I've worked with hundreds of nonprofit leaders over the years, my favorite introductory question hasn't changed: *"What's your fundamental unit of impact?"*

The answers I've received vary widely. Many nonprofit leaders cobble together something vague about changing lives. Some describe a warm feeling that they themselves (or volunteers or beneficiaries) want to have. Others point to a donation dollar. The sobering truth is that very few of the nonprofit leaders I've encountered can identify a fundamental unit of impact that they've carefully determined. In all fairness to them, they simply may have never thought to ask the question.

But then again, isn't that just a restatement of the problem? Ask any professional football, basketball, soccer, curling, or synchronized swimming coach what their fundamental unit of impact is, and you'll get a ready answer:

"A win."

Athletes and coaches aim to win. We may, of course, elaborate with qualifiers—to win the right way, to win with character, to win with good sportsmanship. But the fundamental unit that competitors aim to multiply is clear: they seek wins.

Think about this for your own organization. In order to know what to do to fulfill your reason for existing (see Law 1), your nonprofit needs a practical definition of a win: a fundamental unit of impact.

Although you may not realize it, you operate using fundamental units of impact every waking hour of the day. A healthy food choice, a safe mile driven toward a destination, a dollar saved—all wins. These represent a series of small victories that advance you on your journey toward your long-term goals.

Should our nonprofits be any different? Consider a fictional nonprofit whose mission is "To conserve public nature trails in North and South Carolina." Although this mission statement is terrific, it says little of a practical nature about what the organization counts as a win.

A wise executive director realizes this. She calls a special meeting with the board with one item on the agenda: defining the organization's fundamental unit of impact. What's more, she calls it on a Saturday when the board can meet her at one of the local trails. Where better to decide what constitutes a trail conservation win than on a trail?

After some discussion, the decision is unanimous. The organization's fundamental unit of impact is *a mile of walkable trail that is free of manmade trash and natural debris*.

Note that the fundamental unit of impact is both *concrete* and *repeatable*. It is concrete, as the win can be observed using the five senses; any conscientious volunteer would be able to assess whether a stretch of trail is walkable, free of trash, and free of debris. It is repeatable, because one mile can be replicated, multiplied, stacked. If a single mile is one win, ten miles equal ten wins.

Harken back to our introductory story—what were Koinonia Farm and Habitat for Humanity's fundamental units of impact? For Koinonia, perhaps the peaceful integration of a poor migrant into the fabric of the farm community.

For Habitat, maybe the twelve-month mark after a family has settled into their new home. Both definitions are specific, detectable, repeatable.

Reflecting on your own context, what is your organization's fundamental unit of impact?

Your Vision Statement

While defining a win is helpful to guide a single day's work, it's not enough to define a long-term organizational win.

Instead, you need a way to convert that *micro*-win into a clear vision, a definition of your organization's *macro*-win. Recall once again our trail conservation nonprofit. The executive director and the board (still on the trail) begin to debate how many impact units to aim for over the next three to five years. Stacey says 4,000. Rajeev is more cautious, suggesting 1,000. After much discussion, consensus forms around a vision statement:

In 20xx, there will be 2,500 miles of walkable, trash-free, debris-free public nature trails in North and South Carolina.

And just like that, right there on the trail, magic happens. The group unifies around a common definition of winning. Their efforts become increasingly coordinated. Quite a few will look back on that conversation as a watershed moment worth honoring with the highest solemnity and gratitude.

Note that the only things needed to transform a fundamental unit of impact (a micro-win) into a vision statement (a macro-win) are a *horizon* (typically three to five years) and a *quantification* (ideally an exact number). Taken together, the vision statement starts to align with S-M-A-R-T, a well-known framework for effective goal-setting.

- **Specific:** *Vague goals don't focus your efforts on an end point. Create clear, highly specific goals to keep you on track for success.*
- **Measurable:** *Tracking your progress is an important element of goal-setting. You need to know what efforts are working, what can be improved, and how close you are to achieving your goals.*

- **Attainable:** Unreachable goals not only keep you from becoming successful, they're bad for morale. Set goals that are realistic and motivating.
- **Relevant:** Aim for goals that align with your mission and help propel you toward serving your community as effectively as possible.
- **Time-bound:** Setting a deadline holds you accountable and gives you checkpoints to track your progress.

A S-M-A-R-T vision fuels your nonprofit leadership with intention and purpose. Together with your organization's mission, your vision is the foundation of your nonprofit's identity.[4]

Summary

Clarence Jordan, founder of the groundbreaking and then-controversial interracial community Koinonia Farm in the 1940s, demonstrated what it means for a nonprofit organization to define a win. Following his lead, thirty years later Millard and Linda Fuller transformed the community's housing project into Habitat for Humanity. Today's nonprofit leaders can apply the same principles in their own nonprofits by identifying a fundamental unit of impact (micro-win) and a vision statement (macro-win). An effective fundamental unit of impact is concrete and repeatable. An effective vision statement aligns with the S-M-A-R-T acronym.

The key to the second law of nonprofit impact—*define the win*—is clarity on your nonprofit's vision.

Recommended Further Reading

Downing, Frederick L. *Clarence Jordan: A Radical Pilgrim in Scorn of the Consequences.* Macon, GA: Mercer University Press, 2017.

Grant, David. *The Social Profit Handbook: The Essential Guide to Setting Goals, Assessing Outcomes, and Achieving Success for Mission-Driven Organizations.* Hartford, VT: Chelsea Green Publishing, 2015.

K'Meyer, Tracy Elaine. *Interracialism and Christian Community in the Postwar South: The Story of Koinonia Farm*. Charlottesville: University Press of Virginia, 1997.

Pink, Daniel H. *Drive: The Surprising Truth about What Motivates Us*. New York: Riverhead Books, 2011.

Scott, S. J. *S.M.A.R.T. Goals Made Simple: 10 Steps to Master Your Career and Personal Goals*. Cranbury: Old Town Publishing LLC, 2014.

---

1 Tracy Elaine K'Meyer, *Interracialism and Christian Community in the Postwar South: The Story of Koinonia Farm* (Charlottesville: University of Virginia Press, 1997), 6.

2 Joyce Hollyday, "A Scandalous Life of Faith," *Sojourners* 8, no. 12 (December 1979).

3 Hollyday, "A Scandalous Life of Faith."

4 Les MacLeod, "Making SMART Goals Smarter," *American Association of Physician Leadership* 38, no. 2 (2012): 68.

LAW 3:

Know who you are when you're winning.

> *You will find it will almost always be more comfortable to sit on the sidelines and critique the builders from afar. But at the end of the day, the people who make a difference, the people who shape history, are not the haters.*
>
> **Wendy Kopp (1967–)**

In 1989, Princeton senior Wendy Kopp had a life-changing epiphany.

Since she had been raised in an affluent Dallas neighborhood with a stellar school system, Kopp didn't understand the extreme disparities among people of different, less-privileged backgrounds.[1] It wasn't until she attended Princeton to pursue a degree in public and international affairs that Kopp experienced diversity among her peers.

As she met first-generation college students of a variety of backgrounds and life experiences (including her own roommate), Kopp realized that the place you're born determines whether you'll receive a quality education.

That's when it hit her. The United States, which claimed and aspired to be a place of equal opportunity, really wasn't one.

Kopp organized a conference on campus focused on improving the nation's education system. Student leaders from across the country responded with intense interest in making a positive impact in public education. The conference's success gave Kopp an even bigger idea. What if there was a program that trained college graduates to become teachers specifically hired by rural and urban public schools?[2]

Kopp devised a plan to channel the energy of the rising generation to teach for a minimum of two years in underprivileged public schools. She set out to create a movement to ensure that America lived up to its promise to be a place of equal opportunity.

Kopp's senior thesis served as a proposal for the creation of a national teacher corps. She outlined her intention to build a diverse pool of college graduates who were trained to combat implicit and explicit biases common in education, for example, that a child's socioeconomic status predetermines their success or failure. Using the Peace Corps as a model, Kopp calculated that she would need 500 teachers and $2.5 million to accomplish her mission.

Kopp contacted leading corporations and eventually secured $26,000 in funding from a Mobil executive. This enabled her to found Teach for America (TFA), and she began recruiting hundreds of college students for the program. In the spring of 1990, Kopp convinced billionaire and philanthropist Ross Perot, a fellow Dallas native and supporter of education reform, to contribute $500,000. The credibility that Perot's name gave to the project enabled Kopp to secure the remaining $1.5 million she needed to reach her goal.

One year later, 489 TFA graduates were hired by some of the country's most impoverished schools. Although the program was successful, TFA received withering criticism from the education community. Education leaders complained TFA teachers weren't receiving enough training. Or they were stealing positions from more experienced teachers. Or the short two-year commitment for TFA teachers was disruptive to the school districts. The list went on.

Kopp considered these criticisms, but evidence showed that the organization was making significant impact on communities.[3] She decided the only thing to do was improve the model.

TFA began training college students earlier in their careers to give them more education before graduating and entering public schools.[4] Today, the nonprofit has a $300 million budget, more than 8,000 teachers currently working in urban and rural public schools, and more than 50,000 alumni, most of whom still work in education.

What helped Kopp and Teach for America achieve such world-changing impact?

Defining and fiercely guarding a set of *core values* that were essential to the organization.

Defining Your Core Values

Your core values are the principles you believe that support your organization's vision and philosophy. They serve as a set of standards that dictate how your team members interact with each other, with the community, and with other nonprofit partners. They also bring greater clarity and self-awareness about your purpose and help orient your organization toward its goals.

Defining core values is a step every nonprofit must take before it can reach its full potential. Your organization's core values should answer the question: *Who are we when we're winning?*

When your organization is running at peak performance and experiencing success after success, what are the things about these efforts that bring everyone involved joy, pride, and fulfillment? These are your core values.

Identifying the essential values and principles at the heart of everything you do takes honesty, introspection, and self-reflection. Because your organization thrives on the efforts of many, defining core values can't be left up to just one person.

Begin the process by surveying your staff to gain an understanding of who the nonprofit is at its best.[5] Look for commonalities that allow you to represent the feedback in three to seven main ideas. (Any more than that and the essence of the nonprofit starts to get fuzzy.) After creating this list of values, define what those words mean to your organization and consider ways your nonprofit has lived up to those principles.

Remember, core values are not who you *want* your nonprofit to be. They're who you *already are* when you're winning.

If you need help identifying your organization's values, try this exercise I use when coaching nonprofits. Divide a representative group of your stakeholders (e.g., staff, board, volunteers) into thirds. Have each subgroup name two people associated with the nonprofit who they believe embody the best qualities of the nonprofit and its mission. Then, in a full-group discussion brainstorm a list of attributes for each of the six people you've named. The themes that emerge during this discussion are strong candidates for the organization's core values.

This exercise provides three main benefits. First, it promotes self-reflection among the team as each person considers who to recommend. Second, it rewards the people who fully embrace your organization's core values. Third, it reveals any disconnects in what your team members perceive as your organization's purpose and drive. These insights can be extremely beneficial in aligning your nonprofit's mission, vision, and values.

Stating Your Core Values

Ideas or themes are helpful, but they do not yet fully answer the question *Who are we when we're winning?* To do so, you must clearly state your core values in a way that gives everyone within your nonprofit a method of checking themselves.

Here's one effective formula for stating your core values:

Core Value [word or short phrase] + Check Question [to confirm you're living by your values]

In Law 2 we imagined a nonprofit that conserves nature trails. Here are what they might take as their five core values along with questions that nonprofit leaders can occasionally ask themselves to check if their actions are so aligned:

- **Safety first:** *Am I taking responsible precautions to protect myself and others?*
- **People always:** *Am I seeing our work as a way of connecting people with nature?*
- **Big team:** *Am I working to grow the number of people involved in this effort?*
- **Small wins:** *Am I paying close attention to the tiny details?*
- **Stay weird:** *Am I letting my crazy, rad, nature-loving flag fly?*

This process of confirmation allows you to identify areas within your strategies, processes, and procedures which may not align with your core values. If that's the case, brainstorm ways to cultivate better alignment. Again, the goal is to ensure you're remaining authentic by staying true to your core values.[6]

Once you've stated your core values and are certain you're living by them, you must guard them fiercely. Above all else, stay true to who you are when you're winning. Don't let the actions of others cause your organization to compromise its essence. When Teach for America faced harsh criticism, they could have folded under the pressure and shut down the entire program. Instead, the organization stood by their core values and used them to guide their response. As a result, TFA improved their training process and hired even more quality teachers to help improve the public education system and society as a whole.

It's not enough to know why you exist (Law 1) or what is a win (Law 2); to have impact, you need to know who you are when you're winning.

Summary

Wendy Kopp, founder of Teach for America, a nonprofit that changed the face of the public education system in urban and rural communities, demonstrated the importance of knowing who you are when you're winning. Despite harsh criticisms that threatened to destroy the program she had built, Kopp remained true to her organization's core values and guarded them in the face of adversity. Nonprofit leaders can maximize their impact if they follow this same principle. Seek input from your team to define your nonprofit's core values. Ask yourself how your organization measures up to those values and look for areas to improve. Ensure you're living by the standards you've set for yourself. Above all else, guard your core values against external pressures and forces that may try to derail you from living by them.

The key to the third law of nonprofit impact—*know who you are when you're winning*—is defining and guarding your core values.

Recommended Further Reading

DEVERO, AMIE J. *Powered by Principle: Using Core Values to Build World-Class Organizations.* Bloomington, IN: AuthorHouse, 2007.

KOPP, WENDY. *One Day, All Children..: The Unlikely Triumph of Teach for America and What I Learned Along the Way.* New York: PublicAffairs, 2003.

MIRSHAHZADEH, DARIUS. *The Core Value Equation.* Austin, TX: Lioncrest Publishing, 2020.

---

1 Wendy Kopp, *One Day, All Children....: The Unlikely Triumph of Teach for America and What I Learned Along the Way* (New York: PublicAffairs, 2003), 4.

2 Kopp, *One Day, All Children*, 6.

3 Adam Maier, "Doing Good and Doing Well: Credentialism and Teach for America," *Journal of Teacher Education*, 63, no.1 (2012): 10–22.

4 Olivia Blanchard, "I Quit Teach for America," *The Atlantic*, September 2013.

5 Johan Van Rekom, Cees B. M. Van Riel, and Berend Wierenga, "A Methodology for Assessing Organizational Core Values," *Journal of Management Studies*, 43, no. 2 (2006): 175–201.

6 S. Sai Manohar and Shiv R. Pandit, "Core Values and Beliefs: A Study of Leading Innovative Organizations," *Journal of Business Ethics* 125 (2014): 667–80.

LAW 4:

Plan a strategy to win.

> *Vision isn't enough. Charismatic, entrepreneurial leaders who have game-changing ideas will fail if they don't surround themselves with people who can help convert their vision into strategy, funding, and programs.*
>
> **Laura Deaton (1965–)**

Laura Deaton was puzzled.

It was early 2013, and she had recently taken a position as executive director at Trust for Conservation Innovation (TCI), a nonprofit public benefit corporation that focused on helping organizations engaged in conservation efforts.

TCI helped a small number of nonprofits with a handful of services, including administrative support, navigating 501(c)(3) status, fiscal sponsorship, and basic human resources assistance.

As Deaton reviewed the projects in TCI's limited portfolio, she began to notice that many were not seeing the impact they should have been experiencing.

Deaton had decades of senior leadership experience in operations, strategy, communications, program development, communications, and investor relations. But it didn't take her expertise to see there was a breakdown in TCI's services; many of the nonprofit projects they supported weren't getting the resources necessary to succeed. Deaton knew something had to change.

After doing some research, TCI discovered that the nonprofits that were successful were, beyond sufficient funding and innovative ideas, benefiting from a group of advisors who helped steer strategic decisions. Could it be that all of TCI's projects needed the same wide-ranging capacity-building support? Deaton decided that TCI's purpose was not to simply act as a back-office service provider—they must help organizations create long-term growth.

TCI's new mission would be to help launch and scale new enterprises that worked to save the planet. They felt this would help achieve their vision of ensuring that all people, despite income level or geography, have access to adequate health and sanitation systems, nutritional food, and clean drinking water and air. These were lofty goals, but the group was passionate. The only question was...how would they do it?

Deaton began to build a strategy that would put nonprofits on the fast track to impact.

TCI committed to a three-part strategy. First, they would recruit humanitarian visionaries whose projects aligned with their sustainability mission. Then, they would develop strategies and provide resources for those projects to succeed. Finally, they would return 9% of project revenue to their own organization. By investing in their projects, the nonprofits would bring in more revenue, thus delivering money back to TCI.

If it worked, this cycle would benefit everyone.

TCI worked on their new and improved accelerator model of service delivery for two years before formalizing their strategy. Once they began to see the impact of their new focus, TCI expanded their reach to include nonprofits beyond environmental protection.

In mid-2018, TCI rebranded as Multiplier, with a mission to foster a world that is sustainable, healthy, equitable, and resilient. Multiplier now manages more than fifty projects that span four program areas: health, sustainability, resilience, and equality. Projects range from nonprofits who manage land conservation areas in Peru to organizations that secure worker cooperatives for retirees. Multiplier views every project as essential to collective success, not only among nonprofits, but also with for-profits and government agencies. Multiplier is selective about which new projects to add to their portfolio, staying aligned with a mission of promoting sustainability and conservation. While their project locations include Indonesia and the Pacific Islands, the California-based organization also prioritizes needs in their own backyard.

After just a few years of implementing their new strategy, Multiplier went from a $5-million nonprofit service provider to a $23-million accelerator. Despite challenging economic times, the organization has grown. Today, Multiplier works on projects tackling the global challenges listed in the United Nations Sustainable Development Goals. These societal issues include inequality, poverty, environmental degradation, climate change, justice, and peace.[1]

Multiplier's remarkable efforts have been rewarded by some of the country's deepest pockets, especially those concerned with environmental issues. The Rockefeller Foundation, the William and Flora Hewlett Foundation, and the MacArthur Foundation have all been major supporters of the organization.

How did Deaton take Multiplier from ineffectively serving a handful of nonprofits to sustainably helping humanitarian visionaries?

She worked backward from Multiplier's vision statement to develop a simple *three-part strategy* for how they would win.

Your Three-Part Strategy

There comes a point when every team asks themselves an important question:

How do we win?

Whether it's an army battalion wanting to defeat their foe, a sports team competing for a championship title, or a nonprofit organization aiming to effectively support their constituency, everyone has to develop a strategy to outline the steps they will take to accomplish their objectives. You must plan a strategy to win.

However, before you can map out a plan, you must identify your preferred destination; developing a strategy without purpose is like creating a map to nowhere. To build an effective strategy, you must first define your vision statement.[2] Then, you can work backward to arrive at a three-part strategy to achieve that vision.

While your mission statement defines your nonprofit's goals and how to achieve them, your vision statement defines the desired long-term results and future position of your organization.[3] This statement serves a multitude of purposes: guiding your nonprofit's direction and decision-making, defining performance and ethical standards to gauge your progress and ensure your actions are in alignment with your goals, attracting external support, and serving as a public relations tool.[4]

Law 2 was all about writing your nonprofit vision statement as an answer to the question *What is a macro-win?* In the case of our nature trail conservation nonprofit, that was *In 20xx, there will be 2,500 miles of walkable, trash-free, debris-free public nature trails in North and South Carolina.*

Once you have your mission, vision, and values in place, it's time to define your strategy statement. This statement outlines your long-term direction and serves as a blueprint for how you will bring your organization closer to making your vision a reality.[5]

A highly effective strategy statement highlights the three most important actions that your organization will perform again and again. In other words, if you could only do three things in your organization to make your vision a reality, what would they be?

Begin with your vision statement, then work backward. Think first about your keys to success—what practical, intermediate *outcomes* need to be true on an ongoing basis? Once you have these, you're ready to articulate a strategy—the three *actions* you'll do over and over again to make the keys to success happen. Your threefold strategy is nothing more than those three actions.

What would this look like for our nature trail conservation nonprofit? Their vision is that in five years there will be 2,500 miles of walkable, trash-free, and debris-free public nature trails in North and South Carolina. Taking one step backward from that vision, keys to success include:

- *Weekly patrolling all 2,500 miles of public nature trails.*
- *Enough volunteers to do the weekly trail-walking and conservation.*
- *Training and oversight to make sure conservation is effective.*

All three of these things will need to be true in order to realize the vision. Now, if we could only do three practical, repeatable actions to manifest the above outcomes, what would they be?

- *Recruit trail heroes from the local outdoor enthusiast population.*
- *Train and deploy trail heroes to conserve one trail mile per week.*
- *Celebrate the impact of trail heroes on social media.*

Creating a three-part strategy not only makes achieving your vision more manageable, it also helps you say no to the many good-but-not-best things that tempt you along the way.

When Laura Deaton took on the challenge of shifting TCI's focus to becoming the capacity-building services provider that Multiplier is today, she began by defining their vision. They wanted to be an organization who helped secure healthy living conditions for people of all backgrounds. From there, she worked backward to determine how they could make this impact.

Multiplier's three keys to success were:

- *An increase in the number of successful nonprofits who are focused on conservation and sustainability.*
- *Fully functioning organizations who are not only thriving but continue to grow and expand their impact.*
- *A boost in resources to hire more talent and bring in even more projects.*

As a result, their three-part strategy was to:

- *Bring in humanitarian entrepreneurs who contribute to solving the social challenges we face today.*
- *Provide the necessary advisors and resources they need to succeed.*
- *Return 9% of each project's profits back to Multiplier to fund the addition of new projects to further support the vision.*

By limiting your strategic actions to just three, you can more easily focus the nonprofit's resources and manpower on what matters most to achieve your vision.

Summary

Multiplier is an organization that helps nonprofits turn game-changing ideas into planet-saving impact. As executive director, Laura Deaton demonstrated the value of planning a strategy to win. She knew that when it comes to working for sustainable, systemic impact, there's no time to waste. The same is true for your own organization's vision. Gather input to develop a concise and memorable vision statement. Then work backward from outcome to actions to create a strategy statement. Define the three practical intermediate outcomes that will bring you closer to your vision. Then identify the three repeatable actions that will generate these outcomes.

The key to the fourth law of nonprofit impact—*plan a strategy to win*—is finding the three repeatable actions that are essential to realizing your nonprofit's vision.

Recommended Further Reading

Dym, Barry, Susan Egmont, and Laura Watkins. *Mission, Vision, and Effective Nonprofit Leadership.* Upper Saddle River, NJ: FT Press, 2011.

Gottlieb, Hildy. *The Pollyanna Principles: Reinventing "Nonprofit Organizations" to Create the Future of Our World.* Richardson: ReSolve Inc., 2009.

Herold, Cameron. *Vivid Vision: A Remarkable Tool for Aligning Your Business Around a Shared Vision of the Future.* Austin, TX: Lioncrest Publishing, 2018.

---

1 Tomás Hák, Svatava Janousková, and Bedrich Moldan, "Sustainable Development Goals: A Need for Relevant Indicators," *Ecological Indicators* 60 (2016): 565–73.

2 Sooksan Kantabutra and Gayle C. Avery, "The Power of Vision: Statements That Resonate," *Journal of Business Strategy* 31, no. 1 (2010): 37–45.

3 Michael E. Raynor, "That Vision Thing: Do We Need It?" *Long Range Planning* 31, no.3 (1998): 368–76.

4 Mark Lipton, "Demystifying the Development of An Organizational Vision," *Sloan Management Review* 37, no. 4 (1996): 86

5 Ian Wilson, "Realizing the Power of Strategic Vision," *Long Range Planning* 25, no. 5 (1992): 18–28.

LAWS OF COMMUNITY

LAW 5:

Your network is everything.

> *It's not enough to simply join a group. You must become involved. If you're active and engaged, you're prepared. That's when opportunities come your way.*
>
> **David Peña Jr. (1967–)**

For David Peña Jr., one opportunity made all the difference.

As a Latino boy growing up in South Texas, Peña's life was fraught with obstacles. He and his family were third-generation migrant farm workers. They spent their days toiling in the fields, trying to get by on the meager wages they earned. Peña accepted that this would be his future, as he could not afford college tuition. Then something happened that would change the trajectory of his life.

Peña received a migrant farm worker scholarship that sent him to Saint Edwards University. In 1990, he earned a Bachelor of Arts in political science, becoming the first college graduate in his family. The gift of higher education set Peña on a path toward a successful career.

Peña began working in insurance, eventually becoming owner of a medical transport company. When he sold the business to investors, he took a job as the first executive director of the Valley Alliance of Mentors for Opportunities and Scholarships (VAMOS), a scholarship program in the

Rio Grande Valley. This is where Peña saw firsthand the need for a support group for Latinx students.

As a Latino himself, Peña was acutely aware of the lack of opportunities for young leaders in the Latinx community. Receiving a college scholarship was a lucky break that many people don't experience. Peña decided to do what he could to change the future for other young Latinos by helping students create opportunities for themselves.

Peña felt that if students had a network of people to learn from and share information with, they would be better positioned to find and land successful jobs. Peña has dedicated his life's work to creating such pathways for young people nationwide.

Over the past twenty years, he has advanced numerous nonprofits by developing partnerships and programs to help students overcome obstacles. As president of colleges and universities for the Association of Latin Professionals for America (ALPFA), he has served as a mentor and counselor to hundreds of students, entrepreneurs, future lawyers, and business leaders. Peña gives one recommendation to every student he works with: become involved in a networking group.

Peña feels that developing authentic, meaningful relationships with other Latinos empowers students with skills, knowledge, and resources to boost their success and support their growth. Networking helps to build connections among like-minded people who can educate, refer, and guide you toward a path of success. If you can make those connections, be present in those groups, and engage with others, you're apt to learn about—and be in the position to benefit from—numerous opportunities.

How has Peña used networking to achieve a successful life for himself and help hundreds of students aspire to brighter futures?

By understanding that networking isn't simply a means to accomplish your goal, *networking is your goal.*

Two Kinds of Networks

While there are many kinds of opportunities to make personal and professional connections, networks can be generally categorized into two groups. The first is *internally oriented networks*. These are communities that focus primarily on the network's members and their needs. Examples include business networking groups, like Business Networking International, trade associations, and (to some extent) religious organizations.

Think of internally oriented networks as a circle of people facing inward; they're concerned with the issues happening within the group. Internally oriented networks address things like how to help their members promote their businesses or how to boost member enrollment.

Joining an internally oriented network can provide the following benefits:

- *You are empowered to cultivate your own support system that helps meet your needs.*
- *You can share knowledge in a more streamlined way, allowing you to solve problems more efficiently.*
- *The group makes you feel more connected and builds a strong sense of community.*[1]

From the vantage point of a nonprofit leader, one potential drawback of internally oriented networks is that their members tend to perceive networking as a means to reach their own private goals. For example, a businessman who needs to sell more products might decide to join a trade association so he can meet more people in his industry and expand his target audience. He's focused on his own needs, both in his goals and in his methods.

The other kind of network is *externally oriented networks*. The focus of these communities is more "out there" on some shared objective in the world. Think about the avid fan bases of sports teams, active members of political parties, or the marchers in the civil rights movement. Externally oriented networks are like a circle of people facing outward, or even standing in a line shoulder to shoulder; they're less concerned with their own individual aims and instead seek solutions to a more widespread issue.

Committing to an externally oriented network provides numerous advantages:

- *You gain an awareness of the world around you.*
- *You can raise global awareness about a particular cause.*
- *Economies of scale amplify the impact of the group's resources.*
- *You can identify and coordinate more opportunities for the betterment of an organization, a civilization, or society as a whole.*
- *You can have a more far-reaching impact than you would by simply looking inward to the needs of your network's members.*

Externally oriented networks also enable you to be more proactive. With internal focus, a member mentions they have a need, and everyone reacts. By looking outward, you can innovate new ideas and take the initiative to make them a reality.

Members of externally oriented networks tend to realize that networking itself is a primary goal. Networking amplifies their cause, enables members to develop relationships based on generosity, and builds connections that work together toward a greater good.

Your Nonprofit as a Network

A nonprofit organization is, in and of itself, a network. The question is, then, which kind of network is your nonprofit? The best nonprofit leaders cultivate an externally oriented network. They gather people with a shared vision to realize a meaningful change (or set of changes) in the world.

Externally oriented groups can turn into movements as they can spur needed policy and societal shifts. From passing new laws and seeking justice for marginalized groups to changing a culture's behavior, social movements have played a key role in shaping America. A successful movement takes strong leadership, loyal grassroots support, reliable partners, and a shared plan for desired outcomes. All of these can only be achieved through effective external networking.

A nonprofit acting as an externally oriented group is just as driven as an internally oriented group to create, cultivate, and utilize interpersonal relationships.[2] The difference is, an externally oriented group is able to see those relationships as a driver for impact. By mapping the community and identifying needed connections, nonprofits can bridge groups of people and create opportunities for individuals to participate in activities outside of their own circle of contacts. An external focus helps strengthen their connections with the community and find solutions to collective challenges.

A single nonprofit rarely has all they require to serve every need of their constituency. By networking externally, organizations can partner with other groups who may be able to offer resources they lack, and vice versa. By prioritizing building relationships with other suppliers, government officials, community leaders, and even "competing" nonprofits, groups can gain widespread advocacy while achieving organizational effectiveness.[3] This only helps them better serve their communities.

For professional networking to be successful, organizations must work to cultivate their networks. People have to make the effort to foster mutually beneficial exchanges between groups and individuals.[4] This takes time, but is a worthwhile investment. The question is, how much time should you spend each week cultivating your networks?

You will only get out of networking what you put into it. Best-selling author and networking expert Ivan Misner has found that people who commit at least six and a half hours a week to developing their network see the most noticeable results.[5] Whether you meet people in person or connect with them online, nurturing those relationships will only help your cause.

Summary

From humble beginnings as a migrant farm worker to a successful career creating opportunities for young Latinx leaders, David Peña Jr. understood the value and importance of networking. He knew that cultivating relationships and engaging with a diverse team of people was essential to maximizing his impact. Viewing networking as a goal, rather than as a means to achieve a goal, Peña built a successful life for himself, as well as hundreds of young people with backgrounds like his. The same can be true for your nonprofit. By understanding the difference between an internally oriented network and an externally oriented network, you can adjust your approach to cultivating world-changing relationships. Looking outward and partnering with others will enable you to create a self-sustaining movement for lasting change.

The key to the fifth law of nonprofit impact—*your network is everything*—is external orientation.

Recommended Further Reading

GRANT, ADAM. *Originals: How Non-Conformists Move the World*. New York: Penguin Books, 2017.

KANTER, BETH, AND ALLISON H. Fine. *The Networked Nonprofit: Connecting with Social Media to Drive Change*. San Francisco: Jossey-Bass, 2010.

MISNER, IVAN, DAVID ALEXANDER, AND BRIAN HILLIARD. *Networking Like a Pro: Turning Contacts into Connections*. Irvine, CA: Entrepreneur Press, 2010.

---

[1] Shelly Y. McCallum, Monica L. Forret, and Hans-Georg Wolff, "Internal and External Networking Behavior: An Investigation of Relationships with Affective, Continuance, and Normative Commitment," *Career Development International* 19, no. 5 (September 2014).

2 Carter Gibson, Jay H. Hardy III, M. Ronald Buckley, "Understanding the Role of Networking in Organizations," *Career Development International* 19, no.2 (May 2014).

3 Morgen Johansen and Kelly LeRoux, "Managerial Networking in Nonprofit Organizations: The Impact of Networking on Organizational and Advocacy Effectiveness," *Public Administration Review* 73, no. 2 (2012): 355-63.

4 Mary Jo Goolsby and Joyce M. Knestrick, "Effective Professional Networking," *Journal of the American Association of Nurse Practitioners* 29, no. 8 (2017): 441-45.

5 Ivan Misner, "How Much Time Should You Spend Networking?" *Entrepreneur Magazine*, January 2017.

LAW 6:

Give to gain.

> *When we began receiving private donations and state support, I knew people realized they needed us. We provided a valuable human service and I knew our programs were finally regarded as leading in this field.*
>
> **L. Vincent Strully Jr. (1947–)**

Vincent Strully Jr. dropped out of school at the height of the Vietnam War.

A recent Hamilton College graduate with a degree in government, Strully was in his first year in a political science graduate program at Syracuse University. Antiwar movements were raging across the country. Civil unrest reached unprecedented heights in May 1970, when the Kent State shooting sent a shockwave through America. People couldn't believe the National Guard had opened fire on college students. That's when Strully decided he no longer wanted a career in political science.

Unsure of his next steps, Strully moved to the Albany area and took a job at a childcare center. There, he discovered a passion for teaching children, especially those with severe behavioral issues. Realizing this was his life's calling, Strully relocated to New Hampshire to work with autistic and emotionally disturbed children at the Spaulding Youth Center. At that time, autistic children were often permanently institutionalized. Strully and his colleagues knew there had to be a better way to treat and care for these individuals. As a result, they created the first behavior modification unit to treat children with autism.

After years of painstaking research, Strully determined that a science-centered educational approach based on positive reinforcement was the most effective way to help his students. With this method, he hoped to teach children how to communicate and control their behavior so they could live successful, semi-independent lives.[1]

Seeing a need for a private school for young people with emotional and behavioral disabilities, Strully helped draft a proposal for a contract with Massachusetts. In the summer of 1974, when the government agreed to fund the school, he relocated to oversee the project. With a staff of eight (plus six residential students), Strully began a program of behavior analysis, the only one of its kind, where students learned invaluable life skills in a caring environment.

In 1980, with the school ready for growth, Strully decided to take over a nearby foundering institution. It was a risk, but Strully was determined to rescue the program (and its residents) from failure.

For its first two years, Strully lived at the school full-time. A grueling five years later, the school finally began to receive the state and private donations it needed to continue. With the support of the Commonwealth of Massachusetts, Strully was able to unite his two programs into the New England Center for Children (NECC). His modern facilities enabled him to recruit world-renowned senior clinicians and provide the absolute best in behavioral analysis for autistic children.

Strully's decades-long focus on high-quality autism treatment research was a main driver of NECC's success. Today, he serves as the organization's chief executive officer. The NECC is internationally recognized as a leader in autism research, intervention, and professional development, receiving numerous national awards and millions of dollars in grants.

How did Strully manage to build a successful program and merge with a struggling school to emerge as one of the finest autism and behavioral analysis facilities in the world?

He understood and lived by the philosophy that fruitful relationships result from a steady diet of *vulnerability* and *generosity*.

Relationship Weed Killer and Lawn Fertilizer

Relationships, like lawns, are complicated. Things may look healthy at first glance. But a closer look can reveal self-oriented motives, unexpressed hurts, and unmet expectations lurking like weeds just beneath the surface. By the time the weeds are visible, you've got a ton of work on your hands to get your lawn back to a healthy condition. Most relationship weeds can be neutralized—and most relationship lawns can be fertilized—by two kinds of action: *vulnerability* and *generosity*.

Regarding vulnerability, the best relationship-builders are always wondering (perhaps without even being conscious of doing so), "What can I share of my experience that encourages, entertains, or educates the other person?" This is a *them-focused* vulnerability that helps, calms, and builds others at a modest cost to one's own ego. It's a sacrificial vulnerability that laughs outwardly at one's own mishaps to lighten the burdens of others. This kind of vulnerability is like weed killer—relationship weeds don't live long in this environment.

Strully is a prime example of someone who lives life with *them-focused* vulnerability. From his approach to results-driven behavioral analysis to his work developing and reinvigorating programs for children with autism, he always aims to provide the best care and development for his students.

When asked about the secret of his success, Strully says with self-deprecating humor, "I've always recruited people much smarter than I am."[2] He doesn't take credit for the amazing accomplishments of the NECC. Instead, he remains vulnerable as he continues to create programs, raise funds, and construct facilities to better serve the children in his programs.

Generosity is closely related to vulnerability. The very nature of giving is focusing on the needs of others. The more you give—of yourself, your talents, your time—the more you're likely to receive. This is the ancient "Rule of Reciprocity": people are compelled to support those who support them.

For decades, Strully has dedicated himself to the cause of helping children with autism lead productive lives. This kind of selflessness helped create a program that became so well-recognized, it received funding from state and individual donors. Strully didn't receive that level of investment at the beginning of his journey. He had to give in order to gain.

The Trust Equation

The idea of a *them-focused* perspective in both vulnerability and giving is instrumental in building trust between nonprofits and their constituencies. A theory known as the Trust Equation posits that an individual's or organization's trustworthiness is based on four factors:

- **Credibility:** *How knowledgeable you are in your field.*
- **Reliability:** *How well you follow through on your promises.*
- **Intimacy:** *How much you and they reveal to each other.*
- **Self-orientation:** *How much you focus on yourself.*

High scores in credibility, reliability, and intimacy strengthen trust; but a high level of self-orientation can destroy it.[3] The equation links closely to vulnerability and generosity. Vulnerability, as long as it remains *them-focused*, can significantly increase credibility and intimacy. Similarly, generosity can improve reliability and dramatically reduce self-orientation.

The most impactful nonprofit organizations demonstrate high levels of vulnerability and generosity. The virtue of their actions, drive, and purpose help to instill trust in others.[4] Their very missions are to serve and provide resources that a group or community needs to flourish. They take a *them-focused* perspective, always striving to do what they can to help others.

Your nonprofit likely doesn't have all the resources it needs to fully support your constituency. That's why you have campaigns to raise awareness, funds, and volunteers to serve your beneficiaries. Vulnerability allows you to ask for the help you need to achieve your mission, and enables you to build a relationship between you and your community to work together toward a common goal. People's lives are changed by the passion of a small group for the greater good, tempered by their vulnerability to admit that impact depends on the contributions of others.[5]

As a nonprofit leader, you continually give, not just to your community, but also to your organization. You give your talents, knowledge, experience, and time to create opportunities for your nonprofit and the people you serve. This generosity inspires reciprocity for others to meet your own needs as well as the needs of your beneficiaries. From volunteer hours to manpower to supplies to funds, the right people will respond to your generosity by coming alongside you.

Some of the best professional relationship advice I ever received went something like this: "Immediately following every professional interaction you have, look for a way to give the other person something they value by the end of that workday."

This rarely involves money, and almost never more than $15. So, what kinds of things should you give to a professional contact? It could be a favorite book shipped to their home, or an email introduction to a colleague you think they should meet. It could even be a social media message linking an article that relates to something you recently discussed. If this sounds like work...it is. And so are beautiful lawns.

Summary

At a time when the United States was torn apart by a war happening thousands of miles away, Vincent Strully Jr. found his life's passion while working with children with autism and emotional disorders. He devoted himself to helping these young people live independent and fruitful lives through a groundbreaking program of behavioral analysis based on positive reinforcement. Driven by his passion for helping these children, Strully not only built his own school but revitalized a failing institution. Through a life of vulnerability and giving, Strully earned the trust of state and community partners who helped fund his vision. Eventually, he was able to form the New England Center for Children, now one of the leading autism research and professional development facilities in the world. Strully's example of giving to gain has led to the care and treatment of countless children. Nonprofit leaders who give freely with vulnerability and generosity are able to cultivate trust-based relationships and fertilize them with the care they need to grow and thrive.

The keys to the sixth law of nonprofit impact—*give to gain*—are vulnerability and generosity.

Recommended Further Reading

BROWN, BRENÉ. *Daring Greatly: How the Courage to Be Vulnerable Transforms the Way We Live, Love, Parent, and Lead.* New York: Avery, 2015.

DONVAN, JOHN. *In a Different Key: The Story of Autism.* New York: Crown, 2017.

MAISTER, DAVID H., Charles H. Green, and Robert M. Galford. *The Trusted Advisor: 20th Anniversary Edition.* New York: Free Press, 2021.

NOUR, DAVID. *Relationship Economics: Transform Your Most Valuable Business Contacts into Personal and Professional Success.* Hoboken, NJ: Wiley, 2011

---

1 William H. Ahearn, "The New England Center for Children: Applied Behavior Analysis for Treating All Levels of ASD Severity," in *Comprehensive Models of Autism Spectrum Disorder Treatment: Points of Divergence and Convergence*, ed. Raymond G. Romanczyk and John McEachin, 63–80 (New York: Springer, 2016).

2 Sharon T. Rippey, "The New England Center for Children," *Hamilton Alumni Review*, Winter 1998–1999.

3 Carsten Schultz, "A Trust Framework Model for Situational Contexts," *Proceedings*

of the 2006 International Conference on Privacy, Security and Trust (2006): Article 50.

4 Barry Dym and Harry Hutson, *Leadership in Nonprofit Organizations: Lessons from the Third Sector* (Thousand Oaks: SAGE Publications, Inc., 2005), 20.

5 Peter Shabad, "The Vulnerability of Giving: Ethics and the Generosity of Receiving," *Psychoanalytic Inquiry* 37, no. 6 (2017): 359–74.

LAW 7:

Assemble your dream team.

> *We are trying to change, one person at a time, society's attitudes toward mental illness. We are trying to level the playing field to improve job opportunities, access to housing, and the chance to live in the community instead of being warehoused in an institution.*
>
> **Harriet Shetler (1917–2010)**

Harriet Shetler felt lost, angry, and afraid.

Her beloved son Charles, a freshman at the University of Wisconsin-Madison, had just been diagnosed with schizophrenia. She didn't know where to turn.

She was upset at herself and felt responsible for her son's illness. But she couldn't determine the cause of the diagnosis.[1] Was it her parenting style? Was it something she had said or done during his childhood? She had no one to look to for answers.

Harriet needed someone to share this experience with, someone to confide in and help her sort through her feelings. But she didn't know anyone who would understand.

Seeing Harriet's predicament, a church friend remembered another member of their congregation, Beverly Young, whose son had recently received the same diagnosis. She introduced the two mothers. One afternoon in 1977, they met for lunch to share their stories. The women found in each other a confidant, someone able to relate to their experience.

They became instant friends. As they talked about the challenges of raising a child with mental illness, they found comfort, relief, and peace in their new support system. When they met for lunch a second time, they realized the importance of connecting with people navigating similar journeys who needed this kind of support.

Shetler and Young, who were both active in charitable organizations, decided to form a group for caregivers to individuals with mental illness. In April 1977, they held a meeting at a local nightclub. Thirteen people attended, and they agreed to form the Alliance for the Mentally Ill (AMI). It seemed an appropriate name, given that the acronym AMI is also the French word for "friend." Within six months, the group's membership had grown to seventy-five people.

Young and Shetler learned of a similar group based in California. Realizing there were more people who could benefit from this kind of moral support, the women decided to host a national conference. They hoped to attract as many as thirty-five people. But in September 1979, their conference welcomed 284 people from 59 groups in 29 states. Family members, friends, and mental health professionals attended to learn, share, and discuss the societal impacts of mental health.

Before the conference was over, the group had created a national organization, the National Alliance for the Mentally Ill (NAMI). Now based in Arlington, Virginia, NAMI has over 1,000 local affiliates and 48 state organizations working to reduce the stigma and discrimination surrounding mental illness. The nonprofit is represented in all fifty states, Washington, DC, and Puerto Rico.

What began as a friendship founded on empathy has grown into the leading voice on mental health in the United States. So how did two moms with no experience establishing national nonprofit organizations successfully build NAMI?

They recognized early on that it was up to them to *cultivate a dream team for maximum impact.*

The Power of Events

Finding quality people to join the work is essential to nonprofit impact. Whether you're looking for volunteers or seeking donors to fund your efforts, flying solo isn't an option. As we can see from the development of NAMI, parents and family members meeting at a nightclub helped lay the foundation for a group of people on mission. However, it wasn't until they hosted a national conference that they connected with people on a larger scale.

Events are a highly effective way to cultivate community. An event can serve as both a launchpad for developing a community and a cultivator for generating a greater depth of connectivity. Because they gather people and provide common space for interaction and sharing, events have a special power to accelerate networking and decision-making, both during the event itself and for weeks or months after.[2] Events create opportunities for individuals to make meaningful connections with people doing adjacent and complementary work, which inspires post-event collaboration.

Events with others who are working toward similar visions are an efficient way to expand your contact list, educate yourself further about topics of interest, and build stronger alliances. Your nonprofit's vision depends on it. It's up to you, nonprofit leader, to develop a trusted team of people that understands the challenges you're facing and brings solutions.

My work with nonprofits has convinced me that the primary reason the vast majority of nonprofit leaders have marginal impact—even those with breathtaking missions, visions, and values—is that they try to make an impact alone. Beat the odds by assembling a talented, committed, and close-knit group of people who can support your efforts.

Two Names Per Day

Building a dream team takes work and careful attention. After all, your dream team won't include everyone on your contact list. It's a trusted "cabinet" of leaders who share your values, believe in your mission, get things done, and have fun together. These are relationships that you've developed, nurtured, and hand-selected to help achieve your goals.

How do you form such a team?

Introvert that I am, I've designated a trusted member of my team to be the Keeper of The List. The List is a select group of people with whom, after careful deliberation, I've decided to pursue a trust-based, long-term, mission-driven relationship. This is my impact dream team. Every morning, the Keeper of The List sends me two surprise names. That day I'll reconnect with them by phone call (ideal), text, or email.

By focusing on just two names per day, I can build deep relationships with the people I care about and who care about me. Building a dream team doesn't happen overnight. It takes time—regular, informal, casual, and personal interaction—to yield lasting, fulfilling relationships.[3]

I've come to learn that as the years go by, my dream team tends to change—and that's okay. As relationships and interests among team members transition into new seasons, the composition of your cabinet will shift accordingly.[4] For this reason, I try to be mindful of potential future team members, always keeping an eye out for talent, passion, and fit with the current dream team.

How would this idea apply to you and your mission? Who would you put on The List?

Productive Passion

A natural question follows: *What makes a dream team member?* As nonprofit leaders, we ought to look for people who have what I like to call *productive passion*. Anyone can be passionate about a cause, but it's the combination of *passion* and *action* that yields long-term results.

Gathering passionate people who lack productivity leads to a group of ineffective noisemakers: people who want to talk about their cause but have no motivation to act on it. Conversely, productivity without passion generates a team of coldhearted number-chasers. Such a group only cares about the end-result facts and figures with little regard for the purpose behind their work.

Dream teams are comprised of passionate producers. These are people who feel deeply for your cause *and* get things done. They're creative dreamers *and* proactive go-getters. Because they believe in your mission and goals, they're driven to do whatever it takes to have impact. These are the kinds of people you want on your dream team.

You can spot a passionate producer by looking at what they do when no one is telling them what to do. In the absence of guidance, they attack the problem they deem most pressing. You catch them sweeping the floor, applying for a grant, or organizing the donations, all of their own initiative. Deep down, you sense an intrinsic motivation that empowers them to identify a need, take ownership of the solution, and push cheerfully through any obstacle to have impact.[5]

To be clear, not everyone associated with your nonprofit needs to meet this high bar. Not everyone will be a passionate producer, and that's okay; almost anyone willing to pitch in can be an asset to your mission. From stocking shelves to passing out flyers, nearly every person can do something. These contributors and their involvement are all welcome! They just might not be a good fit for your cabinet—*your dream team*.

Summary

When Harriet Shetler and Beverly Young met for lunch in 1977, they had no intention of starting a nationally recognized nonprofit. They simply needed someone they could trust to share their concerns about living with a mentally ill son. By expanding their circle to include other families in similar situations, the two women built a dream team. That core group made it their mission to create a world where people with mental illness can lead healthy, fulfilling lives supported by a caring community. Hosting a national event brought even more people together, further cultivating a community of leaders with whom they could all share, learn, and connect. As a nonprofit leader, you can develop your "cabinet" of trusted confidants also, cultivating relationships with a select inner circle. By hand-selecting quality people with productive passion, you can unleash a talented team of world-changers united by a shared mission and a deep concern for one another.

The key to the seventh law of nonprofit impact—*assemble your dream team*—is selectively reaching out to passionate producers.

Recommended Further Reading

COVEY, STEPHEN R. *The 7 Habits of Highly Effective People: Powerful Lessons in Personal Change.* New York: Simon & Schuster, 2013.

DUCKWORTH, ANGELA. *Grit: The Power of Passion and Perseverance.* New York: Scribner, 2018.

PARKER, PRIYA. *The Art of Gathering: How We Meet and Why It Matters.* New York: Riverhead Books, 2020.

SNOW, SHANE. *Dream Teams: Working Together Without Falling Apart.* New York: Portfolio, 2018.

---

1 Diana E. Mark, "Experiences of Caregivers for Relatives with a Chronic Severe Mental Illness: Riding the Roller Coaster: A Descriptive Study," PhD diss., (Smith College, 2013).

2 Abraham Carmeli, Batia Ben-Hador, David A. Waldman, and Deborah E. Rupp, "How Leaders Cultivate Social Capital and Nurture Employee Vigor: Implications for Job Performance," *Journal of Applied Psychology* 94, no. 6 (2009): 1553–61.

3 Tanise L. Chung-Hoon, Julie M. Hite, and Steven J. Hite, "Organizational Integration Strategies for Promoting Enduring Donor Relations in Higher Education: The

Value of Building Inner Circle Network Relationships," *International Journal of Educational Advancement* 7, no. 1 (2007): 2-19.

4 Cara Margherio, Kerice Doten-Snitker, Elizabeth Litzler, Julia M. Williams, Eva Andrijcic, and Sriram Mohan, "Building Your Dream Team for Change," *American Society for Engineering Education Annual Conference*, June 2019.

5 Laurent Sié and Ali Yakhlef, "Passion and Expertise Knowledge Transfer," *Journal of Knowledge Management* 13, no. 4 (2009): 175-86.

LAW 8:

Run with achievers of character.

> *If you want to reach your potential and live meaningfully and make a contribution to the world, then find something you care about. Surround yourself with supportive people who will give you honest feedback. And practice, practice, practice.*
>
> **Angela Duckworth (1970–)**

Angela Duckworth was no stranger to hard work and perseverance.

The child of Chinese immigrants, she witnessed her parents strive for prosperous careers in America. Duckworth had to live up to the high standards of her culturally sensitive father who held a doctoral degree in chemistry. At his behest, Duckworth attended Harvard to pursue a degree in neurobiology.

She enjoyed science, but was most fulfilled by her volunteer work with various charitable organizations. During her sophomore year, she became a tutor in a university-wide after-school enrichment program that paired Harvard students with neighborhood schools. This experience ignited a new passion for Duckworth.

Tutoring not only gave her a sense of purpose, but also allowed her to see firsthand the reality of failing students in struggling urban public schools. She knew then that she wanted to devote her life to changing the way society approaches children's development in public education.

Duckworth developed an award-winning tutoring program at Harvard that served as a model for public schools nationwide. Despite having found her passion and made an impact, Duckworth's father shunned her for focusing on teaching. Despite his refusal to talk to her for six months, she remained unwavering in her passion. After earning a master's degree in neuroscience from Oxford, Duckworth spent the following five years teaching in urban schools.

The more she interacted with students in the classroom, the more she realized children consistently fell short of their abilities and did not apply themselves. She observed that, while many of her students had talent, only the ones who combined talent with effort had academic success. What was it, Duckworth wondered, that made some students work harder and longer than others?

Duckworth enrolled in the psychology doctoral program at the University of Pennsylvania and led pioneering studies of how character relates to achievement. She earned her doctorate studying the importance of self-control, grit, passion, and sustained persistence toward long-term goals. She confirmed that, while people can build grit from the inside out by cultivating and practicing interests, they can also grow their grit from the outside in by relying on teachers, mentors, and friends. Duckworth concluded that a persistent drive depends on finding a tenacious group of people and joining them for the long haul.[1]

Duckworth's research led her to believe that, regardless of socioeconomic background, character development impacts achievement in all areas of life. By focusing on elements like self-control, perseverance, and passion, educators can help their students realize their full potential.

After making this discovery, Duckworth and two educators founded the nonprofit Character Lab. This organization focuses on the merits of students' characters and provides teachers with scientific insights to better understand the conditions that lead to the overall well-being of young people.

How was Duckworth able to change so many students' lives?

She realized that running with people of strong character enables you to have the impact you desire. She believed in the idea *"Show me your friends and I'll show you your future."*

Dunbar's Number

While academic, corporate, and social impact careers have their differences, they share one key dependency: your network can predict future success or failure. That being the case, should we run around trying to be best friends with anybody and everybody? Some nonprofit leaders try this approach, but they soon discover there are limits to the number of relationships the average person can maintain.

British anthropologist Robin Dunbar studied the social behavior of nonhuman primates and discovered a correlation between the size of the animal's neocortex (the part of the brain that handles communication and cognition) and the size of the animal's social group.

When Dunbar applied this idea to humans and studied both historical and contemporary data about group sizes, he discovered that social circles can grow to around 150 people before they began to collapse. This figure, known as Dunbar's Number, applies to early hunter-gatherer societies as well as present-day workplaces, organizations, and even online social networks.[2] Whatever the setting, once a group surpasses 150 members it loses cohesion, and members will likely leave or form subgroups.

To build stronger relationships, Dunbar suggests depth over breadth. By focusing on a smaller, tighter community, you can forge deeper, more meaningful relationships. This is crucial because, according to entrepreneur and motivational speaker Jim Rohn, you are the average of the five people you spend the most time with.[3]

Psychologist David McClelland agrees. His findings show the people with whom you habitually associate affect up to 95% of your life's successes or failures.[4] Your closest social circle influences your decisions, your behavior, and your outcomes. Some people hold you back, while others propel you forward. Thus, it's important to think carefully about the people in your network.

If you spend your time with individuals who lack drive and motivation, chances are you will also. However, if you surround yourself with people who do hard world-changing work and find joy in solving tough problems, it's likely that you will too.

When it comes to your nonprofit organization, think carefully about who you run with. Even if you don't have more than 150 in your camp, you may want to consider who to prune from your list of closest relationships. Selfless, talented world-changers who share your passion and drive get to stay.

Proximity and Identity

There are two major factors that impact the influence of the people around you. These are *proximity* and *identity*. Think about times in a classroom or professional setting when you've been assigned to sit beside someone whose character traits were the exact opposite of yours. At the time, you may have dreaded having to sit near that person. But did it occur to you that your seating assignment may have been the work of a wise teacher?

When we are in close proximity to someone every day, we begin to take on some of their character traits (and vice versa). This contagious-character effect can have positive or negative results. If you have a high-performing neighbor, chances are you too will become a high performer. Studies have shown that, when paired together, individuals rarely suffer on their area of strength and instead improve their area of weakness.[5] However, in the case of a group member who is truly toxic, the impact and rate of change is much more pronounced. Severe negativity can infect a group in a fraction of the time it takes positivity to impact others.

Placing people with different strengths in creative configurations is one of the most overlooked tools in nonprofit leadership. By identifying the strengths that they hope to replicate, leaders can determine how best to assign people with complementary skills to work near each other. These kinds of symbiotic pairings can improve performance by as much as 15%.[6]

This concept can be applied in your nonprofit. Assess your team's skill sets and strengths. Identify two or three qualities you'd like to see more of, and think about which team members are strong in those qualities and could boost others' performance. When it comes to organizational impact, creative team-building is a widely underutilized resource. Group your team members thoughtfully to harness the power of proximity and identity.

Summary

Harvard undergrad Angela Duckworth found her true passion while tutoring failing students in struggling urban public schools. Witnessing her pupils' commitment and productivity levels, she realized that talented students weren't progressing as well as hardworking students. To understand what made some students work harder than others, Duckworth sought a PhD in research psychology. Through studies correlating character and achievement, she determined that surrounding yourself with individuals who are determined and committed to succeed will increase your commitment level. This is supported by Dunbar's Number, which reveals that the quantity and quality of our relationships have a finite upper limit. By placing ourselves in close proximity to achievers of strong character for an extended period of time, we experience a halo effect that draws us upward to new levels of impact.

The key to the eighth law of nonprofit impact—*run with achievers of character*—is long-term, close proximity to the right people.

Recommended Further Reading

JINKINS, MICHAEL, AND DEBORAH BRADSHAW JINKINS. *The Character of Leadership: Political Realism and Public Virtue in Nonprofit Organizations.* Hoboken, NJ: Wiley, 1998.

MISCHEL, WALTER. *The Marshmallow Test: Why Self-Control is the Engine of Success.* New York: Little, Brown Spark, 2015.

MISNER, IVAN, AND BEN GOTHARD. *How to Build Your Inner Circle.* Independently published, 2019.

ROHN, JIM. *7 Strategies for Wealth & Happiness: Power Ideas from America's Foremost Business Philosopher.* New York: Harmony, 1996.

---

1 Angela Duckworth, *Grit: The Power of Passion and Perseverance* (New York: Scribner, 2016), 245.

2 Bruno Goncalves, Nicola Perra, and Alessandro Vespignani, "Modeling Users' Activity on Twitter Networks: Validation of Dunbar's Number," *PLoS ONE* 6, no. 8 (2011): Article e22656.

3 Jim Rohn, "The Law of Averages," *Building Your Network Marketing Success*, read by the author (CD Baby Pro, 2000), audiobook.

4 David C. McClelland, "Toward a Theory of Motive Acquisition," *American Psychologist* 20, no. 5 (1965): 321–33.

5 Michael Housman and Dylan Minor, "Toxic Workers," *Harvard Business School Working Paper*, No. 16-057, October 2015.

6 Michael Housman and Dylan Minor, "Organizational Design and Space: The Good, the Bad, and the Productive," *Harvard Business School Working Paper*, No. 16-147, June 2016.

LAWS OF CAPABILITY

LAW 9:

Unleash your unique strengths.

> *Understanding your own blind spots and knowing how to build a team of individuals who can compensate for them is critical to being an effective leader.*
>
> **Aaron Hurst (1974–)**

Aaron Hurst had a problem with details.

In fact, he had a problem with focus of any kind. Hurst struggled constantly in school.

One summer during his junior year of college, Hurst managed to secure a job with the Aspen Institute, setting up and tearing down meeting spaces. Hurst soon found himself in the midst of many gatherings of international nonprofit thought leaders. A daily update helped him keep track of his responsibilities. If a meeting was ending, Hurst was responsible for clearing the tables and disposing of what was left behind. If a meeting took place over several consecutive days, he would leave the items in place.

That summer, the organization hosted a forum on global security. Nearly every living former US secretary of defense was in attendance, along with top US politicians and their counterparts from around the world. Hurst was in awe of the group and felt honored to play a role in their efforts to tackle important issues.

After the forum's third consecutive day, Hurst read on his daily update that it was time to set up for the next conference. He got to work clearing the tables, sweeping the handwritten notes and half-empty coffee cups into a large trash bag, and setting up the room for the next meeting.

Only after all the notes the leaders had been taking for the past three days were in a soggy, crumpled mess at the bottom of a trash bag, drenched in coffee, inked words bleeding together, did Hurst realize he'd made a tremendous mistake.

He'd read the schedule incorrectly.

The forum wasn't finished. The world leaders had one more day to go.

As horrified as Hurst was at the time, there would come a day when he would look back on this event as the best thing that could have happened to him. This life-changing moment caused him to acknowledge his shortcomings and find ways to maximize his strengths.

Hurst realized that to be successful he needed help. He was eventually diagnosed with attention-deficit/hyperactivity disorder (ADHD), which shed fresh light on his focus issues. With a new comprehension of his learning disability, Hurst recognized that he needed to be part of a team. He wasn't good at implementing detailed plans, but he was a strong leader. He knew he could successfully delegate responsibilities to groups of detail-oriented people who could help keep him focused and grounded.

And that's exactly what he's done. With a better understanding of his weaknesses, Hurst built a successful career as a founder and CEO of organizations like the Taproot Foundation, a national nonprofit that connects social change organizations with pro bono business services, and Imperative, a peer-coaching resource for businesses and organizations to build culture, accountability, and a sense of belonging.

As the author of *The Purpose Economy* (2014), Hurst is now considered a leading expert on the science of purpose and fulfillment at work. He's been featured in *The New York Times*, *Wall Street Journal*, and Bloomberg TV.

How did Hurst go from nearly ruining a global leadership conference to becoming a world leader himself?

He realized that individuals and organizations can have more significantly more impact by *improving on their strengths* than by remediating areas of weakness.

The Case for Strengths

We're conditioned from an early age to identify and correct weaknesses. When a child brings home a report card showing good grades in all subjects but one, that "opportunity for improvement" attracts a well-intentioned parent's focus. Whether this fixation is conscious or not, it's an extension of the human inclination toward improvement. By filling a perceived gap in achievement, the argument goes, we help a person become more complete.

Out in the wild, animal life is ruled by survival of the fittest. Weaker animals are prey while the strong survive. The more global and competitive the people landscape gets, the more we see this behavior among humankind as well. No one wants to be the one at the "bottom," so we focus on the weaknesses we worry could put us there. Organizations tend to use this same mentality, often focusing their efforts on addressing team members' weaknesses rather than capitalizing on their strengths.

No matter how good our intentions may be, focusing on the weaknesses of our nonprofit team creates deep insecurities and feelings of inadequacy that have the opposite of the intended effect. Weaknesses are often made worse, not better, when we focus on trying to fix them. The effort to fix weaknesses also allows other negative emotions like anger, anxiety, and fear to invade mindsets, impeding motivation and disrupting progress. The brain goes into survival mode, creativity is blocked, and impact is lost.

Studies show that people who are aware of and coached on improving their strengths have significantly more impact. When they use their strengths, especially in new and different ways, people are happier and more fulfilled.

They're also more confident in their capability to achieve their goals, which leads to higher self-esteem, more positivity, and less stress.[1]

Individuals whose managers emphasize the importance of strengths rather than the eradication of weaknesses perform better in their roles.[2] This is because they're more engaged, more encouraged, and more effective at self-development and personal growth. For these reasons, effective nonprofit leaders play a key role in helping staff and volunteers unleash their strengths. Be forewarned that this can be a difficult task, as many people are unclear about what their strengths are, much less how to unleash them.

By definition, a strength is the ability to consistently produce a nearly perfect positive outcome in a specific task.[3] It consists of three elements:

- **Talent:** *A natural way of feeling, thinking, or behaving.*
- **Skill:** *The natural or acquired ability to complete fundamental steps of a task.*
- **Knowledge:** *The information learned about a topic.*

Accordingly, developing a strength works as follows:

Strength Development = Talent [natural way of feeling, thinking, or behaving] x Investment [time spent practicing skills and expanding knowledge]

Mindset is a major factor in addressing weaknesses and maximizing strengths. Individuals with a *fixed mindset* believe weaknesses and strengths are innate and unchanging, so effort shouldn't be made to alter them. Those with a *growth mindset* believe that skills and understanding can be developed, so weaknesses can be mitigated and strengths improved. People with a growth mindset put more energy into learning and developing their skills, so they tend to achieve more than those with a fixed mindset.[4]

When we focus on correcting weaknesses, we may achieve (at best) average capabilities. But identifying strengths and developing them to their utmost potential results in significantly more impact.

Being a Strengths-Based Leader

If all of this is true, then why do so many organizations focus on improving weaknesses rather than capitalizing on strengths? The focus on weakness takes hold when we confuse the worthy goal of gaining basic mastery of essential skills with the impossible goal of gaining full mastery of every skill. We must replace a pursuit of perfection with a satisfaction in strengths.

A strengths-based leader identifies and maximizes the best aspects of their team. The most impactful teams possess a diverse range of abilities; knowing every person's key strengths enables you to apply them in a way that yields the greatest impact.

It's up to each of us as leaders to reverse the weakness-focused trend in our nonprofits. Here are some discussion prompts to help identify core strengths in yourself and others:

- *Tell me a story of a time when you were at your best.*
- *What gives you energy? When do you create "contagious" energy that infects your whole team?*
- *What do you yearn to do? In what environment?*
- *What comes naturally to you that's hard for others? Why?*
- *Are there situations when you lose track of time because you are so immersed in your work?*

The power of these prompts is that they focus on what's already working. Reflecting on moments when we're at our best empowers us with confidence and suggests ways to make those moments occur more frequently.

However, it isn't enough to simply know our strengths. Once strengths have been detected, we must coach ourselves and our team into capitalizing on them. Here are some key questions leaders can ask to help achieve this:

- *What kinds of assessments can we give you on this team to help you further develop that strength?*
- *Who currently has a higher level of mastery in that strength? Can we connect the two of you?*
- *What skills could you develop that complement that strength?*

Strengths-based leadership creates an environment where people feel free to operate in their zone of genius.[5] As a leader, you spend more time and energy where you and your team excel, and you delegate tasks to individuals whose strengths complement your weaknesses. This approach strengthens cohesion, celebrates diversity, and creates a fun environment where every team member sees how their uniqueness fuels the organization's world-changing impact.

Summary

When a learning disability caused Aaron Hurst to overlook important details at a high-stakes event, the result was disastrous. The mistake caused Hurst to reevaluate his weaknesses and focus on his strengths. Hurst began to delegate tasks to teams of detail-oriented people. This is how he built a successful career as a world-renowned entrepreneur and CEO of global nonprofit organizations. By focusing on strengths rather than weaknesses, people are happier, more fulfilled, and more productive. Understanding the difference between a fixed mindset and a growth mindset helps leaders take a strengths-based approach to driving impact. As strengths-based leaders, we can help others discover and improve upon their unique strengths.

The key to the ninth law of nonprofit impact—*unleash your unique strengths*—is understanding who you and your nonprofit team members are when you're at your best.

Recommended Further Reading

BUCKINGHAM, MARCUS. *Now, Discover Your Strengths.* Washington, DC: Gallup Press, 2020.

DWECK, CAROL. *Mindset: How You Can Fulfill Your Potential.* London: Robinson Publishing Company, 2012.

TRUNK, PENELOPE. *Brazen Careerist: The New Rules for Success.* New York: Business Plus, 2009.

1 Tom Rath and Barrie Conchie, *Strengths Based Leadership: Great Leaders, Teams, and Why People Follow* (Washington, DC: Gallup Press, 2008), 14.

2 Timothy D. Hodges and Jim Asplund, "Strengths Development in the Workplace," *Oxford Handbook of Positive Psychology and Work*, ed. Nicola Garcea, Susan Harrington, and P. Alex Linley, 213–20 (Oxford: Oxford University Press, 2010).

3 He Ding, Enhai Yu, and Yanbin Li, "Strengths-Based Leadership and Its Impact on Task Performance: A Preliminary Study," *South African Journal of Business Management* 51, no. 1 (2020): Article 1832.

4 Carol Dweck, "What Having a 'Growth Mindset' Actually Means," *Harvard Business Review*, January 13, 2016.

5 María Josefina Peláez, Cristián Coo, and Marisa Salanova, "Facilitating Work Engagement and Performance Through Strengths-Based Micro-Coaching: A Controlled Trial Study," *Journal of Happiness Studies* 21, no.4 (2020): 1265–84.

LAW 10:

Mitigate your limiting weaknesses.

> *4-H is about building better citizens, teaching values and developing skills. It doesn't matter if you're from a farm environment or from a big city. 4-H worked for me, and I've continued to work for it.*
>
> **Orville Redenbacher (1907–95)**

You can't teach an old dog new tricks.

At least, this seemed to be the case for American farmers in the 1890s. As far as they were concerned, farming was an ancient profession that originated in the earliest human civilizations. Surely there was no need to entertain the newfangled agricultural discoveries being developed on university campuses. What had worked for generations would continue to work far into the future—or so they thought.

Meanwhile, major advancements were emerging from academic research. Hybrid seed corn was developed to resist drought and withstand other harsh conditions. Improvements in milk sanitation and home-canning procedures resulted in safer, healthier products for families and consumers. But as researchers were making great strides in revolutionizing farming practices, lifelong farmers remained steadfast in their ways. Their resistance to agricultural innovations proved to be a weakness so severe that it negated their many strengths.

Over time, researchers and education professionals began to realize that, while older farmers refused to accept new agricultural developments, the younger generation seemed more open to the new methods advocated by universities. As they were willing to experiment, these up-and-coming farmers would learn about and implement revolutionary farming techniques, then share their experiences with their families.

In 1902, a country schoolmaster named A. B. Graham founded the first agricultural youth group in Ohio as part of a new effort to propel the industry forward. To foster support, their meetings were held in the basement of the county building on Saturday mornings while parents were in town on their weekly shopping trips.[1] In the same year, T. A. Erickson, the son of Swedish immigrants and a Minnesota farm boy who thoroughly loved his land and country, initiated agricultural after-school clubs and fairs in Douglas County, Minnesota. These project-oriented groups began popping up all over the country; by 1910, they developed into 4-H Clubs.

Four years later, Congress passed the Smith-Lever Act, which created the Cooperative Extension System, a new partnership between the USDA, more than 100 land-grant universities, and more than 3,000 county offices that would support the work of agricultural youth clubs. The act combined the resources of federal, state, and local governments to meet the growing need for research, knowledge, and educational programs. This nationalized the 4-H organization, which soon became a household name.

4-H is now integrated into rural, urban, and suburban communities, and has expanded to include an International Farm Youth Exchange. With a new focus on members' personal growth, the organization builds life-skills development into its projects, activities, and events to produce productive members of society.

What does the resistance of the 1890s farmers to new agricultural developments have to do with today's nonprofit impact?

It reflects the contemporary issue that, for 30% of leaders, *one or two severe weaknesses—"fatal flaws"—negate their many strengths.*

Fatal Flaws

Everyone has weaknesses. Some are small, others not so small.

While most people are aware of their shortcomings, leaders and organizations are all too often oblivious to the one or two weaknesses that pose the greatest threat to their impact. These are *fatal flaws*, weaknesses so extreme that they can have a significant effect on a leader and seriously hinder their contribution to their organization, not to mention their overall career.

A leader doesn't have to be great at everything. After all, mild weaknesses don't typically impact a person's overall effectiveness. On the other hand, a leader cannot be totally lacking in a key area of competency and still succeed.[2] A fatal flaw left unchecked can damage all other efforts, no matter how many strengths an individual may possess. The biggest challenge with fatal flaws is that they are notoriously difficult to self-diagnose.

Strengths are a direct result of behavior; it is easy to identify them because you can see their effects. With fatal flaws, however, the results aren't always directly attributable to a specific action. More often than not, fatal flaws are a result of a leader's *inaction*, such as failing to build strong relationships, lack of strategic planning, or skirting responsibility for negative outcomes. These sins of omission are difficult to recognize in ourselves. But the sooner we can identify and address these severe weaknesses, the better our chances of improving our future impact.

So how can you, as a nonprofit leader, determine whether you have a fatal flaw? Research suggests that one-third of leaders possess such a flaw.[3] To determine if you're one of them, seek the help of a *truth-teller*. This is a trusted coworker who is assured there will be no repercussions from speaking up, and has the courage and freedom to share hard-to-hear truths.

Leaders with fatal flaws have many people around them who are aware of the issue. However, these would-be counselors lack the license from the leader to voice their observations in a private and safe setting. Seek these people out and give them the place and time to share honestly. By keeping you grounded and holding you accountable, they play a critical role in maximizing your long-term impact. The key to an effective truth-teller is that they believe that you genuinely want honest information. As a leader, it's your responsibility to set the climate of openness to their feedback.

Perhaps you've identified a trusted peer who can provide you with honest input, but they need some ideas for areas where you may be failing. Consider giving them a list of capabilities that are essential to impact in your nonprofit, a sort of "fatal flaws menu." As they review the list, they can circle any areas that might be weaknesses so severe that they neutralize your many strengths.

If you can't find a trusted colleague who can serve this function, consider bringing in an external set of eyes and ears, perhaps an organization that offers 360-degree feedback, a life coach, or an occupational therapist.[4] A thoughtful and thorough third party can interview your colleagues, distill key themes, and share feedback in a way that you can process it and respond accordingly. Self-awareness is the chief prerequisite to fixing a fatal flaw.

Fixing a Fatal Flaw

So a truth-teller has helped you to identify your fatal flaw. How do you fix it?

Leaders fix their fatal flaws by refusing to let them live in the dark.

Practically speaking, this means first accepting the fact that your fatal flaw will never be a strength. It's unrealistic to expect to turn a deep-rooted weakness into one of your greatest assets. Instead, aim to improve your fatal flaw to the point where it is merely a mild weakness. Mild weaknesses aren't nearly as devastating as fatal flaws, and they're easier to complement with others' strengths.

Next, create a measurable plan for change. This plan could simply be to do the opposite of your fatal flaw. It should include focusing on the thought patterns or behaviors that need modification. Here again, reflection with the help of a third party can help you isolate what causes the flaw. Discover what triggers your typical response, identify what constitutes a better response, and develop cues that will help you adjust your behavior in real time.

For example, if your fatal flaw is that you leap to directly to solutions when faced with complicated challenges instead of involving your team, implement a framework of questions that you must ask your team before you allow yourself to implement any new solution. This standard question sheet will help slow your thought process and make time for the collaborative problem-solving that you used to skip over.

In addition to these heat-of-the-moment strategies, set overall goals and devise ways to track progress in this area. As we've already acknowledged, your colleagues are aware that you struggle with a severe weakness. Include them in your self-improvement journey. Not only does this help you remain accountable and encourage you along the way, but the vulnerability of asking for help serves to build trusting and supportive relationships.

Reward yourself as you make improvements. This is an important step, but one that is often overlooked. Overcoming a fatal flaw isn't easy; it's likely a trait you've exhibited for a long time, so much so that it's become a deeply ingrained habit. Mitigating it will take time, effort, and the support of colleagues and friends to keep you on track.

Consider your own nonprofit organization. As a leader, what fatal flaw do you think is holding you back? Who on your team could you trust to help you identify your greatest weakness? And, more importantly, are you ready to hear the truth, if it means more impact for your mission? The sooner you can mitigate your fatal flaw, the sooner you can make a lasting impact.[5]

Summary

In the 1890s, researchers identified a fatal flaw in the leadership of many long-time farmers: they were unwavering in their resistance to new agricultural developments. Despite the fact that these advancements were benefiting consumers and the industry overall, the farmers weren't interested in this agricultural revolution. By building relationships with the younger generation, universities were able to spread information into farms across the world. The 4-H organization was born, enabling agricultural developments to impact global issues in new and exciting ways. A fatal flaw, if left unchecked, can severely curtail a nonprofit's impact. Relying on truth-tellers to help you identify your greatest weakness is the first step in self-improvement. By developing heat-of-the-moment mitigation tools along with long-term mitigation strategies, you can convert a fatal flaw into a minor weakness.

The key to the tenth law of nonprofit impact—*mitigate your limiting weaknesses*—is your willingness to see your fatal flaws through another's eyes.

Recommended Further Reading

ERICKSON, T. A., with Anna North Coit. *My Sixty Years with Rural Youth.* Minneapolis: University of Minnesota Press, 1956.

SHAW, ROBERT BRUCE. *Leadership Blindspots: How Successful Leaders Identify and Overcome the Weaknesses That Matter.* San Francisco: Jossey-Bass, 2014.

TOPPING, ROBERT W. *Just Call Me Orville: The Story of Orville Redenbacher.* West Lafayette, IN: Purdue University Press, 2011.

ZENGER, JOHN H., and Joseph R. Folkman. *The Extraordinary Leader: Turning Good Managers into Great Leaders.* New York: McGraw-Hill Education, 2009.

---

1 Thomas Wessel and Marilyn Wessel, *4-H: An American Idea 1900–1980* (Chelsea: BookCrafters, 1982), 4.

2 Joe Folkman, Kurt Sandholtz, and Jack Zenger, *Leadership Under the Microscope*, Zenger Folkman, December 2016.

3 Joseph Folkman and Jack Zenger, "Most Leaders Know Their Strengths—But Are Oblivious to Their Weaknesses," *Harvard Business Review*, February 21, 2018.

4 Marcus Buckingham and Ashley Goodall, "The Feedback Fallacy," *Harvard Business Review*, March–April 2019, 92–101.

5 Clinton O. Longnecker and Laurence S. Fink, "Fixing Management's Fatal Flaws," *Industrial Management* 54, no. 4 (2012): 12–17.

LAW 11:

Hire with ruthless selectivity.

> *Employers hire for skills and fire for behavior. We spend at least half of our time focused very, very clearly on making sure our young adults have the attitudinal, behavioral, and communication skills they need to be professionals in the knowledge-based economy.*
>
> **Gerald Chertavian (1965–)**

Gerald Chertavian found his calling early in life.

The son of a dentist, Chertavian was raised in a middle-class neighborhood in Lowell, Massachusetts. Opportunities for advancement were not hard to come by. He attended Bowdoin College and earned a degree in economics, after which he immediately landed a job with Chemical Bank in New York City. During his time there, he decided to try his hand at volunteering with the local Big Brothers Big Sisters program, a nonprofit organization that matches adult mentors with young people facing adversity.

Through this volunteer experience, Chertavian found his true calling.

Chertavian was paired with David Heredia, a ten-year-old boy growing up in a low-income housing project in Manhattan's Lower East Side. Immediately, Chertavian realized that Heredia had work ethic and talent, but Heredia's circumstances made him doubt his own abilities. Chertavian was troubled by the idea that a person's background, income, or zip code would outweigh their talent and skills when it came to finding employment. Then Chertavian had an idea.

He applied to Harvard Business School and submitted an outline for an organization that would provide talented disadvantaged youth with six months of training and six months of apprenticeship, and then place them in meaningful jobs with partnering companies.

Chertavian's definition of a win was helping a young person rise from poverty to a professional career in a year's time. This was a huge goal, a giant dream—and at the time, Chertavian didn't have the resources to see it through.

After graduating from Harvard Business School, Chertavian became the marketing manager for a financial services firm in London. Soon after, he cofounded Conduit Communications, a consulting firm specializing in virtual marketing services. Through years of effort, Chertavian developed Conduit into one of Europe's fastest-growing technology companies; the firm employed 130 people worldwide and made $20 million in annual revenue. In 1999, Chertavian and his business partners sold the company to i-Cube for $80 million.

Finally, Chertavian had the financial freedom to focus on his true passion of supporting disadvantaged youth. The following year, he moved his family to Cambridge, Massachusetts, and founded the nonprofit organization Year Up. Originally serving just twenty-two students, the nonprofit has expanded to twelve cities across America, employs four hundred people, and has an annual budget of $170 million.

Even more impressive than this growth are the outcomes for the eighteen- through twenty-four-year-olds that Year Up has assisted. More than 10,000 young people have completed the year-long training program. Within four months of graduating, 85% have become full-time students or begun their professional careers. The program has a 90% satisfaction rating from its corporate partners, confirming Chertavian's theory that the young people they serve are not social liabilities but economic assets.[1]

Chertavian's hiring policy within Year Up is ruthlessly selective. People who want to work for Year Up must love to serve young people. Once they show this, applicants must demonstrate what they can bring to the organization functionally. As a result of its rigorous recruitment systems and standards, Year Up hires only the most motivated candidates, who go on to deliver as top performers.

How did Chertavian build a successful program for disadvantaged youth that helped them rise from poverty to the middle class in a single year?

By realizing that *the nonprofit organizations that make the biggest impact are those that obsess over talent.*

The Onus Is on Hiring

For a long time, the fashionable topic in human resources has been professional development of the existing workforce. In one year alone, companies across America spent more than $87.6 billion on corporate training and development.[2]

Can people change? Maybe. But if the employee does not embrace the will to improve, prospects for even the best professional development approaches are bleak. So why chance it? Even nonprofit leaders who are optimistic about professional development should be ruthlessly selective about who they bring into their organizations.

Instead of "hire and fix," organizations should instead adopt a policy of "hire the unicorn." Unicorns, albeit hard to find, don't need fixing. Because of their unique mix of skill, will, and harmony with the existing team, unicorns are ready to step into an organization and be a tremendous force for impact from day one.

Too often, I see nonprofits try to fill a position with a clone of the previous staff member. By hiring "the next so-and-so," you set your organization on a path that will likely repeat past performance. Maybe that's a good thing, and maybe it isn't. Instead of trying to replace a previous employee, consider hiring a strong performer who fits your organization's future plans.[3] Every new hire is a chance to make a significant step-change in your nonprofit's talent.

In the for-profit sphere, talent is a top concern for today's CEOs. Many report that the lack of necessary talent and skills is the largest threat to their business.[4] The hard truth is that talent deserves as much (or perhaps even more) attention in the nonprofit sector. It isn't enough to simply fill an open position with "good enough for now." No hire is better than a good-enough hire. I recognize that following this advice will make you something of a pariah in the nonprofit leadership community. That doesn't matter—your cause is too important to be hiring turkeys.

The Best Way to Hire

Organizations often partner with external recruiters to track down candidates. Perhaps they scan recruiting mega-sites like LinkedIn, Indeed, and Glassdoor to find potential matches based on education and experience. In many cases, people on these sites aren't looking to change jobs, but external recruiters aren't picky; their goal is to attract as many applicants as possible with the hope that at least one will work out.

Sometimes recruiters will contact individuals directly to try to persuade them to submit an application. Other times they'll rely on electronic applications so tracking software can scan online profiles for keywords to see if they might be a match for certain positions. The problem with this approach is that on-paper credentials make poor predictors of day-to-day workplace habits and behavior.

It's time to reevaluate our hiring processes. Instead of relying on third-party companies who don't appreciate our missions and values, consider the alternative: *cultivating a pipeline of referrals from a diverse cross-section of star employees and volunteers.* Star performers know other star performers. And your current star performers already know your organization, understand what you're trying to accomplish, and have the best interests of the nonprofit in mind. They're an invaluable resource when it comes to helping you find candidates who they'd love to work alongside for many years.

Choosing candidates referred by people you trust offers numerous benefits, including lower turnover, lower recruitment costs, and stronger alignment with the nonprofit's core values.[5] Applicants who are referred by current team members and volunteers are more likely to accept job offers. They have lower safety incidents, higher productivity, and yield higher profits than non-referred workers.[6]

The easiest way to spread the word about a job opening is to simply let your highest performing staff and volunteers know about it and invite them to share the information with their contacts. For a more formal approach, you could create an employee referral program in which anyone whose recommendation results in a hire is eligible to receive a bonus. If the employee lasts beyond a certain amount of time, the person who referred them may receive an additional perk. This type of program encourages people to think carefully about their recommendations and suggest only candidates who they truly feel would be an asset to your organization.

Relying on your best staff and volunteers for hiring suggestions also shows that you trust and value them as individuals, workers, and resources. Referrals not only improve your organization's future—they help solidify your organization's present.

Summary

Gerald Chertavian had a successful career on Wall Street, but it was his time spent as a volunteer for Big Brothers Big Sisters that ignited his passion. He witnessed firsthand the "opportunity divide" that leaves talented, disadvantaged youth at the bottom of the corporate ladder. In response, he founded Year Up, a nonprofit organization that provides these individuals with a year of training and then places them in meaningful jobs with corporate partners. As for Year Up's hiring practices, interested candidates must pass rigorous screening in order to get hired. In contrast, many nonprofit organizations focus on filling positions with good-enough hires and hope improvement comes over time. Nonprofit leaders seeking to maximize their impact need to look carefully at their hiring practices. Rather than relying on recruiters to attract a pool of good-on-paper candidates, nonprofits should consider obtaining referrals from their top-performing staff and volunteers.

The key to the eleventh law of nonprofit impact—*hire with ruthless selectivity*—is to obsess over filling your nonprofit with the world's best talent.

Recommended Further Reading

KHOR, CHRISTINE. *Hire Love: How to Hire Passionate People to Make Greater Profit.* Surrey Hills Victoria: Michael Hanrahan Publishing, 2015.

MURPHY, MARK. *Hiring for Attitude: A Revolutionary Approach to Recruiting and Selecting People with Both Tremendous Skills and Superb Attitude.* New York: McGraw-Hill Education, 2016.

SCOTT, LYN. *From Passion to Execution: How to Start and Grow an Effective Nonprofit Organization.* Boston: Cengage Learning PTR, 2012.

---

1 Gerald Chetavian, *A Year Up: Helping Young Adults Move from Poverty to Professional Careers in a Single Year* (New York: Plume, 2013), 35.

2 Dan Pontefract, "The Wasted Dollars of Corporate Training Programs," *Forbes*, September 15, 2019.

3 Cathy Fyock, Matha I. Finney, and Stephen P. Robbins, *The Truth About Hiring the Best* (Upper Saddle River, NJ: FT Press, 2007), 2.

4 Peter Cappelli, "Your Approach to Hiring is All Wrong," *Harvard Business Review*, May–June 2019, 48–58.

5 Mitchell Hoffman, "The Value of Hiring Through Employee Referrals in Developed Countries," IZA World of Labor, 2017.

6 Stephen V. Burks, Bo Cowgill, Mitchell Hoffman, and Michael Housman, "The Value of Hiring Through Employee Referrals," *The Quarterly Journal of Economics* 130, no. 2 (2015): 805–39.

LAW 12:

Cultivate super-volunteers.

> *One touch of human nature makes the whole world kin. And that kinship, which human suffering evokes, is perhaps the closest of all, for we know that those who work to help the suffering find true spiritual fellowship in that labor of love.*
>
> **President Franklin D. Roosevelt (1882–1945)**

Franklin Delano Roosevelt was just thirty-nine years old when he lost the use of his legs.

In August 1921, after a strenuous day of activity and a stressful week giving testimony to the Senate on a Navy scandal, Roosevelt came down with polio.[1] At that time the virus spread through contaminated food and water, primarily among American children. Polio affected the central nervous system and left its victims paralyzed into adulthood.

Roosevelt nearly died from the disease. Doctors said that his wife, Eleanor, and her attentive nursing care were responsible for Roosevelt's survival.

A mere eleven years later, the disabled statesman won the US presidency in a landslide. Roosevelt was able to collaborate with his Secret Service team, the media, and event planners to keep his disability hidden from the public. But he eventually realized it couldn't be hidden, and his mindset changed completely. Roosevelt realized that his experience gave him tremendous empathy for others affected by illnesses and disabilities.

Realizing he could use his platform to make an impact on medical research and the support of polio's victims, Roosevelt formed the National Foundation for Infantile Paralysis (NFIP) in 1938. The organization consisted of health researchers and volunteers working together toward a vaccine and aiding victims' rehabilitation. Unfortunately, the foundation couldn't raise enough money to keep up with polio's toll on the nation's children.

Roosevelt knew he needed help, so he turned to the biggest group of supporters he could think of: the American people. Roosevelt's popularity and a feeling of unity that came with World War II gave the NFIP an instant foothold. Roosevelt's close associate Basil O'Connor headed the NFIP's efforts. He knew he needed to build an organization that could reach people anywhere in the country, so he developed a network of local chapters that could deliver aid and raise funds.

These chapters were so relentless in their efforts that celebrity entertainer Eddie Cantor joked that everyone should send dimes to the president for his cause. But the American people took him seriously; in the first "march of dimes," the White House received 2,680,000 dimes and thousands more dollars in individual donations.

By 1950, the NFIP had 3,100 chapters, run primarily by volunteers. What later came to be formally known as the March of Dimes was truly a grass-roots movement. Millions of tiny donations funded cutting-edge research to discover how poliovirus functioned and how it might be stopped. Thanks to the efforts of countless volunteers, a breakthrough occurred at the University of Pittsburgh, where a young physician and March of Dimes grantee named Dr. Jonas Salk developed a vaccine that would end the spread of the virus. Following the generosity of the March of Dimes, Salk refused to pursue patents, making the vaccine available to all. As a result, polio dropped from tens of thousands of new cases per year to just a few.

The dreaded disease had been virtually eradicated, all due to the work of a nonprofit's volunteers.

The March of Dimes has historically been one of the few nonprofits to use volunteers effectively. Today, volunteers work to raise money to help fund research, awareness, and education regarding the prevention and care of children with birth defects.

How did President Roosevelt catalyze an organization that would eradicate the epidemic that crippled his legs?

He oversaw the creation of an organization where *super-volunteers could easily recruit and inspire more super-volunteers.*

Match Volunteers' Skills with Assignments

When they are recruited, trained, and deployed well, volunteers can be a powerful asset to a nonprofit organization. They donate their time and energy to help with various essential tasks, but they also serve higher-level functions as fundraisers, ambassadors, and advocates. To maximize the potential value of volunteers, nonprofits need to be committed to using them effectively.

Tragically, many nonprofits don't see their volunteers for the strategic assets they are. As a result, many people who give their time to nonprofits don't return the following year. Some nonprofits, however, like the March of Dimes, have realized the significance of cultivating dedicated volunteers. They invest in recruitment efforts that help recognize and develop super-volunteers, and *align volunteer talent with the assignments that maximize their skills.* When people with specialized abilities are asked to do manual labor instead of capitalizing on their talents, they don't feel valued or fulfilled. Volunteer experience should result in a successful outcome for both nonprofits and volunteers.

Recognize Volunteers' Contributions

Although volunteers don't donate their time for honors and accolades, everyone likes to be appreciated for their involvement. Nonprofits who recognize their volunteers' contributions instill a sense of pride in their helpers and increase the likelihood that those volunteers will return year after year.[2]

Recognition doesn't have to be in the form of a formal ceremony or event. Simply developing an organizational culture that values volunteers through public recognition can have positive results. In most annual reports, nonprofits list the individual names of significant financial donors, but they rarely provide a similar list for people who have donated their time.

Smart nonprofit leaders realize that donations of time and talent can just be as valuable as those of money. Whether it is published in an annual report or posted on the organization's website, a recognition list of the names of volunteers and the impact they've made shows volunteers that they're appreciated. People who feel appreciated will continue to contribute to the overall success of the organization.

Measure the Value of Volunteers

To truly maximize your volunteers as a resource, you must be able to measure their value. There are three common ways to do this:

- *Multiply the amount of volunteer hours by the national average hourly wage.*
- *Calculate the cost of paying employees to complete the volunteers' tasks.*
- *Determine how much volunteers would be paid at their full-time job for the hours they devote to your organization.*

These figures help an organization realize how much money they save by asking a volunteer to do the work of a full-time employee. They also reveal the overall impact a volunteer has on the nonprofit's bottom line.

By measuring your volunteers' value, you gain a greater appreciation for their services. The more appreciated your volunteers feel, the more committed they are to your organization. And the more committed they are, the greater the impact and the potential for more super-volunteers and donations.[3]

Invest in Volunteers' Capacity

Proper volunteer management is an important factor in creating a successful nonprofit organization. Volunteers need a baseline amount of training in order to be helpful to the mission they are supporting, but staff and board members also need to learn how to work effectively with volunteers. This kind of education takes an investment of time and resources that many nonprofits underestimate.

Volunteers who don't receive any reception, onboarding, or training tend to feel uncertain and undervalued in their roles. We've all had that feeling as a volunteer: standing, waiting, and wondering if the nonprofit staff we're working with bothered to make even the slightest effort to plan for our arrival. And as a rule of thumb, the more talented the volunteer is, the less patient they will be with an underprepared nonprofit.

An effective nonprofit leader will create opportunities for staff and volunteers to receive the formal indoctrination and training they need to best serve their constituency. Management practices like coordinating refresher courses, enhancing interpersonal contacts, and training and supervising volunteers directly correlate to satisfaction, commitment, and duration of service.[4] Increase the likelihood of your volunteers' having a great experience by investing in them heavily on the front end.

Foster Admiration among Volunteers

Volunteer retention is essential to nonprofit success. Volunteers who feel deep admiration for the organization they're serving are not only likely to keep donating their time. They're also more likely to encourage other super-volunteers to join the cause.

Fostering admiration among volunteers helps people feel as though they are a part of something special. Proactive volunteer stewardship efforts have been shown to increase a volunteer's involvement and contribute to the long-term impact of the nonprofit.[5] The same body of research points to admiration as the leading factor in developing a positive volunteer-nonprofit relationship. Generating an environment of admiration leads to increased trust, commitment, and satisfaction among both volunteers and employees.[6]

The object of volunteers' admiration can vary. Depending on the nonprofit's specific mission, vision, values, strategy, and history, the objects of volunteers' admiration can include beneficiaries (e.g., survivors of human trafficking); current staff members (e.g., a pioneering executive director); past staff members (e.g., the executive director who originally founded the organization); a distinguished track record of impact (say, eradicating polio); a bold stance on a controversial subject (e.g., equal rights for a marginalized group); and the list goes on.

As a nonprofit leader, your objective should not be to over-architect what volunteers will find admirable about your organization. Rather, you should work to identify what your existing super-volunteers find admirable and become more intentional about recruiting other super-volunteers who will resonate with that same admiration.

Summary

A victim of the debilitating polio virus, President Roosevelt used his position to form a nonprofit organization that raised funds for polio research and rehabilitation. Realizing that the virus was outpacing the organization's capacity, Roosevelt appealed to the American people to volunteer. As a result, the March of Dimes eventually funded the research needed for Dr. Jonas Salk to create a vaccine that eradicated the disease in America. Unlike many nonprofits, the March of Dimes recognized the world-changing power of local volunteers. To maximize their impact, nonprofits must match volunteers with assignments that are aligned with their unique strengths. Only by measuring the financial value of their volunteers can organizations truly appreciate the incredible assets they are to the organization. Nonprofits that invest in volunteer orientation and training will see higher volunteer satisfaction and less turnover. By fostering admiration, organizations can rapidly grow a large base of super-volunteers.

The key to the twelfth law of nonprofit impact—*cultivate super-volunteers*—is being an organization worthy of a talented volunteer's admiration.

Recommended Further Reading

KIZER, DARREN. *The Volunteer Project: Stop Recruiting. Start Retaining.* Atlanta, GA: 181 Publishing, 2015.

MCKEE, JONATHAN, AND THOMAS W. McKee. *The New Breed: Understanding and Equipping the 21st Century Volunteer.* Loveland, CO: Simply Youth Ministry, 2012.

ROSE, DAVID W. *March of Dimes.* Charleston, SC: Arcadia Publishing, 2003.

---

1 David Amy Berish, "FDR and Polio," Franklin D. Roosevelt Presidential Library and Museum, November 2011.

2 David Eisner, Robert T. Grimm Jr., Shannon Maynard, and Susannah Washburn, "The New Volunteer Workforce," *Stanford Social Innovation Review*, Winter 2009, 32–37.

3 Mark Groza and Mya Pronschinske Groza, "Enhancing Volunteer Pride and Retention Rates: The Role of Organizational Reputation, Task Significance, and Skill Variety," *Journal of Nonprofit & Public Sector Marketing* (May 2021).

4 Amanda Beck, Sarah Garven, and Michelle Yetman, "Do Donors Value Volunteer Commitment in Assessing Nonprofit Effectiveness?," (February 8, 2021), available at SSRN.

5 M. Carmen Hidalgo and Pilar Moreno-Jiménez, "Organizational Socialization of Volunteers: The Effect on Their Intention to Remain," *Journal of Community Psychology* 37, no.5 (July 2009): 594–601.

6 Virginia S. Harrison, Anli Xiao, Holly K. Ott, and Denise Bortree, "Calling All Volunteers: The Role of Stewardship and Involvement in Volunteer-Organization Relationships," *Public Relations Review* 43, no. 4 (2017): 872–81.

LAW 13:

Act quickly when it's not working.

> *If you aren't willing to let go of people who aren't performing at the level you need them to, you'll never accomplish what you otherwise could. It's the toughest part of building a talent-rich organization, but it's critical.*
>
> **Jerry Hauser (1968–)**

Jerry Hauser faced a tough decision.

As the COO of Teach for America, a nonprofit organization that places teachers in low-income schools, Hauser was working with a struggling regional director.

The new director was underperforming and under-delivering. At first, the solution seemed simple; Hauser should invest more time and resources into her professional development. So that's what he did. Hauser supported multiple site visits to observe her techniques, phone calls to discuss the challenges she was facing, and in-depth coaching from a senior leader.

Unfortunately, none of these seemed to improve her performance and help her reach her fundraising goals. Hauser began to think he was expecting too much of her. After all, she was working in a challenging region with difficult circumstances. Anyone would have a hard time succeeding in that situation, right?

Ultimately, the resources Teach for America invested into this manager's development failed to generate the necessary improvements. Hauser was forced to fire her.

Considering what to do next, he decided to take a risk. He filled the position with a young woman who was already part of the Teach for America network, but had little experience.

In her first year, working independently with less supervision than the previous manager had received, she boosted fundraising in her area from $43,000 per year to $285,000. Within two years, it was up to $1 million. Not only was she bringing in more money, she wasn't costing the organization the expenses of professional development. She didn't need extensive training. Nobody had to guide her through the facets of performing her job. She was simply a better performer. This was a huge improvement for the nonprofit.

Through this experience, Hauser learned an important lesson. He realized that one high performer can have the same impact as five or more lower performers. It was more economical (in terms of time, money, and other resources) to invest in that single top performer than to try to improve the results of several low performers. Hauser knew that many nonprofits fail to see this, and decided to create an organization to guide other organizations in effective management.

He founded The Management Center in 2006 with the goal of helping social justice leaders build and run effective, successful, and sustainable organizations. The Management Center trains managers on practices that deliver lasting results. From hands-on coaching for executives to training courses and other tools and resources, Hauser wanted to provide managers with practical information that could help them succeed. Part of that advice is the importance of knowing when to let people go.

To that end, The Management Center provides specific, actionable suggestions. They don't just prod clients to have a difficult conversation; they provide talking points and rehearse the conversation so that it goes as smoothly as possible. The ultimate goal is increased capacity to serve the nonprofit's constituency.

How did Hauser improve fundraising results for Teach for America and help over 1,000 organizations see better results through stronger management?

He understood that *the most important capability-building activity that nonprofit leaders do, second only to hiring, is firing.*

Stars Attract Stars

Financial upside isn't the only reason nonprofit organizations should focus on firing low performers and hiring star players. It's true that a top performer will increase department-level output. But even more important than the work they do is the talent they attract.

Just one year after a star player joins a department, the average talent that subsequently joins the department increases significantly.[1] Hard workers don't want to be responsible for carrying others' workloads; they want to be surrounded by other hard workers. Stars want to feel like they're on the varsity team.

The best nonprofit leaders have an eye for discerning top-10% from bottom-90% talent. They can identify superstars and act quickly and creatively to draw them in. Superstar employees possess qualities that make them priceless assets to your organization, including:

- *They believe that quality work is a top priority.*
- *They have a self-directed growth mindset that seeks ways to improve.*
- *They welcome feedback in the hopes of improving their performance.*
- *They possess strong people skills and a large social network.*

After a sustained period of attracting people with these qualities, there comes a point when you reach critical mass and the organization does the work of attracting great people on its own. But this is not the case in most nonprofits. So how does a nonprofit leader attract top-level talent when it's not already inside the organization?

High-caliber employees know their worth, and they want to invest in an organization where they can thrive. Value alignment is an important factor for quality workers—they want to work for an organization they believe in. They also want to know what sets your nonprofit apart from others in your field. Do you offer advancement opportunities and competitive pay? Your organization's external and internal reputations are motivators for driven employees. People rely on testimonials and feedback within their personal networks.

If you're looking to hire superstars (and why wouldn't you be?), it's time to take a close look at your organization to determine whether you're the kind of nonprofit that attracts high performers. All it takes to gain momentum is that first star, and more stars are sure to follow.

Return on (Talent) Investment

Leadership development takes time and energy. The most effective nonprofit leaders strive to ensure that these expenditures yield an impact return. Resources spent month after month on persistently poor performers (who will eventually leave or be removed anyway) could have been spent on top performers. Therefore, there is a double developmental benefit to acting quickly to remove poor performers: (1) you mitigate loss of development time and energy that you would have wasted; and (2) you compound the return on development time and energy that you spend on the right people.

The moment you realize that an employee isn't going to work out, it's best to give them notice to begin looking for another job immediately so you can make room for a star performer.[2] Like Teach for America, countless nonprofits have provided training and growth opportunities for workers who will never improve and will eventually leave. This is beyond tragic.

An effective way to ensure you're pushing the envelope on talent development is to always be hiring. Don't wait until a position is open or your budget is flush to go on the hunt for high-caliber talent.[3] Every interaction—from drive-thru pickups to church small groups—presents an opportunity to find the next star for your organization. Job descriptions and organizational charts have their place. But it's far better to scramble with your board to hack out a place in the budget for a newly discovered superstar than accept another year of mediocrity out of respect for the approved budget. The best nonprofit leaders solve for impact, not politeness.

A Word on "Family"

Most leaders with a heart have found themselves, at one time or another, referring to their department or organization as a "family."

We're more than just a group of coworkers here at the Big Heart Foundation—we're family.

I've been known to say this kind of thing myself. Over the years, however, I've learned that it's best to reserve this term for your long-in-the-tooth, proven circle of top performers. *Family* refers to those who have stood the test of time. This is not to say that newcomers to the organization should be treated as less-than or viewed with squint-eyed scrutiny. It's only natural that the people who have been with you through the crucible and lived to tell the tale should enjoy your trust in an elevated way. The distinction gives newcomers something to appreciate and aspire to.[4]

Those of us at the Big Heart Foundation who have survived and thrived through some hard times have come to consider each other family. We'd like to give you an opportunity to earn your place in that legacy.

Who wouldn't admire such a sentiment? By reserving the term "family" for a select group of veterans, you give yourself the maneuverability to act quickly when a new hire isn't working out.

Summary

When Jerry Hauser realized the time, money, and resources he was investing in his regional manager weren't improving her performance, he knew he had to fire her. Her replacement, with far less supervision, was able to increase fundraising results five-fold in just one year. This was an invaluable lesson for Hauser. When it comes to building a successful team, nonprofit leaders need to be prepared to fire low performers to make room for top performers. After all, stars attract stars, and top talent can increase productivity, revenue, and the quality of future candidates. If you are going to invest resources into the professional development of your staff, it must provide a good return on (talent) investment. Training a top performer will get you much higher rewards than training an underperforming staff member or volunteer. Reserving the term "family" for a select cohort of grizzled veterans will give you the maneuverability to act quickly to remove underperforming team members.

The key to the thirteenth law of nonprofit impact—*act quickly when it's not working*—is caring more about maximizing impact than about avoiding a tough conversation.

Recommended Further Reading

FALCONE, PAUL. *101 Tough Conversations to Have with Employees*. Nashville, TN: Thomas Nelson, 2009.

GREEN, ALLISON, AND JERRY HAUSER. *Managing to Change the World: The Nonprofit Manager's Guide to Getting Results*. San Francisco: Jossey-Bass, 2012.

SHWALUK, LAURA, AND JERRY KEZHAYA. *Hiring a Superstar: Save Time and Money When Hiring Support Staff for Your Small Business*. Hampton: Fun Stuff LLC, 2017.

---

1 Ajay Agrawal, John McHale, and Alexander Oettl, "Why Stars Matter," *National Bureau of Economic Research Working Paper 20012*, March 2014.

2 David Siegel, "A More Humane Approach to Firing People," *Harvard Business Review*, August 21, 2018.

3 Kirk Kramer and Preeta Nayak, *Nonprofit Leadership Development: What's Your 'Plan A' for Growing Future Leaders?* (Scotts Valley, CA: CreateSpace Independent Publishing Platform, 2013).

4 Ethan R. Burris, Matthew S. Rodgers, Elizabeth A. Mannix, Michael G. Hendron, and James B. Oldroyd, "Playing Favorites: The Influence of Leaders' Inner Circle on Group Processes and Performance," *Personality and Social Psychology Bulletin* 35, no. 9 (2009): 1244–57.

LAW 14:

Win while you're sleeping.

> *People who say it takes money to make money are using the worst excuse ever. Create massive value for others by providing a solution where no other exists.*
>
> **Matt Mickiewicz (1983–)**

Matt Mickiewicz was fascinated with the idea of building websites.

The year was 1997, and Mickiewicz was fourteen years old. The internet was a budding new technology, but there wasn't much information on how to use it, let alone on how build websites. Even though he was just a kid, Mickiewicz began to spend endless hours researching and teaching himself how to create a website from scratch.

He kept excellent records, making note of useful resources and documenting the intricacies he learned. It occurred to him that there must be other people who wanted to build websites but didn't have the know-how—perhaps they could benefit from the answers he'd found and discoveries he'd made. Mickiewicz was inspired and established his first successful business, Webmaster-Resources.com. Later renamed SitePoint, the website served as a helpful resource for developers, designers, programmers, and entrepreneurs that answered questions and provided information on building and developing new websites. As more individuals and companies became reliant on SitePoint for its invaluable information, something interesting began to happen.

Designers chatting in the SitePoint forum started challenging each other to become better at their craft. They created fictitious contests to see who could design the best graphics for web use. These friendly competitions were great opportunities to practice their skills, increase their experience, and build rapport.

As designers posted their entries, other SitePoint members began to see the talent in their network. If these designers put this much time and effort into a free contest, imagine what they could create if they were designing for cash prizes!

Professionals began posting challenges for graphic design needs, and forum members submitted their work in the hopes of earning pay. What first began as a need for simple logo design and graphic elements evolved rapidly into demands for shirt designs, car wraps, wine labels, and billboards. When Mickiewicz realized the potential of this market and the need for this kind of resource, he decided to create a spinoff brand. In 2008, he established 99designs.com, a crowdsourced marketplace for graphic design projects. The company encouraged customers to submit a project description and set a contest prize amount. Then, designers could present their creations for consideration. Essentially, 99designs.com created an open invitation for bordered organizations to take advantage of the collective effort of a borderless community.[1] The organization minimized risk by letting customers see a finished product first; it also provided people with several design options while giving graphic designers opportunities to bid for work.

How has the crowdsourcing approach of 99designs.com become so successful at helping for-profit and nonprofit organizations do better work for less cost?

Mickiewicz understood that *a global team of freelancers can help ambitious leaders make the most of all twenty-four hours in a day.*

Where to Find Freelancers

Nonprofit leaders often struggle to stretch limited budgets to cover everything they need to get done. As a result, the staff members that nonprofits can afford typically wear multiple hats, often taking on responsibilities that aren't aligned with their strengths. And the budget gets the blame.

There's another way. Far-flung freelance workers who you can find online are a fairly recent innovation. They give leaders an economical and efficient way to distribute some of the nonprofit's workload to people with a real talent for the work. Instead of hiring a salaried full-time employee, you can pay an expert by the hour or by the project. There are millions of people providing freelance work in the United States, and tens of millions more around the world. But how do you find them?

Much like hiring full-time staff, it's important to work with freelancers whose values and abilities align with your mission. It's helpful to cast a wide net and then whittle down your options to the person whose skills and experience best meet your needs.[2] You might start with word-of-mouth referrals from people you trust who value your organization and won't recommend someone who would negatively impact your mission.

There are also several online resources you can use to connect with freelancers. These sites enable you to provide a price and a description of your needs and allow workers to bid on your project. This process gives you a variety of experience and talent to choose from; thus, you're more likely to receive a final product you're happy with.

Depending on your needs, you might look into the following websites for freelance workers:

- **99designs.com**—*ideal for graphic design needs.*
- **Freelancer.com**—*a popular platform for a variety of freelance projects. Have your assignments bid on or create a contest to select a winning worker.*

- **CollegeRecruiter.com**—*college students interested in entrepreneurship are a terrific resource, since they're learning the latest in industry skills and trends.*
- **Upwork.com**—*available in a variety of niche markets, these workers can handle short-term and long-term projects.*
- **Fiverr.com**— *freelancers advertise what they do (their "gig") and you reach out to them one at a time.*

On these sites you can see freelancers' profiles, explore their experience levels, and discover their pricing structures. Whether you need a graphic designer, translator, virtual assistant, or data entry specialist, freelancers can be working while you sleep to give you excellent work for as little as $5 per hour.

One of my personal favorite alternatives for finding freelancers is going straight to social media. Nearly every self-employed individual now has one or more social media accounts to promote their business.[3] Instagram makes searching for freelancers easy; hashtags such as #writersofinstagram or #emailcopywriting make it easy to find specialized talent. This works by location as well. For example, if your Chicago-based nonprofit needs an event photographer, you could search #chicagophotographer on Instagram. Not only will you find plenty of results, but you can evaluate their portfolio of work directly on their social media page.

How to Use Freelancers

The downside to these online resources is that they enable anyone to create a profile and claim to be an expert. It's important to do your research, conduct interviews, and perhaps even run a paid mini-project to get a feel for a freelancer's work. While hiring freelance workers provides new ways to reach peak performance in the face of uncertainty, it takes a fair amount of due diligence to find a gem.[4]

The first step toward using freelancers effectively is to identify freelance-friendly tasks that will advance your nonprofit's mission. My favorite question along these lines is *"What tasks would I love to have completed over the next few nights while I'm sleeping?"* Maybe it's a new one-pager you'd like to put on all the business bulletin boards around town. Or maybe it's a list of all the family foundations in your area who donate to nonprofits like yours. Or maybe it's research of other nonprofits around the country who are doing similar work to find out their fundraising best practices. The number and scope of tasks that freelancers can do for you is limited only by your creativity.

True story: I was working with an organization that fights human trafficking to develop deeper relationships with executives in large companies. Pursuing a guerilla marketing idea to reach a senior HR executive at a Fortune 50 company, I had a freelancer create an illustration of a little girl handing the executive a bouquet of flowers with a company storefront in the background. The caption read, "Thank you, Miss Donna. Thank you for saving me." We turned it into a canvas and sent it as a gift to the executive in the mail. The entire project cost less than $100.

"Thank you, Miss Donna. Thank you for saving me."

Before you hire a freelance worker, ask to see samples or a portfolio of completed projects. Here as always, be ruthlessly selective. Evaluate their work and consider contacting some of their past clients. Their candid feedback could make the difference between your next great freelancer discovery or many weeks spent spinning your wheels.

Once you've chosen a freelancer to hire, provide them with the context they need to achieve your desired outcomes. Share your company values, branding guidelines, business strategy, or any other information that would help them deliver to your expectations.[5]

Track the progress of their work through a series of milestones. By breaking a large project into smaller phases, you can ensure the quality of their work meets your standards. Consider releasing portions of the total payment as each milestone is reached. The first milestone should be small, so you can check their work before they've gone too far in the wrong direction. This enables you to make quick corrections and steer them on the right course from the start.

Once you've found a rock-star freelancer, take steps to bring them into the fold as a semi-permanent member of your team. Having a deep bench of freelancers who do great work at low cost will be an organizational asset that compounds in value rapidly over time.

Summary

Fourteen-year-old Matt Mickiewicz loved building websites from scratch, but had few resources to guide him. To help other developers, designers, and entrepreneurs, Mickiewicz created SitePoint, a website where he published his research findings. Through SitePoint's forum, designers challenged each other to fictional contests to practice their skills. As other users saw the talent in this online community, they began offering real project requests for cash prizes. Mickiewicz realized people valued freelance workers, so he created 99designs.com, where individuals could post design contests and designers could submit their contest entries. Mickiewicz understood that a fleet of freelancers can help for-profit and nonprofit leaders make the most of every hour. Freelance workers can be found on several online platforms. You can review profiles, see samples of work, and check references to find the worker that best fits your needs. Through clear project descriptions and ruthless selectivity, you can build a bench of low-cost talent that you rely upon for years.

The key to the fourteenth law of nonprofit impact—*win while you're sleeping*—is creatively leveraging freelancers to make the most of every hour of each day.

Recommended Further Reading

Coutu, Jim. *The Employer's Guide to Hiring Freelancers and Managing Outsourced Projects.* Lutz: Gator Data Press, 2013.

Mottola, Matthew, and Matthew Douglas Coatney. *The Human Cloud.* New York: HarperCollins Publishers, 2021.

Phillips, Kim Walsh. *Ultimate Guide to Instagram for Business.* Irvine, CA: Entrepreneur Press, 2017.

Smart, Geoff, and Randy Street. *Who: The Method for Hiring.* New York: Ballantine Books, 2008.

---

1 Silvia Avasilcai and Elena Galateanu, "Emerging Creative Ecosystems: Platform Development Process," *Annals of the University of Oradea: Fascicle of Management and Technological Engineering*, no.3 (December 2017).

2 Melody Barlage, Arjan van den Born, and Arjen van Witteloostuijn, "The Needs of Freelancers and the Characteristics of 'Gigs': Creating Beneficial Relations Between Freelancers and Their Hiring Organizations," *Emerald Open Research* 1, no. 8 (February 2019).

3 E. S. Bondarovich, G. G. Karlova, and V. S. Lomakina, "Instagram: Entertainment or a Source of Revenue?," *ECON: World Economy and International Business*, no. 2 (2017): 98–99.

4 Michael Solomon and Rishon Blumburg, "5 Key Ways Freelancers Help Companies Stay Nimble," *Strategic HR Review*, February 2021.

5 David Schwartz, "Embedded in the Crowd: Creative Freelancers, Crowdsourced Work, and Occupational Community," *Work and Occupations* 45, no. 3 (2018): 247–82.

LAWS OF DIVERSITY

LAW 15:

Look like your beneficiaries.

> *I know how transformational an exceptional hire can be for a team and for an organization…Each of the hires we are engaged in can and should be part of a broader organizational strategy for our clients.*
>
> **Katie Bouton (1973–)**

Katie Bouton had a plan.

In four years, she would graduate from college, move to New York City, and become a magazine editor.

At least, that's what the University of New Hampshire student told herself. She was a brand-new freshman in 1992. But soon, life began to take her down a different road. An active member of the swim team, Bouton found herself going to school full-time while training thirty hours a week. This rigorous schedule immersed her in several different communities in the school and brought her face-to-face with a diverse group of people.

Her transformation accelerated when she enrolled in an introduction to women's studies course. Bouton encountered ideas she had never imagined and had conversations about topics she had never discussed before. Bouton immediately changed her major and spent the next four years earning a degree in English, journalism, and women's studies.

The lessons she learned from her courses, as well as the experiences she had with her diverse group of friends, helped Bouton uncover a wholly redefined passion. Bouton enrolled at Towson University, where she earned a master's degree in human resource development.

After graduation, Bouton's sense of civic and women's leadership landed her a position as a human resources generalist at the Institute for Teaching and Researching on Women and the Women's Law Center of Maryland. She enjoyed working in the public sector, but her strong belief in "doing good by doing right" ultimately led her to a career of serving nonprofit organizations. There, she found a sense of fulfillment that she hadn't experienced in her previous roles.

The more Bouton interacted with nonprofits, the more she began to recognize a distinct difference in how for-profit and nonprofit organizations approached their talent and hiring strategies, and the results these differences had on staff diversity. It was clear to her that nonprofits needed the expertise and guidance of recruitment firms to ensure they were focusing on mission and culture fit in their candidate searches.

In 2004, from a small desk in the corner of her bedroom, Bouton started Koya Leadership Partners, founded on the idea that the right person in the right place can change the world. She had seen firsthand how a good hire could positively impact an organization and the lives it touched.

Koya identifies executives with successful corporate track records and matches them with nonprofits who can benefit from their expertise. By helping organizations find and retain exceptional talent, Koya helps make a positive impact on the communities their clients serve.

Why does Bouton believe so strongly in the importance of recognizing culture fit and Koya's careful placement of diverse talent for their nonprofit clients?

She understands that *a nonprofit's impact depends on its board and staff members reflecting the diverse populations they serve.*

The Data on Diversity

One of the greatest challenges nonprofits face is developing and sustaining diverse organizations. After all, a group's ability to attract, retain, and advance people from a multitude of ethnic, socioeconomic, geographic, and other kinds of backgrounds impacts the quality of talent they hire and their ability to achieve their missions.

People feel connected to an organization when they see themselves represented within it. For this reason, diversity is an important aspect for nonprofits to consider, both in the people they serve and the staff they develop. According to the most recent US Census, nearly 30% of the population is comprised of people of color; this percentage is rapidly growing.[1] Unfortunately, the nonprofit workplace isn't keeping pace with these demographic shifts.

In the nonprofit sector, this gap is most pronounced at the leadership level. More than 84% of nonprofits are led by whites.[2] This is due in large part to widespread and significant obstacles barring minorities from reaching nonprofit senior management.[3]

A lack of diversity among nonprofit organizations isn't due to a lack of interest. On the contrary, most nonprofits realize that having a diverse staff is critical to the success of the organization. The problem arises in attracting and retaining a diverse workforce.

Nonprofits experience obstacles in three main aspects of hiring new talent: *recruitment, retention,* and *prioritization.* Nonprofits find that it's nearly two to three times as challenging to recruit people of color in programs, fundraising, and other areas.[4] Recruitment challenges include:

- *Little to no access to diverse networks.*
- *Interview tactics that don't accurately portray a nonprofit's commitment to diversity.*
- *Hurried hiring process that doesn't provide time to build diverse candidate pools.*

Even after a person of color is hired at a nonprofit, they often experience injustices that cause them to leave their position.[5] High turnover rates impact organizations in manpower, morale, and the cost of filling vacancies.

For the best results, a nonprofit's commitment to diversity of all kinds (as diversity is not limited strictly to race or ethnicity) must come from its leadership. When diversity isn't a top priority, the issue isn't given the attention it deserves and resources aren't allocated to support such efforts. It takes significant top-team focus and effort to consider concepts of identity and address shortcomings in diversity.[6] A values-driven approach that recognizes the importance of diversity in a nonprofit is essential to real change that results in a nonprofit looking more like the beneficiaries it serves.

Diversity isn't just essential among a nonprofit's staff and volunteers; board members should also reflect the demographics of an organization's beneficiaries. Recent studies have shown a direct correlation between the expertise of a diverse board and the overall performance of a nonprofit.[7] After all, who better to make important decisions for the benefit of their community than people who truly understand the issues and concerns it faces?

The more varied the backgrounds of an organization's staff, volunteers, and board members, the more perspectives can positively influence a nonprofit's direction. Improved decision-making, increased creativity, and enhanced innovation all help an organization achieve its mission.

Strategies for Increasing Diversity

It's one thing to say you support diversity as a nonprofit leader. It's quite another to take real steps toward making your nonprofit team of staff, directors, and volunteers more diverse. The challenges are real and difficult. They culminate in a single, critical question:

How can my nonprofit do more this month to recruit, retain, and celebrate diversity while instilling a culture where all employees feel empowered and valued?

To build a diverse and inclusive nonprofit, we must first *maintain open communication* with candid conversations. Any time we focus on our differences, whether it be education or gender or race, discussions can grow uncomfortable to the point they feel offensive. An open conversation that welcomes the free-flowing exchange of ideas regarding issues like diversity, bias, and inclusion can help bring transparency and a general understanding to these topics.

The Race Matters toolkit developed by the Annie E. Casey Foundation provides numerous resources to kick-start such conversations. You might create a committee to coordinate trainings, guide staff conversations, or conduct organizational assessments. An objective third party can also help identify existing areas for improvement and mediate difficult conversations.

An important result from these open conversations should be an *organizational diversity statement and plan*. Much like a mission statement helps keep staff focused on the purpose of the organization, a diversity statement helps communicate your beliefs and practices to volunteers, employees, donors, and members of your community. Use this statement to address your definition of diversity, how you value diversity, your goals in relation to diversity, and how you plan to achieve those goals.

It's important to build networks and partnerships who *facilitate effective recruiting*. Identifying talent takes time and resources, so partner with people who know the community you serve and can help locate potential candidates more effectively. Explore professional associations, alumni networks, clubs, and publications.

Consider building and leveraging advisory committees of staff, volunteers, and community members to assess and execute recruiting strategies. Utilizing these champions helps form a plan and gives credibility to your diversity effort.

Make sure your *hiring process is inclusive and equitable*. Review your policies and practices to confirm they're not unintentionally insensitive, unfair, or offensive.

To avoid employee disengagement, nonprofits must abide by their values and actively work to *embrace, develop, advance, and retain their employees.* Continue to have open conversations. Conduct surveys to measure employee satisfaction and learn about areas for improvement. Stay attuned to your staff, and communicate that opportunities to advance to senior leadership positions are open to all.

Summary

Diverse friendships, new conversations, and a well-rounded education changed the trajectory of Katie Bouton's future. With a master's degree in human resources, Bouton worked in the for-profit sector before discovering her passion for nonprofits. She soon realized there were significant differences in how for-profit and nonprofit organizations approached their hiring strategies and, as a result, the diversity of their staffs. In 2004, Bouton formed Koya Leadership Partners, a recruitment agency that matches for-profit leaders with nonprofit organizations. Her goal was to create a positive hiring process that made successful matches while bridging the diversity gap in nonprofit organizations. By maintaining open conversations, developing a diversity statement/plan, facilitating effective recruiting, ensuring their hiring process is inclusive, and actively working to embrace, develop, advance, and retain employees, nonprofits can build a culture that demands diversity.

The key to the fifteenth law of nonprofit impact—*look like your beneficiaries*—is making diversity a top priority, starting with the most senior leadership of your nonprofit organization.

Recommended Further Reading

BROWN, JENNIFER. *How to Be an Inclusive Leader: Your Role in Creating Cultures of Belonging Where Everyone Can Thrive.* San Francisco: Berrett-Koehler Publishers, 2019.

BURLINGHAM, BO. *Small Giants: Companies That Choose to Be Great Instead of Big*. New York: Portfolio, 2016.

WOODS, ARTHUR. *Hiring for Diversity: The Guide to Building an Inclusive and Equitable Organization*. Hoboken, NJ: Wiley, 2021.

---

1 Robert Schwartz, James Weinberg, Dana Hagenbuch, and Allison Scott, *The Voice of Nonprofit Talent: Perceptions of Diversity in the Workplace*, Commongood Careers and Level Playing Field Institute, 2014.

2 R. Patrick Halpern, "Workforce Issues in the Nonprofit Sector," *American Humanics*, May 2006.

3 Annie E. Casey Foundation, *Change Ahead: The 2004 Nonprofit Executive Leadership and Transitions Survey*, 2004.

4 Johns Hopkins Institute for Policy Studies, *A Nonprofit Workforce Agenda: Report on Listening Post Project Roundtable on Nonprofit Recruitment and Retention*, 2008.

5 Level Playing Field Institute, *Corporate Leavers Survey*, 2007.

6 Judith Y. Weisinger, Ramón Borges-Méndez, and Carl Milofsky, "Diversity in the Nonprofit and Voluntary Sector," *Nonprofit and Voluntary Sector Quarterly* 45, no. 1 (2016): 3S–27S.

7 Erica E. Harris, "The Impact of Board Diversity and Expertise on Nonprofit Performance," *Nonprofit Management & Leadership* 25, no. 2 (2014): 113–30.

LAW 16:

You get more of what you platform.

> *If you don't have an idea that materializes and changes a person's life, then what have you got? You have talk, research, telephone calls, meetings, but you don't have a change in the community.*
>
> **Eunice Kennedy Shriver (1921–2009)**

Eunice Kennedy Shriver had had enough.

She had received not one, but two phone calls from troubled mothers in the northeast United States who could not find a summer camp for their children with intellectual disabilities. The year was 1960, and neither mainstream camps nor the public education system knew how to serve children with special needs.

Something had to be done—and soon.

Since she grew up alongside a sister with intellectual disabilities, Shriver was acutely aware of the injustices such people faced and the inhumane ways they were often treated. She had already begun devoting her life to serving as an advocate for children's health and disability issues.

As a social worker and member of the famed Kennedy dynasty, Shriver was instrumental in bringing mental health to the forefront of governmental concern. She served on government and hospital committees that paved the way for research and treatment. Shriver even urged her brother, newly elected President John F. Kennedy, to make intellectual disabilities a priority for his administration.

So when she received those phone calls from two desperate mothers, Shriver decided that she would create a summer camp for children with disabilities on her own farm in Maryland. Local schools and clinics provided her with names of potential campers. She contacted high school and college students to serve as counselors. By the time summer began, Shriver had enrolled thirty-four children, ranging in age from six to sixteen, and enlisted twenty-six counselors. The first Camp Shriver was in session.

While many of the counselors were initially hesitant about the program, everyone quickly realized these children were nothing like stereotypes that were widespread at that time. Like any child, they simply wanted to have fun—ride horses, swim, and kick soccer balls.

Word quickly spread, and local community members were invited to visit Camp Shriver. Everyone was amazed by its success and the results they could see in the campers, who were thriving on the attention and inclusion they were receiving.

Camp Shriver continued to grow and flourish for the next four years. Seeing the correlation between physical activity and improvement in learning skills, Shriver proposed a nationwide sports contest to be held for young people with disabilities.

On July 20, 1968, the first International Special Olympics Summer Games were held at Soldier Field in Chicago. Over two hundred events were offered, from softball and water polo to broad jump and swimming. The athletes were thrilled to be in an environment where they could have fun, spend time with friends, enhance their physical fitness, and test their limits.[1] The event was a huge success and widely publicized, playing a major role in changing the public's opinion about people with intellectual disabilities.

Today, Special Olympics is the world's largest sports organization for individuals with intellectual and physical disabilities. In addition to reaching 172 countries and providing year-round training and activities to five million participants, Special Olympics instills social confidence and self-esteem in its athletes.[2]

How did Camp Shriver and, ultimately, Special Olympics help to shift an entire population's opinion of individuals with disabilities?

Shriver understood that *whoever nonprofit leaders want to attract should be who they prominently feature.*

The Faces of Your Nonprofit

As I look around the present nonprofit landscape, I see far too many nonprofit leaders following their corporate counterparts as they strain to craft a signature "brand" using their own faces. It's rare to find a nonprofit leader carefully curating the nonprofit's brand through the faces of their constituents. Shriver's legacy of Special Olympics is a shining example of this approach.

Nearly every image the public ever sees related to Special Olympics shows a volunteer and an athlete sharing a moment of authentic, exultant joy. These moments exemplify the experience of practically every Special Olympics event. To their great credit, the leaders of Special Olympics predicted that the secret to getting more volunteers and athletes like those in the pictures was giving them a platform.

Unlike so many corporate and nonprofit leaders, the team at Special Olympics understands that people aren't nearly as interested in the organization's leaders as they are in the people it serves. Storytelling with real-life program participants is extremely powerful. To capitalize on this, Special Olympics partnered with ESPN on a global short-film initiative to showcase some of its participants and game-changing moments in the organization's effort to promote inclusion.[3]

Stories range from volunteers making life-changing discoveries to children overcoming stereotypes and becoming athletic superstars. Through compelling video clips, Special Olympics volunteers, coaches, parents, and athletes share their experiences in their own words and reach the nonprofit's audience on a personal level. These videos not only help build positive attitudes toward individuals with intellectual disabilities and promote inclusion, they also enable Special Olympics participants to connect with the public on a deep emotional level.

Authenticity in an organizational brand plays an important role in nonprofit engagement, from volunteerism to donor contributions.[4] By showcasing actual participants, a nonprofit can paint a clear picture of its mission, its values, and its beneficiaries. It can provide living proof of the impact its efforts and portray the difference volunteers make on individuals' lives and the community as a whole. Authenticity is a powerful tool for inspiring new support.

Through their partnership with ESPN and the Game Changers campaign, Special Olympics has increased participation by more than 172% and boosted coach certification by more than 464%.[5] When people see the tremendous impact the organization has on the lives it touches, they want to be part of that mission and become the volunteers shown in the videos and photos.

When associating with a brand, people seek to relate to the individuals they see portrayed. Given the choice between campaigns using models or everyday people, audiences tend to prefer everyday people because they are more relatable and give an organization more credibility.[6]

As a nonprofit leader, it's imperative that you take a close look at your own organization's marketing efforts—whose faces do they feature? Highlighting real beneficiaries and volunteers helps you connect with your audience and inspire them to join your efforts.

Surprise and Delight

There's something else, perhaps a bit less obvious, to learn here. The young counselors at Shriver's first backyard summer program were wary at first; they had heard that children with disabilities were "difficult" and "belligerent." The counselors had already formed an opinion about what to expect from the campers. But what they witnessed at the camp were happy, engaged children who just wanted to have fun.

The representatives from the parks department and public schools who visited had their own predetermined ideas about children with disabilities as well. They, too, were stunned by what they saw. The truth didn't need to be said. It was shown. And that's when the camp really began to catch on.

There's a pressing question here for every nonprofit leader:

What's true about your work that would surprise and delight most people?

Whatever the answer to that question is, *that* is what you should feature in your images, videos, and in-person events. For Shriver, it was the eagerness of children with disabilities to run and jump and play. What is it for your nonprofit?

People often approach nonprofits with deeply entrenched perceptual frameworks, causing them to view your organization in a static way.[7] Understanding the public's take on your mission can help guide your marketing efforts. When you can identify inaccuracies in their perceptions, you can find ways to overcome those stereotypes with delightful revelations about your impact.

For example, if you lead a homeless shelter, you may find there are many people who think of such places as full of forlorn and hopeless individuals. Perhaps the key to surprising and delighting these people is showing the good-natured, cheerful, everyday humanity of the neighbors who reside in your shelter each night.

If you lead a cancer research institute, your challenge may be the common image of sick people being poked and prodded by medical staff. You might overcome this by showing the close connections between the scientists, families, and patients who fight cancer battles together.

If you lead a home repair ministry, the public may imagine helpless individuals who can't maintain their homes. A surprising and delightful campaign could feature a volunteer praying with a hardworking single mom and her children.

No matter your unique context, there's a way to feature the work that you do in ways that are sure to surprise and delight.

Summary

A lifelong advocate of children with disabilities, Eunice Kennedy Shriver maximized her family's political influence to raise awareness about these misunderstood children. In 1960, when she learned that these children had no summer camp options, Shriver took matters into her own hands. She created Camp Shriver, opening her Maryland farm to local children with special needs. As people saw the camp's positive results, public opinion about intellectual disabilities began to change. The camp continued to grow, eventually becoming Special Olympics. Now the world's largest sports organization of its kind, Special Olympics brands itself through imagery of real-life athletes and volunteers. As a result, people relate to and connect with these stories, and they're compelled to join the efforts of the organization. As a nonprofit leader, you can win hearts and minds for your mission by identifying and featuring the truths about your work that would surprise and delight most people.

The key to the sixteenth law of nonprofit impact—*you get more of what you platform*—is advancing your cause with creatively packaged and beneficiary-focused truths.

Recommended Further Reading

DURHAM, SARAH. *Brandraising: How Nonprofits Raise Visibility and Money Through Smart Communications.* San Francisco: Jossey-Bass, 2009.

GRODZICKI, JENNA. *Eunice Kennedy Shriver: Inspiring Olympics for All.* Huntington Beach, CA: Teacher Created Materials, 2021.

SHRIVER, TIMOTHY. *Fully Alive: Discovering What Matters Most.* New York: Sarah Crichton Books, 2015.

---

1 Deborah R. Shapiro, "Participation Motives of Special Olympics Athletes," *Adapted Physical Activity Quarterly* 20, no. 2 (2003): 150–65.

2 Elisabeth M. Dykens and Donald J. Cohen, "Effects of Special Olympics International on Social Competence in Persons with Mental Retardation," *Journal of the American Academy of Child & Adolescent Psychiatry* 35, no. 2 (1996): 223–29.

3 Teri Couch, "*ESPN* and Special Olympics Launching Multimedia Initiative, Special Olympics: 50 Game Changers," ESPN, July 26, 2018.

4 Nina Michaelidou, Milena Micevski, and John W. Cadogan, "An Evaluation of Nonprofit Brand Image: Towards a Better Conceptualization and Measurement," *Journal of Business Research* 68, no. 8 (2015): 1657–66.

5 Rebecca Simon, "ESPN and Special Olympics Expand Relationship," http://www.SpecialOlympics.org, 2021.

6 Danasue Amber Remke, "The Effects of Using 'Real Women' in Advertising," master's thesis (Oklahoma State University, 2011).

7 Stephen R. Block, *Why Nonprofits Fail: Overcoming Founder's Syndrome, Fundphobia, and Other Obstacles to Success* (Hoboken, NJ: Wiley, 2003), x.

LAW 17:

Acknowledge past trauma in staff and volunteers.

> *The abduction of a child is a tragedy. No one can fully understand or appreciate what a parent goes through at such a time, unless they have faced a similar tragedy. Every parent responds differently. Each parent copes with this nightmare in the best way he or she knows how.*
>
> **John Walsh (1945–)**

It happened in broad daylight.

While running a quick errand at her local Sears department store, Florida mother Revé Walsh briefly left her six-year-old son Adam to play with a group of boys at a video game display.

When she returned, all of the boys were gone. After searching the store and desperately paging Adam over the intercom with no results, Walsh's heart filled with terror as she realized her little boy had vanished.

A police investigation helped the Walsh family piece together the events of that day. When the boys at the gaming display had scuffled over whose turn it was to play, a security guard had escorted them out of the building.

The other boys went home, leaving Adam alone in unfamiliar surroundings. He was the perfect target for an abductor.

The search for Adam lasted two agonizing weeks. Then, on August 10, 1981, partial remains were discovered in a local drainage canal. They were soon identified as those of Adam Walsh. The search became a manhunt for the boy's killer.

Thanks to eyewitness reports, the police eventually identified a suspect, a drifter with a criminal background. Although he admitted to the crime, he couldn't be convicted due to a recanted confession and lost evidence. Regardless, police were certain they had captured the man responsible for Adam's murder; the man died in prison while serving a life sentence for other crimes. The case was eventually closed.

Revé Walsh and her husband John were infuriated with the way their son's case had been handled. From the initial missing person's report to the misplacing of crucial evidence, the Walshes felt the police department had botched the entire investigation. The couple had no one to fight for them and nowhere to turn for help.

Angry and devastated, they vowed to protect other parents from a similar fate. The Walshes became strong advocates for victims of violent crimes. John created and hosted his own television show, *The Hunt with John Walsh*, and later became the host of the world-famous *America's Most Wanted*. Walsh's media success enabled him to raise much-needed awareness of the victims of violent crimes. In fact, during his time on *America's Most Wanted*, Walsh was credited with helping capture 1,100 criminals, including 17 on the FBI's Ten Most Wanted list, and reuniting 43 missing children with their families.

Across America, parents of missing children were universally frustrated by the lack of available resources and disappointed in poor coordination efforts between law enforcement and government agencies. They joined the Walshes and *America's Most Wanted* in demanding better services for missing children and their families.

On June 13, 1984, their voices were heard. Congress formed the National Center for Missing and Exploited Children (NCMEC) and established a national twenty-four-hour toll-free missing children's hotline. NCMEC assists in the search for missing children and raises awareness about preventing abductions.[1] Since its inception, the nonprofit has helped law enforcement recover more than 348,000 missing children.

How were Revé and John Walsh able to work through their unimaginable grief and help thousands of families by building NCMEC?

They realized that *hurt people hurt people, and healed people heal people.*

Start with Your Own People

As nonprofit leaders, we've stepped forward to help others during their time of need. From child mistreatment to rebuilding communities after a natural disaster, we often see people at their worst. Although there are real rewards for the work we do, they don't come without a cost.

We and our staff are continually exposed to trauma. The challenge is to ensure that this trauma doesn't debilitate our workers and volunteers, and ultimately cycle back to those we serve. Someone who has an extensive, close interaction with an individual who has suffered a terrifying event can begin to exhibit adverse reactions as if they had experienced the trauma themselves.[2] Serious care must be taken to protect your team from this secondary trauma. *Healing needs to begin inside a nonprofit and radiate outward to its beneficiaries.*

Nonprofit workers tend to be uncommonly empathetic, which puts them at a higher risk for secondary trauma and the multitude of adverse effects that go with it.[3] For your organization to build a healthier community, your workers must be resilient to the traumas of others, as well as the traumas they may have experienced in their own pasts.

Be aware of the feelings, memories, and experiences that each of your team members brings to their work. Trauma comes in many forms, and certain individual factors (e.g., race, gender, ethnicity, disability, health history, abuse history, etc.) could make some forms of trauma more likely than others. Consider how those factors could impact the people you serve and whether healing needs to play a bigger role in a team member's journey before they step forward to help others.

Proactive preparation is one of the most effective strategies a nonprofit can use to promote healing from trauma within an organization. Organizational stressors, physical stressors, and triggers from the work itself can retraumatize team members. A plan to promote resilience and healing is essential to ensure your people can continue their work without incurring long-term damage.

One frequently overlooked resource that nonprofits can provide their people is access to mental health resources. I can't imagine any board denying an executive director the latitude to include mental health benefits as part of staff health coverage or keep a counselor on retainer that staff could consult as needed. It is the responsibility of nonprofit leaders to advocate for these benefits on behalf of their people—rarely will staff or boards think to include them until asked.

Consider also creating a committee responsible for discussing and mitigating sources of trauma within the organization. Committee members can help monitor the organization's operations to ensure staff and volunteers get the support they need. Perhaps host qualified speakers who may have experience in healing from traumatic situations; their journey may be relatable for members of your team. Consider also role-playing situations so that team members feel confident they will be able to work through such situations without incurring secondary trauma.

Above all, maintain open communication and create an environment where team members feel comfortable discussing their feelings and concerns. As nonprofit leaders, we must remind ourselves that a happy, healthy team is necessary to maximize our impact.

That Includes You Too

As leaders, we often feel called to a higher standard of selflessness and sacrifice. Still, we don't have to pretend that we're impervious to harm. It's okay to *lead with a limp*—many of the best nonprofit leaders do. The trick is learning how to distinguish a limp caused by a past wound from new trauma—a *present wound*.

The idea that you can serve with passion and remain unaffected by the traumas of your beneficiaries is unrealistic. However, it's essential to remember that your attitude and adaptability serve as examples to those who look to you for leadership. The strategies you use to cope with trauma have a direct impact on your staff and volunteers.[4] Your management of stress and emotion are critical to the effectiveness and success of your organization.

Trauma is an inevitable part of life, both for our constituents and for ourselves. By creating a trauma-informed community, you can promote safety and recovery from life's adversities. Building such an organization doesn't happen overnight. Rather, it's an organic process that occurs gradually. You must first recognize that all people are vulnerable to trauma, and then organize interventions to minimize its impact on your beneficiaries, your volunteers, your staff, and yourself.

Organizations who work with individuals in pain face enormous stresses, which can cause staff members to lose sight of their mission, vision, and values.[5] The Sanctuary Model is an effective tool for such nonprofits. Created by health providers and social scientists in the early 1980s, this model creates safe, healing environments for children, adults, and families who have faced ongoing stress and hardship. The model focuses on three main components:

- *Theoretical foundations that form the basis for the model.*
- *Trauma-informed shared language that focuses on Safety, Emotion Management, Loss, and Future (SELF).*
- *A tool kit of valuable resources.*

A core part of the trauma-informed shared language is the list of Seven Sanctuary Commitments, a set of principles that guide people and organizations away from trauma-reactive behaviors.

- **Nonviolence:** *Build and model safety skills.*
- **Emotional Intelligence:** *Teach and exhibit impactful management skills.*
- **Inquiry and Social Learning:** *Build and model cognitive skills.*
- **Democracy:** *Develop and model civic skills of self-discipline, self-control, and healthy authority administration.*
- **Open Communication:** *Overcome barriers to productive conversations, refrain from acting out, implement self-correction, and teach healthy boundaries.*
- **Social Responsibility:** *Establish healthy relationships and connect with society.*
- **Growth and Change:** *Restore meaning, purpose, and hope.*[6]

The Sanctuary Model is unique in that it teaches leaders how to treat their beneficiaries and create more effective and safer organizations. When nonprofit leaders train their staff with the Sanctuary Model and the Seven Sanctuary Commitments, results include improved outcomes for beneficiaries, higher staff satisfaction, and safer work environments.

Summary

Revé and John Walsh were disgusted by law enforcement's handling of the case of their young son's abduction and murder. As a result, they became advocates for victims of violent crimes and helped establish the National Center for Missing and Exploited Children and a twenty-four-hour toll-free missing children's hotline. The Walshes coped with tragedy by advocating for systematic change that would help hundreds of thousands of families avoid the outcome they endured. The nonprofit sector is fraught with similar kinds of trauma. To ensure your empathetic workers are able to be a force for impact, healing must begin inside the nonprofit and radiate outward to its beneficiaries. As a leader, you must also assess your own well-being and coping mechanisms. While it's okay to lead with a limp, you must be able to distinguish past scars from present wounds. Consider incorporating the Sanctuary Model and its Seven Commitments into your plan for creating a trauma-informed working environment.

The key to the seventeenth law of nonprofit impact—*acknowledge past trauma in staff and volunteers*—is to radiate healing from the inside out.

Recommended Further Reading

VAN DER KOLK, BESSEL. *The Body Keeps the Score: Brain, Mind, and Body in the Healing of Trauma.* New York: Penguin, 2015.

VIVIAN, PATRICIA, AND SHANA HORMANN. *Organizational Trauma and Healing.* Scotts Valley, CA: CreateSpace, 2013.

WALSH, JOHN, WITH SUSAN SCHINDEHETTE. *Tears of Rage: From Grieving Father to Crusader for Justice: The Untold Story of the Adam Walsh Case.* New York: Pocket Books, 1997.

---

1 Cathy Nahirny, "National Center for Missing and Exploited Children: Who We Are and What We Can Do For You," *Sheriff* 52, no. 5 (2000): 20–94.

2 Ijeoma Njaka and Duncan Peacock, "Addressing Trauma as a Pathway to Social Change," *Stanford Social Innovation Review,* January 21, 2021.

3 Anthony Silard, "Interpersonal Leader Responses to Secondary Trauma in Nonprofit Human Service Organizations," *Nonprofit Management & Leadership* 30, no. 4 (2020): 635–53.

4 Jeffrey L. Brudney and Anthony Silard, "The Management of Secondary Trauma in Nonprofit Organizations," *Academy of Management Proceedings* (2018).

5 Sandra L. Bloom, "The Sanctuary Model of Trauma-Informed Organizational Change," *The Source* 16, no. 1 (2007): 12–16.

6 Nina Esaki, Joseph Benamati, Sarah Yanosy, Jennifer S. Middleton, Laura M. Hopson, Victoria L. Hummer, and Sandra L. Bloom, "The Sanctuary Model: Theoretical Framework," *Families in Society: The Journal of Contemporary Social Services* 94, no. 2 (2013): 87–95.

LAW 18:

Celebrate and elevate.

> *Acknowledging someone is an act of altruism in the first place, so converting that act of altruism into a pizza party or company fleece jacket or a gift card is fine. But it's not in keeping with the spirit in which it all began.*
>
> **Charles Best (1976–)**

As a high school student at St. Paul's School, Charles Best appeared to have it made.

The New Hampshire college preparatory boarding school had everything students could possibly want. Squash courts, art supplies, and graphing calculators were readily available. Field trips ranging across the northeastern United States gave students an education informed by firsthand experiences. In this idyllic setting, Best was inspired to become a teacher, wanting to make a difference in the lives of young people as his teachers had done for him.

After graduating from Yale in 1998, Best took a position at a newly constructed high school in the Bronx, teaching children from low-income families. Although he expected to see inequity in the school system, he was surprised to discover the school lacked funds for the most basic and essential supplies.

Best constantly used his own money to purchase materials that would help his students learn.

This wasn't a unique problem. In the teachers' lunchroom, Best and his colleagues discovered they had a mutual complaint—how much of their own personal resources were going into their students' education. The group agreed there must be a way to help students by mobilizing citizen philanthropists to fund those needs.

That's when Best had a revolutionary idea.

In 2000, he created a rudimentary website, the first version of DonorsChoose. Teachers could post simple needs like pencils and microscopes. Donors could browse posted projects and choose which ones to fund. Since the site was unproven and had no donors, Best's colleagues were skeptical. Armed with a delicious pear dessert his mother had made, Best bribed ten of his teacher friends to come up with project needs and post them to the site.

Best's aunt funded the first project. When no other donors came forward, Best anonymously funded the rest himself. His colleagues, thinking the site had worked, spread the news to other teachers and hundreds of projects were added to the site. Now all they needed were donors.

Best's students volunteered to stay after school and help contact potential donors via a letter-writing campaign. Through requests to alumni from Best's high school and college, the campaign eventually received $30,000 in donations.

In 2003, DonorsChoose garnered national attention when it was featured on the *Oprah Winfrey Show*. After the tragic events of 9/11, schools near Ground Zero had uploaded post-disaster project needs; a reporter published a one-paragraph blurb about this in *Newsweek*. Winfrey's producer saw the blurb and booked Best for the show. After it aired, DonorsChoose was flooded with thousands of people wanting to contribute. This enabled the organization to grow; today it serves schools across the country.

Best believes the key to the organization's continued success is the ability of donors to see how their dollars make a difference. When a donor funds a project, regardless of contribution level, they receive digital photos of the project and a handwritten thank-you letter from a student whose life has been impacted by their donation. To date, DonorsChoose has fulfilled more than 1.7 million classroom project requests.

How did Best help reduce financial strain on teachers and empower students to reach their maximum potential regardless of socioeconomic background?

He understood that *the best nonprofit leaders elevate diversity by celebrating wins.*

"Exciting Progress" Beats "Thank You"

While a word of gratitude is always warranted, our people are more likely to find motivation in acknowledgement of progress than in personal thanks. That's why, at some point along the way, I started replacing, "Wow, thank you for that!" with "Wow, that's really exciting progress!" After all, if there's any kind of positive reinforcement that we want motivating our people, it's not the thanks of a certain leader. That kind of reinforcement will only serve to turn our teams into boss-pleasers and approval-seekers.

Instead, we want to be positively reinforcing *impact*. Progress is powerful. Making strides in our work boosts motivation, lifts spirits, and shapes perceptions. The more frequently we experience a sense of accomplishment, the more innovative we tend to be. Even a series of *small wins* can greatly affect how we feel and perform.

Small wins enable teams to divide a large project into individual milestones, creating a more manageable workload that lends itself to frequent feelings of accomplishment. People feel good when they can chip away at a goal. Continual achievements boost confidence and generate momentum. Small milestones also help mitigate the impact of any setbacks that may occur at each checkpoint. While disappointing, these lesser failures are relatively easy to recover from. They give hope that another small win—and a step toward progress—is just over the horizon.

The power of progress is driven by the intrinsic need for *inner work life harmony*. When people are happy, have positive perceptions of their organization, and are motivated by the work they're doing, their performance improves.[1] This same concept applies to nonprofit organizations and their donors. When people are satisfied with (and motivated by) the work an organization does, they're more likely to contribute to the cause. In the case of Best's handwritten thank-you letters to donors, the gratitude was a nice sentiment. But it's really the digital photos of the contribution's impact on progress—the small, visible wins—contained within that letter that resonate with donors and positively reinforce the impulse to give.

Although progress is a fundamental need, few leaders understand how to use it as a motivational tool. It isn't enough for your team to simply achieve small wins; you as their leader must also *celebrate those wins*. Acknowledgment of each step forward, no matter how small the victory, is a catalyst for continued success.

Most managers believe recognition is the key motivator for their workers. Nonprofit leaders have more impact on productivity and success rates than we realize. Understanding how to nurture progress internally is essential to the external impact of your nonprofit. By celebrating small wins, you can positively affect your team members' morale, creativity, and productivity.

As a leader, you can help nourish these feelings by acknowledging the accomplishments and progress your workers are making. Celebrate the small wins. "Ring the bell."

Celebration and Diversity

What does celebration have to do with diversity? Everything. Nonprofit teams are diverse groups of people. When you publicly celebrate the wins of new hires, introverted team members, minorities, and other members of your team who are more likely to be seen as "the other," you accomplish two things at once. First, you reinforce the effort and innovation it took to secure the win. The entire team learns that it's okay to take calculated risks to enhance the organization's impact. Second, the organizational culture begins to identify inclusion with winning. *An integral part of what makes winning possible here at so-and-so nonprofit is the opportunity for people from very different backgrounds to contribute.* When this becomes your nonprofit's ethos, diversity and inclusion quickly come alive as shared values.

Diversity of backgrounds and viewpoints is essential to a nonprofit's overall success. After all, everyone on your team has something to contribute. An experience, a skill, a cultural understanding—something unique that helps serve your beneficiaries in a way that you alone cannot. However, building a diverse workplace will not automatically boost your organization's performance.[2] Simply hiring specific demographics to meet a quota may increase the diversity of your team, but will typically lead to high turnover rates and diminished productivity.[3] To truly maximize the multitude of benefits a diverse workplace brings, you must shift your organization's culture and power structure, and be open to the strengths and skills of everyone on your staff. Celebrating the accomplishments of your team members who are at risk of being seen as outsiders helps build the kind of culture that associates inclusion with impact.

A nonprofit leader who elevates and celebrates everyone not only creates a better work culture and environment, but also casts a wider net for volunteers and donors. Their nonprofit attracts a more diverse range of people who could benefit from their services, creating more opportunities for small wins, celebration, and overall impact.

Summary

After lamenting with his fellow high school teachers about personally funding basic supplies for their classrooms, Charles Best developed a website where teachers could post project-need requests. Individuals and organizations could browse the projects and choose which to support. Now a nationally recognized nonprofit, DonorsChoose has fulfilled more than

1.7 million classroom project requests. Each donor who contributes any amount receives digital photos of the project and a handwritten thank-you note from a student who has been helped by their donation. Similarly, the best nonprofit leaders elevate diversity by celebrating wins. While words of gratitude may feel nice in the moment, long-term motivation in a nonprofit context comes from steady affirmations of progress. Celebrating the small wins provides positive reinforcement for desired actions and builds exciting momentum. By making a point of celebrating the wins of those at most risk of exclusion, nonprofit leaders can infuse their nonprofits' culture with an ethos that associates inclusion with impact.

The key to the eighteenth law of nonprofit impact—*celebrate and elevate*—is constantly finding ways to "ring the bell."

Recommended Further Reading

AMABILE, TERESA M., AND STEVEN J. KRAMER. *The Progress Principle: Using Small Wins to Ignite Joy, Engagement, and Creativity at Work.* Boston: Harvard Business Review Press, 2011.

COYLE, DANIEL. *The Culture Code: The Secrets of Highly Successful Groups.* New York: Bantam Books, 2018.

GALLAGHER, B. J. *A Peacock in the Land of Penguins: A Fable About Creativity and Courage.* San Francisco: Berrett-Koehler Publishers, 2015.

---

1 Teresa M. Amabile and Steven J. Kramer, "The Power of Small Wins," *Harvard Business Review*, May 2011.

2 Robin J. Ely and David A. Thomas, "Getting Serious About Diversity: Enough Already with the Business Case," *Harvard Business Review*, December 2020.

3 Tom Astikainen, "Diversity Management and Team Leadership in a Nonprofit Organization," PhD diss., (Lappeenranta University of Technology, 2006).

*LAWS OF
LEADERSHIP*

LAW 19:

Eat last and get dirty.

> *I am not sure exactly what heaven will be like, but I know that when we die and it comes time for God to judge us, he will not ask, "How many good things have you done in your life?" Rather, he will ask, "How much love did you put into what you did?"*
>
> **Mother Teresa (1910–97)**

While surrounded by utter chaos, Mother Teresa had a distinct moment of transcendent clarity.

Since the age of twelve, she had dreamed of becoming a missionary. Her lifelong journey toward this goal had brought her to Calcutta, where she was extremely concerned by the area's widespread poverty.

In 1943, conditions took a devastating turn with the Bengal famine; almost three million people died of malaria, starvation, and lack of sanitary conditions and proper healthcare. In addition to misery and death, the famine brought violence to the community.

During this tumultuous time Mother Teresa decided to leave her position as a teacher at the Loreta Convent School and go help the poor. She offered no explanation other than she was heeding an inner call from God. Mother Teresa received approval for her resignation, and her mission work began.

Mother Teresa formed Missionaries of Charity, a congregation that cared for people who were disabled, blind, diseased, and shunned by society. They created a hospice to provide free care for the poor and founded an orphanage for the increasing number of homeless children. Word spread about Mother Teresa's work, and donations and support began to pour in. The congregation was able to help more people in India and branch out to other countries.

Today, Missionaries of Charity has a member community in the thousands, and serves communities in more than one hundred countries. Mother Teresa was a humble, yet powerful, world-leading humanitarian who received numerous awards, including the Nobel Peace Prize. She was canonized in 2016 by the Roman Catholic Church as Saint Teresa, and to this day is recognized around the world as a symbol of selflessness and charity.

How did a little girl with a passion for helping others grow up to impact the lives of millions of the world's most impoverished people?

She understood that *leadership is a delicate interplay between self-sacrifice and command.*

Work Martyrs

Team members who have a strong work ethic are essential to any organization's success. However, according to some, there is a fine line between loyalty and martyrdom. A number of authors and commentators have coined the term "work martyrs" to refer to people who, in their eyes, are willing to unnecessarily suffer for their work.

Critics of work martyrs claim that their efforts go to an unhealthy extreme, which can lead to bitterness, resentment, and burnout in the workplace.[1] We're told that work martyrs believe they can't take a day off from work, that they want to be seen as the first to arrive and the last to leave. Some have gone so far as to say that work martyrs are ruining workplaces, industries, countries, and entire societies.[2]

Supposedly work martyrs egotistically think they're the glue that holds the organization together, and they won't entrust tasks to others for fear they won't be done correctly. Opponents of so-called work martyrdom claim this attitude damages feelings of teamwork and equality in the workplace, not to mention destroys trust among coworkers.

Critics claim further that, while dedication is an admirable trait, an individual who feels they need to be constantly available for work doesn't have healthy work-life balance. When a worker is glued to their phone and replies to emails at all hours of the night, the argument goes, they're not sufficiently prioritizing their own personal needs. This unhealthy behavior, it is argued, can lead to negative feelings about the organization and degrade its overall impact.[3]

Pressfield's Leonidas

When it comes to nonprofit leadership, I reject entirely the polemic against work martyrdom.

Leaders have a moral imperative to eat last. To carry the heaviest load. To wake up earliest, open the front doors first, and depart after the rest of the team has gone home.

Are there leaders who operate "successfully" without doing these things? Of course, just as there are wealthy people who accumulate their riches by theft.

Bad winners don't change the definition of good leadership. For the nonprofit leader, work martyrdom isn't something to fix, but something to embrace.

I recognize that this is a controversial position. One of my favorite books on leadership may help illustrate my point.

In Steven Pressfield's historical novel *Gates of Fire* (1999), a Greek prisoner recounts the story of the Battle of Thermopylae, when a few hundred Spartans made their final stand against a vast Persian army. King Leonidas, the head of the Spartan army, understood the value of leading by example.

In preparation for the great battle to come, Leonidas discovered that the Phocian Wall, which was paramount to their defense strategy, lay in ruins.

Engineers and draftsmen assessed the situation. Diagrams were sketched in the dirt; one captain even produced a drawn-to-scale blueprint for the wall's reconstruction. As they discussed, debated, and disagreed about the best way to rebuild the wall, the aging soldier-king stepped forward. Pressfield writes,

> Leonidas simply picked up a boulder and marched to a spot. There he set the stone in place. He lifted a second and placed it beside the first. The men looked on dumbly as their commander in chief, whom all could see was well past sixty, stooped to seize a third boulder.
>
> Someone barked: "How long do you imbeciles intend to stand by, gaping? Will you wait all night while the king builds the wall himself?"
>
> With a cheer, the troops fell to. Nor did Leonidas cease from his exertions when he saw other hands joined to labor, but continued alongside the men as the pile of stones began to rise into a legitimate fortress...
>
> The king stripped, and worked alongside his warriors, shirking nothing, but pausing to address individuals, calling by name those he knew, committing to memory the names and even nicknames of others heretofore unknown to him, often clapping these new mates upon the back in the manner of a comrade and friend.

It was astonishing with what celerity these intimate words, spoken only to one man or two, were relayed warrior-to-warrior down the line, filling the hearts of all with courage.[4]

While others "led" with words, Leonidas led with sweat and toil.

A willingness to get your hands dirty and take the first step toward impact is essential to world-changing nonprofit leadership. Nonprofit leaders face a set of unique challenges that for-profit companies don't experience. For instance, you oversee both paid and unpaid people who serve your mission. Many for-profit workers are motivated enough by salary to perform their duties. In nonprofits, leaders must find additional ways to encourage their team members. This often means making significant (perhaps what some would consider extreme) sacrifices alongside your staff and volunteers.

By sharing the workload, Leonidas compelled others to work together for the greater good. In describing him to the king of the Persians, the story's narrator offers the following description:

> A king does not abide within his tent while his men bleed and die upon the field. A king does not dine while his men go hungry, nor sleep when they stand at watch upon the wall. A king does not command his men's loyalty through fear nor purchase it with gold; he earns their love by the sweat of his own back and the pains he endures for their sake. That which comprises the harshest burden, the king lifts first and sets down last.
>
> A king does not require service of those he leads but provides it to them. He serves them, not they him...A king does not expend his substance to enslave men, but by his conduct and example makes them free.[5]

As nonprofit leaders, we lead, inspire, and show our team members that we don't ask anything of them that we don't first do ourselves. When we take the initiative and put forth the effort we expect from our team, we show ourselves worthy of the label "leader." This identity becomes relationally recognized and endorsed by all who are fortunate enough to serve alongside such a leader.[6] People will follow a strong and sacrificial figure who leads by example.

Summary

When Mother Teresa received a message from God that instructed her to leave her teaching position and serve the poor by living among them, she obeyed. Following her faith led her to create the Missionaries of Charity. During her sacrificial life, she served countless poor and underprivileged people all over the world. Her life's work was successful because she understood that leadership is a delicate interplay between self-sacrifice and command. Throughout the years, some critics have come up with the negative idea of "work martyrdom." By prioritizing work above all else, critics claim, work martyrs create negative workplace environments and damage relationships with colleagues. As nonprofit leaders, we shouldn't see work martyrdom as something to be eradicated in ourselves, but rather, something to be embraced. Like Mother Teresa and Pressfield's King Leonidas, when we lead by unspoken example and work tirelessly and humbly alongside our teams, we inspire greatness and deep devotion.

The key to the nineteenth law of nonprofit impact—*eat last and get dirty*—is to reject the prevailing narcissism of the present age in favor of a life of self-sacrifice.

Recommended Further Reading

Robbins, Mike. *We're All in This Together: Creating a Team Culture of High Performance, Trust, and Belonging.* Carlsbad, NM: Hay House Business, 2020.

Simler, Kevin. *The Elephant in the Brain: Hidden Motives in Everyday Life.* Oxford: Oxford University Press, 2018.

Spink, Kathryn. *Mother Teresa: An Authorized Biography.* San Francisco: HarperOne, 2011.

---

1 Edwin A. Locke and Ellen Kenner, "Burnout and the Battle for Your Own Happiness," in *Coping, Personality and the Workplace: Responding to Psychological Crisis and Critical Events*, ed. Alexander-Stamatios Antoniou and Cary L. Cooper, 83–102 (London: Routledge, 2016).

2 Brigid Schulte, "Are You a 'Work Martyr?,'" *Washington Post*, August 24, 2014.

3 Beth Kanter and Aliza Sherman, "Updating the Nonprofit Work Ethic," *Stanford Social Innovation Review*, September 22, 2016.

4 Steven Pressfield, *Gates of Fire: An Epic Novel of the Battle of Thermopylae* (New York: Bantam, 1999), 304–5.

5 Pressfield, *Gates of Fire*, 492–93.

6 D. Scott DeRue and Susan J. Ashford, "Who Will Lead and Who Will Follow? A Social Process of Leadership Identity Construct in Organizations, *Academy of Management Review* 35, no. 4 (2010): 627–47.

LAW 20:

Embody the nonprofit's values.

> *To be alone as a pioneer, like we were, was difficult. My strategy was not only to help the people, or transform the world, but to do both.*
>
> Bernard Kouchner (1939–)

French doctor Max Recamier was shocked and disturbed by the images on his television.

The Nigerian Civil War of 1968 had culminated with Federal Government troops blockading the province of Biafra. The ensuing stalemate led to severe famine. The media flooded television screens across the globe with images of children dying from starvation.

France, a chief supporter of Biafra, recognized this as a major crisis; the French Red Cross desperately needed volunteers. The Red Cross knew Dr. Max Recamier from previous missions, and reached out to him for help. The first person Recamier recruited was Bernard Kouchner, a doctor so young he hadn't even completed his required thesis. Four other medical personnel volunteered to join the mission, but Recamier and Kouchner were the only doctors.

Nothing could have prepared them for the horrors they experienced in Nigeria.

The war was a much bloodier conflict than many had realized. Civilians were being murdered and starved by the blockading forces. In addition to treating malnourished citizens, the Red Cross medical team was forced to conduct war surgery in makeshift hospitals while under constant attack by the Nigerian armed forces.

Recamier and Kouchner felt the world needed to know what was really happening in Biafra.

On video and in writing, they voiced their condemnation of the Nigerian government and the Red Cross for their complicity in the violence. Over the next three years, Biafran doctors joined, sharing their own concerns. This outcry laid the foundation for a new form of humanitarianism that disregarded political or religious boundaries and placed the needs of people first.

As these doctors worked to form an emergency medical response group, two journalists announced their desire to establish a band of doctors to help those suffering in the wake of major disasters. The Biafran doctors knew this was their chance to provide experience and education about war surgery, public health, and triage medicine. They believed that all people had the right to medical care, and as such, the needs of desperate people should outweigh the restrictions of national borders.

On December 22, 1971, Doctors Without Borders (Médecins Sans Frontières) was founded by Jacques Bérès, Philippe Bernier, and ten additional French doctors and journalists. The organization consisted of three hundred volunteer doctors, nurses, medical staff, and journalists. Their first assignment was to assist the people of Managua after an earthquake devastated the Nicaraguan capital and killed tens of thousands of people. Soon after, the organization helped Hondurans recover from Hurricane Fifi and created a large-scale medical program during the Cambodian refugee crisis of 1975.

Today, Doctors Without Borders employs more than 30,000 people in 28 countries around the world. The organization has treated over 100 million patients, maintains its financial and institutional independence, and upholds a critical view of itself and the broader aid system with the sole purpose of providing timely and effective aid to those who most need it, wherever they may be.

How did Recamier and Kouchner, two doctors thrust into horrific war-torn conditions, help to establish a medical aid organization that has assisted millions of people worldwide?

They believed that leading means *becoming the living embodiment of the values you claim to espouse.*

Values Lived Big

From time to time, leaders have an opportunity to embody their values on a grand stage. Long after the fact, memories of these moments continue to evoke feelings of solemn remembrance, even awe. Lincoln at Gettysburg. MLK at Selma. Christ on the cross. Most of the world's great movements can point to one or more symbolic moments that encapsulate the leader's journey, their cause, and their values.

As a nonprofit leader, this is one of the few activities that you can't delegate to anyone else—it has to be you. You must be the one to testify before Congress. To march at the head of the protest. To write the open letter advocating on behalf of your beneficiaries.

How will you recognize a high-potential opportunity to embody your values in a big way? *If it scares you.* There's always a cost, always a sacrifice. A significant part of what makes such moments so awe-inspiring years, decades, or even centuries after the fact is the high price willingly paid by the leader.

Examples of opportunities to live your values in a big way include:

- *Television or podcast interview with a national audience*
- *Global, national, or local crisis (e.g., pandemic, terror attack, hurricane)*
- *Scandal involving your nonprofit organization or sector*
- *Difficult staff, board, or volunteer situation warranting their removal*
- *Event that draws focus to your city (e.g., political convention, Olympics)*

- *Fundamental disagreement with the direction of national or global headquarters*
- *Tragedy in your personal life that pulls you away from work*
- *Major fundraising setback (e.g., loss of a key donor, event cancellation)*
- *Situation when a team member makes a high-profile mistake*
- *Public criticism from a high-profile source (e.g., organization's founder)*
- *Opportunity to take a stand for diversity and inclusion*
- *Situation when the entire board disagrees with something you know is right*
- *Meeting with a state or federal official with a platform to drive major change*
- *Major anniversary of the organization's founding*
- *Launch of a capital campaign with an ambitious goal*
- *Conversation with a major donor about a record-setting gift*

Note that some of the above might be considered *crisis moments*. Various sources are credited with a quote that sums up the matter nicely: "Let no crisis go to waste." Crisis moments are opportunities to remain calm, remember your values, and act accordingly. These are moments when people on all sides will counsel expediency and equivocation; few or none will advise you to take the harder and often more transparent road. Leaders worth following choose the harder right over the easier wrong in moments like these.

Another subgroup of the above list might be labeled *grand-slam moments*. It's the bottom of the ninth inning, the bases are loaded, and the pitcher hangs one out over the plate in slow motion. *CRACK!* A grand-slam moment is a once-in-a-lifetime opportunity to capitalize on a wonderful confluence of careful planning, hard work, and good fortune. Train yourself to look for these moments, especially when things are going well. Great nonprofit leaders act decisively when the moment is right to seize a colossal win from a favorable situation.

Values Lived Small

The embodiment of values isn't limited to events of high drama. Television appearances, public marches, and major awards may be the stuff of Wikipedia pages, but the stuff of legendary nonprofit leadership often rests in the tiniest of details that (often accidentally) become a celebrated part of an organization's sacred lore.

Examples abound. A volunteer driving by the warehouse sees the founder's car in the parking lot because she's doing warehouse inventory by herself in the middle of the night. A churchgoer looks out her car window and sees her pastor ministering to a homeless family in a superstore parking lot. An executive director notices in database notes that the development director has persuaded twenty of her friends and family members to donate $25 per month to the organization. The urban legends sparked by stories like these may never make headlines. But the bigger, splashier moments that do receive attention probably owe their existence to the culture created by the subtleties of *values lived small*.

In founding Doctors Without Borders, Recamier and Kouchner didn't set out to launch a movement. They simply wanted others to know the truth about what was happening in Nigeria, so they did what they felt was right. They spoke out publicly against the government.[1] They had no way of knowing that other people felt the same way and would also speak up. A large social movement grew from their small act, because they believed desperate and suffering people should receive medical care regardless of their geography, religion, or socioeconomic status.

In 1999, Doctors Without Borders received the Nobel Prize for its pioneering humanitarian work on several continents. Recamier and Kouchner didn't foresee earning accolades and prizes. Their accidental movement created awareness of the need for social action and forged a global community that united individuals, governments, non-governmental organizations, and international institutions.[2]

You want to change the world? Start by picking up the scrap of trash on the sidewalk in the community where you serve. Not so that someone will see you do it (though they may)—do it because you *are* the leader who lives out your values, all the way down to the smallest of acts.

Summary

When doctors Max Recamier and Bernard Kouchner volunteered to care for the sick and injured during the Nigerian Civil War, they were shocked by the horrific injustices that civilians were experiencing. The two men spoke out about what they witnessed, and soon other doctors joined their outcry. They shared the belief that all people everywhere had the right to medical care. With the help of two journalists, the group of medical professionals formed Doctors Without Borders (Médecins Sans Frontières). From natural disasters to armed conflicts, the organization has treated over one hundred million patients around the world. By holding firm to their values, Recamier, Kouchner, and their successors have provided timely and effective aid to those who need it most, wherever they may be. Nonprofit leaders must embody their organization's values through action. Whether in big, high-profile ways or small, internally inspiring ways, effective nonprofit leaders are ever-mindful that the world is watching.

The key to the twentieth law of nonprofit impact—*embody the nonprofit's values*—is a lifestyle of large and small values-driven actions.

Recommended Further Reading

Fox, Renee C. *Doctors Without Borders: Humanitarian Quests, Impossible Dreams of Médecins Sans Frontières*. Baltimore: Johns Hopkins University Press, 2015.

Huetteman, Lisa. *The Value of Core Values: Five Keys to Success Through Values-Centered Leadership*. St. Petersburg: BookLocker Publishing, 2012.

STEARNS, RICHARD. *Lead Like it Matters to God: Values-Driven Leadership in a Success-Driven World.* London: InterVarsity Press, 2021.

---

1 Renee C. Fox, "Medical Humanitarianism and Human Rights: Reflections on Doctors Without Borders and Doctors of the World," *Social Science & Medicine* 41, no. 22 (1995): 1607–16.

2 Robert Dechaine, "Humanitarian Space and the Social Imaginary: Médicins Sans Frontières/Doctors Without Borders and Rhetoric of Global Community," *Journal of Communication Inquiry* 26, no. 4 (2002).

LAW 21:

Know your people.

> *Love and my best intentions have gotten me in a lot of trouble in my life, but they also brought me to create Gone West, a tree-planting company made by the planters and for the planters. Anyone with a passion is welcome to join. Even if they have no money or experience. If they want to plant, we will make it happen.*
>
> **James Hughes**

James Hughes was living in his van.

An experienced logger in the United Kingdom, Hughes had just started his own tree-planting company and was struggling to get his business off the ground. Friends had laughed at him when he'd told them his plan. They said he'd "gone west," a British expression meaning he'd gone crazy. So that's what he named his new business—Gone West. But he was starting to think maybe his friends were right.

Hughes, who didn't have much experience in this particular field, was having difficulty securing new contracts. To make ends meet, he reluctantly accepted jobs from large timber companies that paid him a daily wage to plant trees. Hughes would hire his friends to help him with these jobs, which significantly impacted his profit and left no room to expand his company. Something had to give.

In 2015, after completing a planting project for a timber company during harsh winter weather, Hughes had nearly twenty extra trees. He took them to a well-known market in Glasgow and sold each tree for whatever price people felt was fair. He sold every tree. That's when he realized he could make a profit by selling the trees he planted directly to companies that wanted to offset their carbon footprints.

By focusing on sustainability, Hughes developed exclusive partnerships with ecologically conscious businesses that enabled Gone West to engage in conservation work. Rapid growth followed, and soon Hughes was ready to expand his team. First, he hired Jakub Sutory, a planter who believed in Gone West's environmental work.

Sutory had serious concerns about the environmental effects of the pesticides Gone West used to treat their trees. Hughes listened to Sutory's argument and agreed that they wouldn't do business with companies who wouldn't allow them to plant without pesticides. Hughes promoted Sutory to Gone West's operational manager of forestry services. As business continued to grow across communities and companies around the world, Hughes realized Gone West needed more help.

At the same time, Collin O'Mara, president and CEO of the National Wildlife Federation, was working to solve another problem. The International Labour Organization had reported a serious unemployment issue among America's youth. O'Mara hoped to resurrect a federal program from the 1930s, President Franklin D. Roosevelt's Civilian Conservation Corps, also known as the Tree Army, which employed 3.4 million American youths to plant billions of trees. The program was intended to salvage two of the country's most valuable resources: its land and its youth.[1]

Although the revival wasn't taking hold in America, Hughes loved the idea. Instead of asking people to volunteer their time and expertise, Gone West hires young people who need work and teaches them about the tree-planting profession. Since adopting the program in 2015, Gone West has employed more than two hundred young people and planted more than five million trees.

How did Hughes go from living in his van to building a company powered by a Tree Army that gives back to the environment as well as society?

He recognized that *the best leaders tailor their approach to their people's personalities, histories, and love languages.*

Personality Profiles

To foster an organizational culture that promotes team-driven impact, nonprofit leaders must understand the people they work with. This means calibrating one's leadership approach to each team member's unique personality.

There are, of course, a wide range of options for classifying different personality types. One of the more popular frameworks is known as the Big Five. Using the acronym OCEAN, the framework identifies five components of personality with two options for each component.

- **Openness to experience:** *curious vs. cautious*
- **Conscientiousness:** *organized vs. careless*
- **Extraversion:** *outgoing vs. reserved*
- **Agreeableness:** *friendly vs. critical*
- **Neuroticism:** *nervous vs. confident*

The Big Five framework can be a helpful tool for identifying and understanding the personalities of the people you work with.[2] Knowing someone's profile can reveal their preferred learning styles, which can be important for training purposes, and help you determine whether they would be a good fit for particular roles within your organization. While someone's profile doesn't necessary tell their whole story, it does provide a helpful shorthand for interacting with them in a personality-informed way.

The Myers-Briggs Type Indicator (MBTI) is another way to assess personalities. This framework places people on a spectrum according to four dichotomies:

- **(E)xtraversion vs. (I)ntroversion:** *Do you recharge being with many people or few/none?*
- **(S)ensing vs. i(N)tuition:** *Do you focus on the details or do you reflect more broadly?*
- **(T)hinking vs. (F)eeling:** *Do you more naturally favor reason or emotion in decisions?*
- **(J)udging vs. (P)erceiving:** *Do you tend to go by the book or take more improvisational approach?*[3]

Preferences within these dichotomies (which may be slight or great, depending on the person) result in one of sixteen distinct personality types. (In case you're curious, I'm an INTJ.) One of the advantages of MBTI as a personality assessment tool is that the relatively low number of types—only sixteen—has given rise to an enormous amount of literature about how one type interacts with the other fifteen. From workplace dynamics to sports teams to romantic relationships, MBTI offers the careful student of personalities a chance to interact with others in considerably more informed ways.

Histories

Of course, a person's identity consists of far more than their personality. Their unique history from infancy to the present has shaped them in many ways, perhaps some of which they themselves don't yet fully understand. By understanding a person's backstory, we gain insight into the behaviors they exhibit, decisions they make, and things they prefer. In addition, a person's past contains moments that powerfully shape—for good or for ill—their view of themselves and the world around them.

As a nonprofit leader, it's important to know the histories of your staff, board, and key volunteers. Memories of past negative experiences can affect how they respond to beneficiaries and colleagues. Understanding their positive experiences is just as useful; learning about tools or resources that have benefited them or ideas they've had that yielded positive results can fuel your nonprofit's impact in the present.

With requisite gentleness and deference to their willingness to share, you can learn a lot about a person by asking a few open-ended questions.

- *What was your home like as a child?*
- *Growing up, what school activities or sports did you participate in?*
- *What world event most significantly impacted you in your youth?*
- *How did you choose your career?*
- *What accomplishment are you most proud of?*
- *What's the one thing you most want people to remember about you?*

These questions are of course helpful for team members, but you should seek to gain more insight into the histories of the beneficiaries you serve as well. By understanding their journeys, you can better identify ways to meet their needs in the present, and perhaps even learn insights useful for preventing others from future suffering.

Histories are stories, and storytelling and story-listening are critical to establishing the deep connections necessary to make a difference in people's lives.[4] Understanding histories helps employees, communities, beneficiaries, and donors remember what's so easy to forget in the busy thrum of life: that all of us began as children, all experienced hurt, and all need grace.

Love Languages

Whatever a person's personality or history may be, they likely have another dimension to their identity that's important to learn, namely the way they receive love. Renowned researcher and author Dr. Gary Chapman approached his relationship studies with the simple thesis that all relationships grow better through mutual understanding. His research revealed that people give and receive love in different, yet categorizable, ways. By gaining insight into these differences and acting accordingly, he found, people can more effectively express their love for each other.

Dr. Chapman developed five categories or "love languages" according to which people give and receive love:

- *Words of affirmation*
- *Acts of service*
- *Receiving gifts*
- *Quality time*
- *Physical touch*

In the workplace, and especially in the nonprofit sector, love can be equated with *appreciation* for who someone is and what they're contributing. Motivation for our work is strongly correlated with appreciation shown in a way that aligns with our preferred love language.[5] Feeling valued and cared for in the ways we receive it best unlocks in us new levels of motivation and performance. At an organizational level, a team appreciating its' members in ways aligned with each person's love language can achieve significantly higher impact.

No two people are the same, and that includes the ways individuals prefer to receive appreciation. Love languages help identify which rewards might motivate people and which aren't as meaningful. For instance, giving a pat on the back to someone whose love language is "acts of service" may not result in the desired effect. While that individual may register your effort, it may not result in as big a boost in motivation compared to, say, taking out their office trash or clearing snow off their car.

It's a nonprofit leader's responsibility to keep the organization running and maintain a cohesive, high-impact workforce. When we understand how our workers prefer to receive appreciation, we can create a positive environment where team members expend more of what psychologists call *discretionary energy*—the energy that an employee chooses to exert or not exert in service to their team or clients at work. Unleashing a group's discretionary energy is one of the most important ways that nonprofit leaders can drive world-changing impact.[6]

Summary

When professional tree-planter James Hughes was struggling to launch his new business, he discovered a client base that was interested in minimizing their carbon footprint. By recognizing this trait in businesses and communities worldwide, Hughes shifted his approach and grew Gone West into a successful enterprise. He soon hired Jakub Sutory, who voiced concerns about the environmental effects of the pesticides they used. Hughes agreed to work only with businesses who agreed to refrain from pesticides. The organization's success enabled Hughes to revitalize Roosevelt's Tree Army by providing out-of-work youths with employment and education. Following Hughes's example, it's important that nonprofit leaders know their people. This includes team members, volunteers, donors, and beneficiaries.

The keys to the twenty-first law of nonprofit impact—*know your people*—are identifying their personality profile, learning about their histories, and knowing their love language of appreciation.

Recommended Further Reading

ALEXANDER, BENJAMIN F. *The New Deal's Forest Army: How the Civilian Conservation Corps Worked.* Baltimore, MD: Johns Hopkins University Press, 2018.

CHAPMAN, GARY. *Life Lessons and Love Languages: What I've Learned on My Unexpected Journey.* Chicago: Moody Publishers, 2021.

HOWARD, PIERCE J., and Jane Mitchell Howard. *The Owner's Manual for Personality at Work: How the Big Five Personality Traits Affect Your Performance, Communication, Teamwork, Leadership, and Sale.* Portland: Bard Press, 2000.

---

1 Jerrell H. Shofner, "Roosevelt's 'Tree Army': The Civilian Conservation Corps in Florida," *The Florida Historical Quarterly* 65, no. 4 (1987): 433–56.

2 Deborah A. Cobb-Clark and Stefanie Schurer, "The Stability of Big-Five Personality Traits," *Economics Letters* 115, no. 1 (2012): 11–15.

3 Marcia Carlyn, "An Assessment of the Myers-Briggs Type Indicator," *Journal of Personality Assessment* 41, no. 5 (1977): 461–73.

4 Mary McInerney, "How Nonprofits Can Use Storytelling and Engagement Metrics to Improve How They Share Their Philanthropy Narrative," PhD diss., (University of San Francisco, 2018).

5 Gary Chapman and Paul White, *The 5 Love Languages of Appreciation in the Workplace: Empowering Organizations by Encouraging People* (Chicago: Northfield Publishing, 2019).

6 Janice T. S. Ho, Jirong Huang, and Shakifur Rahman Chowdhury, "The Conditions for Discretionary Energy: Implications for Organizational Business Performance," *Academy of Management Proceedings* 2018, no. 1 (2018).

LAW 22:

Have a grand narrative.

> *The Innocence Project is about freeing as many innocent people as possible, addressing systemic issues, and giving back life and liberty.*
>
> **Peter Neufeld (1950–)**

In 1983, Marion Coakley was in serious trouble.

A jury had just found the mentally disabled twenty-eight-year-old guilty of robbery and rape, and a judge had sentenced him to fifteen years in prison.

There was just one major problem: Coakley was innocent.

Supported by several reliable witnesses, Coakley had a solid alibi. Plus, there were distinct differences between his appearance and that of the man witnesses had observed at the crime scene. Regardless, Coakley had been convicted, and there was little he could do to secure his freedom.

Public defenders Barry Scheck and Peter Neufeld of the Legal Aid Society in the Bronx received word about Coakley's predicament. Fascinated with the intersection of science and criminal justice, the lawyers had been studying a new, state-of-the-art method of assessing crime scenes and proving innocence using DNA. After all, they surmised, if DNA technology could prove people guilty of crimes, perhaps it could also prove their innocence.

In 1986, Scheck and Neufeld appealed Coakley's case. Even though biological evidence from that particular crime had been lost after the conviction, Scheck and Neufeld were able to use other means of testing to compare the rapist's DNA profile to Coakley's. Their tests determined that they did not match. Coakley was proven innocent. With no further evidence to consider, Coakley was released and compensated with $450,000 from the New York Court of Claims.

Seeing how effective DNA technology had been in proving Coakley's innocence, Scheck and Neufeld realized the potential of correcting the speculations and subjectivity of the American criminal justice system with hard science.[1] Coakley was only one case of wrongful conviction—how many more people's freedom could be secured through DNA testing?

In 1992, Scheck and Neufeld founded the Innocence Project at the Benjamin N. Cardozo School of Law in New York to provide legal aid to people who had been wrongfully convicted, reform the criminal justice system, and help capture the actual perpetrators.

As word spread about Scheck and Neufeld's work, a small team of volunteers, students, and lawyers joined their cause. Tackling groundbreaking legal cases to exonerate innocent individuals, the Innocence Project became a nonprofit in 2004. The first of its kind, the organization faced serious hurdles in pursuing its mission.

At the time of its inception, laws supporting the right to obtain post-conviction DNA evidence didn't exist. Therefore, every exoneration was a battle and often required extensive changes to state laws. With each overturned conviction, the Innocence Project revealed flaws in the legal system and opened more doors to claims of innocence. It also inspired policies for systemic improvements, such as laws for mandatory interrogation recordings and the ability for convicted persons to request DNA testing to help prove their innocence.

Today, the Innocence Project has successfully exonerated 375 innocent people—all because two public defenders believed in the power of science and its application to criminal justice.

How did Scheck and Neufeld revolutionize the criminal justice system in ways we are only beginning to understand?[2]

They realized the power of *a grand narrative.*

The Hero's Journey

Storytelling is a critical (albeit often unwritten) part of the job description of every nonprofit leader. The act of telling a story is one of the most powerful means of engaging your nonprofit's stakeholders, connecting with them on a meaningful level, and enabling your nonprofit to distinguish itself from other organizations.[3] As Jesuit priest and psychotherapist Anthony de Mello puts it, "the shortest distance between truth and a human being is a story."[4]

Great leaders don't become great storytellers by accident; they must first become great students of storytelling. One such student was a twentieth-century American professor of literature named Joseph Campbell. Campbell took the typical three-act structure of many stories (the protagonist begins in an ordinary world, visits a special world, then returns to the ordinary world) and expanded it into a framework known as the Hero's Journey.

Campbell's concept has been studied and followed by master authors and filmmakers since it was first published in 1949. The twelve-stage structure develops an in-depth character arc that helps the reader connect with each stage of the protagonist's journey.[5]

1. *Ordinary World*

    Before the story begins, the hero exists in a place of relative safety, oblivious to the journey ahead. Here we learn important details about the hero, like his outlook on life and his true nature. The audience can identify with him, which allows us to empathize with him later in the story.

2. *Call to Adventure*

   A threat to the hero's peace, safety, community, or family sets the story in motion. Perhaps it's a conversation, a phone call, or an act of war. No matter what form it takes, this call to action is the catalyst that sends the hero on his quest.

3. *Refusal of the Call*

   Despite his eagerness to accept the challenge, the hero has second thoughts and serious doubts about the task at hand. He ultimately refuses the call and opts to stay home, where he is safe and his surroundings are familiar. Again, the audience can relate to him, and we bond even further with the reluctant hero.

4. *Meeting the Mentor*

   At this critical point in the story, the hero needs guidance. He meets a mentor who provides some value—an important object, sage advice, expert training—to help him overcome his fears. From this encounter the hero finds the courage and strength needed to begin his journey.

5. *Crossing the Threshold*

   The hero is finally ready to answer the call, and he crosses the threshold between his ordinary world and a world he has never known. We see his commitment to the quest and his willingness to face the challenges ahead.

6. *Tests, Allies, Enemies*

   The hero enters a crucible of difficult challenges that test his mettle. He must overcome various obstacles in an effort to reach his goal. Along the way, he earns allies he can trust and meets enemies set on thwarting his efforts. Every difficulty builds his resilience and provides further insight into his character.

7. *Approach to the Inmost Cave*

   Whether an inner conflict or a physical location, the inmost cave is where a formidable danger awaits. As he approaches the threshold, the hero faces more doubts and reflects upon his journey before mustering the courage to go forward. This pause builds anticipation of the test ahead and allows the audience to grasp the magnitude of the events that are about to transpire.

8. *Ordeal*

   Everything the hero has encountered up to this point culminates in facing his greatest foe. The entire journey hangs by a thread. The hero experiences some version of "death," whether his own, that of an ally, or a previous state of the world around him. This moment represents his one and only chance for victory—if he fails, all will be lost.

9. *Reward*

   Upon surviving death, defeating his enemy, and conquering his greatest personal challenge, the hero emerges with a prize. This could be greater understanding, an object of significance, or an answer to a secret. The time to celebrate is limited, as the hero must prepare for the final leg of his journey.

10. *The Road Back*

    The reverse of his Call to Adventure, the Road Back sends the hero home with his reward and the anticipation of acclaim, absolution, exoneration, or vindication. As he commits to the final stage of his adventure, he must choose between his own personal goal and that of a greater good.

11. *Resurrection*

    Just when we think the hero has faced his ultimate challenge, he has one final scrape with death. This last battle has existential consequences for the Ordinary World he left behind. Should he fail, all that he loved in his previous life will suffer or be lost. This added pressure allows the audience to participate in the hero's tension. The hero ultimately prevails, destroying the villain and arising purified and enhanced.

12. *Return with the Elixir*

In this final stage of the story, the victorious hero returns to his ordinary world with a fresh perspective. The Reward he brings home represents change, success, and proof of his expedition. The story's supporting characters find resolution, and, although the hero has returned to the beginning location of his journey, things will never be the same.

Campbell believed the Hero's Journey isn't just for fictional characters but serves as a path that all maturing people and cultures must follow.[6] As children, we depend on others for our psychological, material, and physical needs. We eventually trade this dependency for responsibility in a story arc similar to the Hero's Journey.[7]

As a nonprofit leader, you can appropriate Campbell's framework to craft a powerful grand narrative that sits at the heart of everything you do. In doing so, however, you may be tempted to make your nonprofit the hero; far better to position your organization as the mentor or the ally. The true hero is, depending on context, your beneficiary (transforming the Ordinary World that was holding them back or causing them harm) or your donor (stepping up to vanquish a foe that was causing great suffering to the vulnerable and helpless). Together, you're all going on the Adventure of adventures to do something legendary.

What's your nonprofit's grand narrative?

Summary

When public defenders Barry Scheck and Peter Neufeld won freedom for a falsely convicted a man using DNA testing, they revolutionized the criminal justice system. Their nonprofit organization, The Innocence Project, continues to provide legal aid to people who have been wrongfully convicted. Its staff and volunteers aim to reform the criminal justice system and help capture the true perpetrators of violent crimes. Since its inception, The Innocence Project has helped exonerate 375 people through DNA technology, as well as inspire new laws for systemic improvements. Like theirs, your nonprofit has a story that deserves to be told, a grand narrative. Telling that grand narrative well can help you inspire conviction in your audience and secure the people and resources necessary to have world-changing impact. Joseph Campbell's Hero's Journey provides a helpful structure for crafting an effective grand narrative for your nonprofit.

The key to the twenty-second law of nonprofit impact—*have a grand narrative*—is becoming a lifelong student of great storytelling.

Recommended Further Reading

CAMPBELL, JOSEPH. *The Hero with a Thousand Faces*. Princeton, NJ: Princeton University Press, 1973.

CRAIG, WILL. *Living the Hero's Journey: Exploring Your Role in the Action-Adventure of a Lifetime*. Boulder, CO: Live and Learn Publishing, 2017.

SCHECK, BARRY, PETER NEUFELD, AND JIM DWYER. *Actual Innocence*. New York: Berkeley Books, 2003.

---

1 Peter Neufeld, "Legal and Ethical Implications of Post-Conviction DNA Exonerations," *New England Law Review* 35, no. 3 (2001): 639–48.

2 Jane Gitschier, "The Innocence Project at Twenty: An Interview with Barry Scheck," *PLOS Genetics* 9, no. 8 (August 2013): Article e1003692.

3 Sarah-Louise Mitchell and Moira Clark, "Telling a Different Story: How Nonprofit Organizations Reveal Strategic Purpose Through Storytelling," *Psychology & Marketing* 38 (2021): 142–58.

4 Anthony de Mello, *One Minute Wisdom* (Portland: Image Publishing, 1998), 23.

5 Clive Williams, "The Hero's Journey: A Mudmap to Wellbeing," in *Heroism and Wellbeing in the 21st Century: Applied and Emerging Perspectives*, ed. Scott T. Allison and Zeno E. Franco, 49–63 (New York: Routledge, 2018).

6 Joseph Campbell, *Pathways to Bliss: Mythology and Personal Transformation* (New York: New World Library, 2004), 189.

7 Joseph Campbell, with Bill Moyers, *The Power of Myth* (New York: Anchor Publishing, 1991), 44.

LAW 23:

Be interested and interesting.

> *I've been a cook all my life, but I am still learning to be a good chef. I'm always learning new techniques and improving beyond my own knowledge. There is always something new to learn and new horizons to discover.*
>
> *José Andrés (1969–)*

In the northern woods of Spain during the 1970s, young José Andrés would help his father prepare paella, a traditional Spanish dish. As a child, he was taught that the quality of the fire would determine the quality of the meals they cooked together.

This fascinated him. Could the heat levels of a fire directly infuse the flavor of a meal? Seeing for himself that fire could instill such flavor into a dish resonated with Andrés. He knew even from that early age that he wanted to become a chef.

At the age of fifteen, Andrés began attending culinary school. He had the good fortune of working in a restaurant often visited by the father of modernist cuisine, Ferran Adrià. Adrià's legendary restaurant El Bulli had a job opening, and he offered the position to Andrés. The young chef worked there until the Spanish navy enlisted him as a cook. As his ship sailed into New York Harbor, past the Statue of Liberty, Andrés knew his future was in America.

Four years later, he returned to the United States with just $50 in his pocket. Almost immediately, he took a position cooking in a Manhattan outpost of a popular Barcelona restaurant. Soon after, Andrés opened his own Spanish-inspired restaurant in Washington, DC. When he was asked to take over another local eatery two years later, Andrés was told by restaurateur Richard Melman that it was time to throw in the anchor and build a real future. And Andrés could think of no place better to do this than the nation's capital.

In just a few years, Andrés was on his way to building a small restaurant empire. He was only twenty-five years old.

Living by the credo that chefs feed the few but have the opportunity to change the world, Andrés believed in volunteering his talents to help others in need. He joined DC Central Kitchen, a nationally renowned community kitchen that recycles food from around Washington, DC, to provide local service agencies with thousands of meals. Although he served on the board and loved the work he was doing, Andrés believed the agency was falling a bit short. He wanted to see an organization that focused on empowering people, not just feeding them.

Then, in 2010, a 7.0 magnitude earthquake devastated Haiti. Andrés rushed there to work with other nonprofits to install clean cookstoves and help provide humanitarian relief. Upon seeing how the area's poverty had been worsened by unsanitary cooking conditions in overcrowded tent cities, Andrés knew this was his moment to create an organization that empowers those in need.

Andrés founded World Central Kitchen, now a world-famous nonprofit organization that uses a chef network to address education, health, jobs, and social enterprise worldwide. From building kitchens in public schools to establishing culinary schools that stimulate the economy, World Central Kitchen has helped millions of people recover from poverty, natural disasters, and even a global pandemic.

How did a young chef from Spain create a restaurant empire that positioned him to develop a nonprofit organization that benefited millions of people around the world?

He understood that *curiosity, eccentricity, and performance are all positively correlated.*

Curiosity

The desire to seek new experiences, gather new information, and explore new possibilities is inherent to human nature. Not everyone, however, exhibits a degree of curiosity high enough and consistent enough to manifest a life story like that of Andrés. Speaking personally, whenever I'm asked who my best teacher in school was, my answer is, "curiosity." Of course, I've had many great teachers. But the real driver of learning—especially learning that leads to world-changing impact—is the impulse to ask "why?" or "how?" or (my own personal favorite) "really!?".[1]

Science is beginning to bear out the benefits of curiosity at the physiological level; as described in one recent study, "curiosity is a condition of increased stimulation whose termination is rewarding and facilitates memory."[2] Nonprofit leaders can capitalize on this trait by cultivating curiosity in themselves and their organizations, with immeasurable benefits for workers, beneficiaries, and the nonprofit as a whole.

Curiosity at all levels enables leaders and staff to adapt to ever-changing circumstances. This is especially true for nonprofit organizations. Whether it's government regulations, constituents' needs, or available funds, nonprofits must be able to think critically and creatively to discover less-than-obvious solutions. Curiosity also inspires collaboration and helps workers share different perspectives. This kind of open communication enables people to trust each other, increase morale, and establish a workplace that runs on respect and teamwork. And at the end of the day, curious nonprofits are just more fun.

Unfortunately, many nonprofit leaders associate curiosity with change, so they stifle creativity in an effort to preserve the status quo. While this impulse is understandable, it reflects a misguided mindset about curiosity. Perhaps, among other things, such leaders worry that empowering workers to question things will make the nonprofit more difficult to manage.[3] But empowerment is essential to continuous improvement, the goal of any distinctive organization.

An over-emphasis on efficiency can also stifle a culture of curiosity. Seeking out ways to streamline processes is a worthy pursuit, but if taken too far it can sacrifice tomorrow's potential impact on the altar of today's metrics. Staff and volunteers can become so intent on watching the scoreboard that they stop asking questions about how to significantly change the game for the better. Consider ways to build "scenic overlook" moments into your nonprofit's annual calendar when, as a full team, you scramble up out of the valley of the day-to-day to look down on it all. *Why are we doing what we're doing? If we were to start from scratch today, would we end up with this? What are we missing that could take us to new levels of impact?*

Curiosity, of course, begins and ends with leadership. By asking "really!?" questions and giving others the space to offer honest answers, nonprofit leaders will be endlessly surprised by opportunities to improve processes, develop programs, and create an organization that better serves its beneficiaries. Modeling an inquisitive nature and admitting that the current way of doing things most likely isn't perfect encourages workers to unleash their curiosity.

Eccentricity

One unfortunate drawback of the extensive literature on leadership "strategies" and "best practices" is a tendency among leaders to try to fit a mold or play a role. Careful study of great leaders past and present, however, reveals not only that many of them were just plain weird, but they also weren't afraid to let their weird flag fly.

As nonprofit leaders, we must ask ourselves what weirdo tendencies distinguish us from others. Of the things that come natural to us, what makes us unique? These eccentricities shouldn't be traded for the world's boring old uniform, but worn proudly. Baseball fan? Wear that favorite jersey to the office on Fridays. Nerd with a sense of style? Rock those colored frames for your glasses. Music lover? Surprise your team by blasting some tunes in the office from time to time. These eccentric little rebellions, small as they may seem, inspire trust as people come to believe they truly know you. They broadcast without words: *This is a place where it's okay to be interesting.*

The dark side of eccentricity is that, taken to an extreme, eccentric people can be a challenge to work with. This is especially true when eccentricities manifest as counterproductive habits or personality quirks—e.g., chronic lateness, poor hygiene, or directness that sometimes strays into harshness of tone. Memories of working with these kinds of leaders should provide sufficient caution to all of us to prevent our own eccentricities from becoming fatal flaws (see Law 10).

The most constructive eccentricities—those that inspire fun, trust, and creativity—are playfully odd expressions of one's personal values.[4] Examples include Amazon CEO Jeff Bezos expressing his frugality by repurposing a door as a desk.[5] Or Tesla and SpaceX CEO Elon Musk expressing his dedication to working alongside his team by sleeping on the factory floor.[6] Or American business and investment tycoon Warren Buffett opting for a simple flip phone over a smartphone.[7] These examples demonstrate a willingness on the part of the leader to allow their values to visibly, publicly, unashamedly make them a little weird. As a result, the members of their organizations feel inspired to embrace that the organization's values will make the it a little weird too.

Summary

When chef José Andrés learned about the devastation that a 7.0 magnitude earthquake had caused in Haiti, he immediately sprang into action. Using his skills and experience, he was able to help create safe and healthy eating conditions for people in need. This experience inspired Andrés to found World Central Kitchen, a nonprofit organization that uses a chef network to address education, health, jobs, and social enterprise worldwide. Since its founding, World Central Kitchen has helped millions of people recover from poverty, natural disasters, and a global pandemic. Andrés's story ought to inspire other nonprofit leaders to embrace curiosity and eccentricity in their own approach to leadership. Curiosity is essential to nonprofit impact because it leads to creative questions and challenges the status quo. A culture of creativity within a nonprofit is complemented by a leader who doesn't hide her eccentricities. By expressing our values in ways that might make us appear slightly odd to a watching world, we inspire the members of our organizations to see themselves as part of a cohesive, values-driven group of happy eccentrics.

The keys to the twenty-third law of nonprofit impact—*be interested and interesting*—are curiosity and eccentricity.

Recommended Further Reading

ANDRÉS, JOSÉ. *We Fed an Island: The True Story of Rebuilding Puerto Rico, One Meal at a Time.* New York: Ecco Press, 2018.

GREENBERG, SARAH STEIN. *Creative Acts for Curious People: How to Think, Create, and Lead in Unconventional Ways.* Berkeley: Ten Speed Press, 2021.

SINCLAIR, BRETT. *Eccentricity: Today's Secret Sauce: The Value of Being Eccentric.* Cambridge, MA: Alpha Academic Press, 2017.

---

1 Zander Lurie, "Bolstering Curiosity to Advance Workplace Equity," *Stanford Social Innovation Review*, January 9, 2019.

2 Marieke Jepma, Rinus G. Verdonschot, Henk van Steenbergen, Serge A. R. B. Rombouts, and Sander Nieuwenhuis, "Neural Mechanisms Underlying the Induction and Relief of Perceptual Curiosity," *Frontiers in Behavioral Neuroscience* 6 (February 2012).

3 Francesca Gino, "The Business Case for Curiosity," *Harvard Business Review*, September–October 2018, 48–57.

4 Louis R. Pondy, "Leadership is a Language Game," in *Readings in Managerial Psychology*, ed. Harold J. Leavitt, Louis R. Pondy, and David M. Boje (Chicago: University of Chicago Press, 1988), 232.

5 Ben Gilbert, "Jeff Bezos and His Early Amazon Employees Used Desks Made Out of Recycled Doors, and the Reason Behind it Helps Explain Why Amazon Became So Successful," *Business Insider*, September 7, 2019.

6 Mark Matousek, "Elon Musk Said He Slept n the Floor of Tesla's Factory Because He Wanted to Suffer More Than Any Other Employee During Model 3 'Production Hell,'" *Business Insider*, July 12, 2018.

7 Brett Molina, "After Years of Owning a Flip Phone, Warren Buffett Finally Has an iPhone," *USA Today*, February 25, 2020.

LAW 24:

Shine in moments of truth.

> *The road to happiness lies in two simple principles: find what it is that interests you and that you can do well. When you find it, put your whole soul into it—every bit of energy and ambition and natural ability you have.*
>
> **John D. Rockefeller III (1906–78)**

John D. Rockefeller III had a passion for nonprofit organizations.

A third-generation member of the renowned industrial, political, and banking family, Rockefeller was expected to take a lead role in his family's legacy of wealth and success. After earning an economics degree with honors, Rockefeller began working in his father's office in Manhattan. He thrived in the family business, serving in prominent roles on various boards and foundations.

But his greatest interest was private philanthropy. Rockefeller quickly became a key leader in fundraising efforts for developing the Lincoln Center in Manhattan. Not only did he raise funds for the project, but he also navigated complex agreements between social leaders, artists, and civic officials to achieve the center's successful completion. His involvement in this project solidified his view that private philanthropy was vital to a flourishing America.

When the government passed the Tax Reform Act of 1969, imposing strict regulations on charitable giving and foundations, Rockefeller felt compelled to take action to protect the influence of private philanthropy. He made it his mission to campaign for public policy that was favorable to charitable giving. Rockefeller gathered people with diverse backgrounds—from business executives and politicians to religious and community leaders—to help him conduct an important study on giving in America.

In 1973, Rockefeller initiated the Commission on Private Philanthropy and Public Needs (also called the Filer Commission, after its chair John H. Filer). His goal was to create a privately supported citizen's board who would study philanthropy as a concept, investigate the role of the private sector in American society, and recommend ways to boost voluntary giving. It sought to gain insight about philanthropy and people's motivations for giving. The commission concluded that donations were critical to life in America, but expressed concerns about the strength of nonprofit organizations and the continuation of charitable tax deductions.

For two years, the commission conducted more than eighty-six research projects on the role of the private nonprofit sector in America. These studies led to important discussions in an advisory panel of more than one hundred cause-driven advocates and specialists in sociology, law, economics. Focusing on areas like health, arts, education, foreign practices, and taxation and regulation, this research helped shape decisions about philanthropy's role in the public and private sectors. The Filer Commission also surveyed three thousand people nationwide to determine whether incentives like tax deductions influenced their decisions to contribute to nonprofits.

In 1975, the commission concluded its research and published its findings in a report called *Giving in America: Toward a Stronger Voluntary Sector*. This project directed public attention to a newly conceived "third sector" beyond business and government. From then on, private entities would be categorized as either for-profit or nonprofit. The commission's work inspired academic research into philanthropy for the next two decades and motivated the formation of the Independent Sector Coalition, one of the country's strongest advocates for nonprofit organizations.

How did the grandson of oil baron John D. Rockefeller change the way the government and society viewed and contributed to nonprofit organizations and philanthropy?

He capitalized on the idea that *certain rare moments have exponentially more potential impact than all others combined.*

The Power of Moments

A third-down pass in the big game against the school rival. A definitive meeting with the CEO. A first kiss with a sweetheart. Some moments have considerably more power than others. Get them right and things can take a distinct turn for the better. Get them wrong and you may lose big and perhaps not recover.

The ability to recognize—and even orchestrate—these "moments of truth" is one of the most important skills of leadership. Our lives tend to consist of a series of defining moments: meaningful and memorable beginnings, endings, and culminations that stand out to us as life's milestones. These moments shape who we are, how we perceive ourselves, and how we view the world around us.[1]

In *The Power of Moments*, Chip Heath explores why some experiences elevate and change us, and how we can create these opportunities in our daily lives. He explains that some moments in our lives are high points, occasionally remarkable moments we want to remember forever. "The 'occasionally remarkable' moments," he writes, "shouldn't be left to chance! They should be planned for, invested in. They are peaks that should be built. And if we fail to do that, look at what we're left with: mostly forgettable."[2] According to Heath, there are four elements to an occasionally remarkable moment:

- **Elevation:** It transcends the normal course of events.
- **Insight:** It changes our understanding of ourselves or the world around us.
- **Pride:** It seizes us at our best.
- **Connection:** It should be shared with others.

When a moment meets these four criteria, it holds tremendous meaning and endures as a lasting memory. These kinds of memories, rare as they are, have disproportionately more power than all others combined to shape our present and our future.

Thinking through your own history of seminal moments of truth may help shed light on what may constitute these moments for others. Perhaps it was when you decided to make a move to a new city, state, or country; the first day at a new job or school; meeting a new boss for the first time; an achievement long in the making, such as a graduation, an exam for a credential, or a major gift to your nonprofit; a cherished occasion shared with a dear friend or colleague; and the list goes on.

The most important opportunity these moments represent for leaders is not their recognition, but their replication. Organizations that learn to multiply these moments and unleash their motivating potential will find that staff and volunteers who experience them become fiercely loyal to the cause and give far more of their talent and energy than they otherwise would.

Imagine a new staff member to your nonprofit arriving for her first day on the job. A senior leader welcomes her with her favorite morning beverage; shows her to her desk where she finds fresh flowers, a card signed by the entire board of directors, and her laptop open and already set up with a screen welcoming her by name; and directs her to a welcome video on the laptop, narrated by the organization's founder, that describes the organization's history, mission, vision, and values. It's not difficult to see how a beginning like this would stand out as a moment of truth not only for the staff member, but for the nonprofit that will benefit from her years or decades of loyal service.

Moments of Truth in Nonprofit Leadership

As busy nonprofit leaders, we can't afford not to make it count in moments of truth—but we have to know what to look for. Below are some archetypal moments of truth that are likely to occur in your nonprofit.

1. *Drafting your nonprofit's founding documents.*

   As the underlying framework for your organization, these essential documents—articles of incorporation, bylaws, policies and procedures, and so on—establish how the organization is governed. Nonprofit leaders who rush through these steps in order to get started may miss an opportunity to capitalize fully on this moment of truth.

2. *Selecting a board member.*

   This is probably the most underwhelming use of a moment of truth I see in nonprofits today. Rather than fight hard for the highest level of values, talent, network, and commitment they can find, a nonprofit leader merely asks a friend or family member who is too polite to say no but too busy or disinterested to serve well. Nonprofit leaders that fight to make this moment of truth count, however, see much more long-term impact.

3. *A staff member's or volunteer's first day.*

   Making someone feel welcomed, valued, and significant on the same day they are feeling most insecure, exposed, and vulnerable can win you a lifelong devotee. Missing this opportunity risks their concluding this is "just another job." Go all out to send the unambiguous message to new staff and volunteers that your organization is special.

4. *Staff or volunteer misconduct or underperformance necessitating their removal.*

   Releasing a staff member or volunteer is one of a nonprofit leader's most difficult responsibilities; making it a succinct, empathetic, confidential, and respectful conversation can help mitigate any negative feelings. Fight for ways to demonstrate a genuine love for the person that wants to see them find a role in another organization that's right for them, while remaining committed to making your nonprofit the distinctive organization your beneficiaries deserve.[3]

5. *Your first statement and/or action following an organizational, national, or global crisis.*

   This is a moment of truth that can completely change the way people view your organization. Consider carefully how you might make a timely, concise statement that genuinely voices an appropriate emotional response (e.g., sadness, frustration, outrage) while also leading people into a mindset of hope, healing, and positive action.

6. *Conversation with a major donor.*

   Not all donor-related moments of truth are about making the Ask. A major donor visit might be a significant moment of truth for reasons of cultivation—to learn about the donor, understand her passion for the organization and its mission, and develop a human-to-human connection that helps you know, like, and trust one another. But at the right time, the Ask does eventually need to be made.

7. *Public speech, video, or other high-visibility event.*

   Any time you have the opportunity to appear in front of the public, you have a chance to shape the way people view your organization. Take advantage of these moments of truth by embodying your nonprofit's mission and values.

There are likely many other examples—hopefully this list help you see more clearly those special moments that can have disproportionately more power to move your mission forward.

Summary

John D. Rockefeller III had a passion for philanthropy. When the government passed the Tax Reform Act of 1969 regulating charitable giving and foundations, Rockefeller appointed himself America's caretaker of philanthropy. Seeing a need to study philanthropy in America, he founded the Filer Commission to investigate the role of the private sector in the United States and find ways to increase voluntary giving. After two years, the commission reported their findings, which revealed the need to differentiate between for-profit and nonprofit private entities. It inspired a coalition to advocate for nonprofits, and changed the way government and society viewed philanthropy as a whole. As nonprofit leaders, we have the ability to follow Rockefeller's example and capitalize on the power of moments—those rare, fleeting opportunities to make huge advances for our nonprofits' missions.

The key to the twenty-fourth law of nonprofit impact—*shine in moments of truth*—is having eyes to see when you're in the midst of a special opportunity for world-changing impact.

Recommended Further Reading

BRILLIANT, ELEANOR L. *Private Charity and Public Inquiry: A History of the Filer and Peterson Commissions.* Bloomington: Indiana University Press, 2001.

RICHT, MARK. *Make the Call: Game-Day Wisdom for Life's Defining Moments.* Nashville, TN: B&H Books, 2021.

SAMIA, YOM TOV. *Leadership in Moments of Truth.* Tel Aviv: Contento Now, 2016.

---

1 Martha Henderson Hurley, "Chapter 1: The Power of Moments," in *Myth and Reality: Reflections on Our Travels Through West Africa* (Dayton, OH: University of Dayton, 2019), 9–16.

2 Chip Heath, *The Power of Moments: Why Certain Experiences Have Extraordinary Impact* (New York: Simon & Schuster, 2017), 258.

3 William K. Hengen Jr., "Managing Moments of Truth," *Management Review* 87, no. 8 (1998): 56.

LAWS OF FINANCE

LAW 25:

Be frugal.

> *Paying attention early on for the unit economics is going to make a difference between having a great idea that maybe inspires people versus an inspiring idea that can actually scale.*
>
> *J. B. Schramm (1963–)*

J. B. Schramm had a high school friend named Tiny.

When Tiny told Schramm in confidence that he'd decided to postpone college, Schramm knew something wasn't right.

The two high school seniors attended an inner-city school in Colorado, where they both excelled in different ways. Schramm got straight A's; Tiny was a talented basketball player, school leader, and student council member.

So Schramm thought it was odd that their school counselor encouraged him to apply to Yale, yet recommended that Tiny focus on applying only to community college. The only real difference between the two students? Schramm's parents had college degrees, and Tiny's did not.

Unsurprisingly, Tiny was accepted to community colleges in their area. However, he confided in Schramm that he'd decided to hold off on continuing his education and would instead get a job. Schramm could tell that Tiny was troubled.

As Schramm went on to excel and become an academic advisor for freshmen at Harvard, he thought often of Tiny. So many of the files for incoming freshmen revealed notes from admissions officers who were looking for low-income talent. He also noticed that students from low-income backgrounds who earned the grades to attend college weren't pursuing the opportunity. That's when Schramm had an idea.

In 1993, Schramm and two friends created a teen education hub in the basement of a community center in Washington, DC. They worked with low-income students who had the resilience, intelligence, and focus to succeed in college, but lacked the knowledge of how to pursue continuing education. The more students they encountered, the more Schramm realized that the most influential person to a seventeen-year-old was another seventeen-year-old.

This program revealed how one student could influence their friends down a path to higher education. In 1996, College Summit was incorporated. Now operating as PeerForward, the organization has grown into a national movement that relies on the power of peer influence to transform the lives of disadvantaged youth.

By training eleventh- and twelfth-graders to manage peer-to-peer coaching, run events, and increase awareness, PeerForward keeps costs low while significantly increasing its impact. As a result, more students are able to complete the Free Application for Federal Student Aid (FAFSA), and more than $13 million has been awarded in scholarships and grants to help students pay for school.

How did a college graduate son of college-educated parents develop a program to create opportunities for qualified low-income students to enter higher education?

He realized that *frugality is more about lowering the cost per unit of impact than about cost elimination.*

The Dangers of Cost Elimination

Expert skills training, effective fundraising processes, and current information technology systems are important tools for any nonprofit today. Unfortunately, most nonprofits cite limited resources and lack of funds as reasons for not investing in such tools. Time and again, I've seen nonprofit leaders go to remarkable extremes to cut costs in all sorts of ways with the noble motive of focusing on the bare essentials needed to support their beneficiaries.

While all this sounds like a responsible approach to money management, more often than not, nonprofit organizations underinvest in the non-urgent but important things. Extreme cost elimination can have far-reaching and disastrous effects that hinder long-term growth and impact. Poor or nonexistent professional development leads to an ineffective workforce. Outdated computers waste time and put mission-critical data at risk. Broken-down equipment and furniture project the image of an organization that doesn't have its act together.

This debilitating trend of underinvestment in organizational infrastructure is jeopardizing the existence of tens of thousands, if not hundreds of thousands, of nonprofits.[1] So why, then, do so many nonprofit leaders continue to poormouth their way through day after day?

Strategists Ann Goggins Gregory and Don Howard with Bridgespan Group, a large management consulting firm for nonprofits, conducted a case study on this very issue:

> *Our research reveals that a vicious cycle fuels the persistent underfunding of overhead. The first step in the cycle is funders' unrealistic expectations about how much it costs to run a nonprofit. At the second step, nonprofits feel pressure to conform to funders' unrealistic expectations. At the third step, nonprofits respond to this pressure in two ways: They spend too little on overhead, and they underreport their expenditures on tax forms and in fundraising materials. This underspending and underreporting in turn perpetuates funders' unrealistic expectations. Over time,*

funders expect grantees to do more and more with less and less—a cycle that slowly starves nonprofits.[2]

It's difficult to overstate the ramifications of this finding. Some researchers predict that this starvation cycle has the potential to bring about the death of the nonprofit sector.[3] The good news is, it's not too late. By educating funders about the realistic costs of running a nonprofit and being transparent about spending needs, nonprofit leaders can set appropriate expectations and begin to reverse this trend back in the direction of operational excellence.

Lowering the Cost Per Unit of Impact

Rather than define nonprofit frugality as eliminating costs (which, per the above, will ultimately starve your organization), consider redefining nonprofit frugality as *lowering the cost per unit of impact*. Doing so shifts focus from reducing spending to *right-sizing investment* in the things that will yield the most long-term impact.[4]

Here are five ways to lower the cost per unit of impact:

1. *Passive impact delivery.*

    Find ways to make an impact through on-demand products or services that have low or no variable cost, e.g., an online course with free 24/7 access for unlimited beneficiaries.

2. *Volunteer-driven execution.*

    Although it's not a viable option for all nonprofits, using volunteers for execution comes with at least three benefits: lowering the cost per unit of impact, cultivating volunteers into donors through involvement in the work, and accelerating product/service innovation.

3. *A few good tools.*

    Investing in a few strategic, high-quality, durable tools that will stand the test of time spreads the higher cost over a number of years of increased productivity and impact. A new $2,000 laptop that saves a staff member an average of twenty minutes per day (over their current 90s vintage dinosaur desktop) results in productivity gains of $2,250+ per year. That estimate does not include other likely gains from recruiting better talent, incurring less turnover, and driving employee engagement.

4. *Fight "subscription drift."*

Subscriptions semi-permanently increase the cost per unit of impact. For this reason, I'm not a big fan. Although that one-off $20/month subscription or membership may not seem like a big deal, ten of them running in the background will cost your nonprofit $2,400 every year. Because those tiny charges run monthly or annually, they can be difficult to detect and shut off.

Once every two months or so, review all of the previous month's transactions for subscriptions and get ruthless about eliminating them. If subscriptions are a must, inquire about discounted pricing for nonprofits, and whether you can save money by paying annually versus monthly.

5. *Freelancers.*

Closely related to subscription drift, the costliest kind of "subscription" is a full-time employee. While there will always be a place for full-time staff in the nonprofit world, it's wise to skew your paid talent strategy as much as possible toward contractors and freelancers. Contract or freelance work can be tailored specifically to what will yield the most impact, perhaps even in a way that directly aligns compensation incentives with impact (see Law 14).

Once you make the mindset shift from cutting costs to minimizing cost per unit of impact, a whole new world emerges. Nonprofit leaders who were once known for moaning to friends and family about the woes of social sector scarcity are suddenly transformed into vivacious, creative problem solvers and shrewd investors in a myriad of bargains sure to amplify their impact.

For example, when the US National Institutes of Health initiated the Diabetes Prevention Program, its one-on-one clinical model was too expensive for most. Thinking creatively, the YMCA devised a way to train its employees to deliver the program to the masses, cutting costs by 75% and making it easier to reach more people. Seeing its effectiveness, insurers reimbursed the cost of the program and opened the door for widespread use.[5]

By lowering the cost per unit of impact rather than cutting costs strictly for the sake of a lower number, leaders can demonstrate to donors and volunteers the worthiness of investing in their nonprofit's long-term growth.

Summary

When J. B. Schramm realized low-income high school seniors weren't prepared for college applications, he decided to help level the playing field. He created PeerForward, a nonprofit that relies on volunteer peer-to-peer coaching to provide students with the most effective kind of support. The strategy carried the added benefit of keeping costs at a minimum. Far too many nonprofits equate frugality with cost elimination, setting their organization on a sure path to starvation and closure. Instead, leaders ought to redefine frugality as lowering the cost per unit of impact. This bang-for-your-buck approach accepts that a requisite level of investment is required to effectively meet the needs of present and future beneficiaries. Nonprofit leaders who train themselves and their people to squeeze every last drop of impact from a donor's sacred dollar position the organization for long-term growth and world-changing impact.

The key to the twenty-fifth law of nonprofit impact—*be frugal*—is defining frugality as impact maximization with your organization's precious financial resources.

Recommended Further Reading

DROPKIN, MURRAY, JIM HALPIN, AND BILL LA TOUCHE. *The Budget-Building Book for Nonprofits: A Step-By-Step Guide for Managers and Boards.* San Francisco: Jossey-Bass, 2007.

SONENSHEIN, SCOTT. *Stretch: Unlock the Power of Less—and Achieve More Than You Ever Imagined.* New York: HarperCollins Publishers, 2017.

WEIKART, LYNNE A., *Greg Chen, and Ed Sermier. Budgeting & Financial Management for Nonprofit Organizations: Using Money to Drive Mission Success.* Washington, DC: CQ Press, 2012.

---

1 Jesse D. Lecy and Elizabeth A. M. Searing, "Anatomy of the Nonprofit Starvation Cycle: An Analysis of Falling Overhead Ratios in the Nonprofit Sector," *Nonprofit and Voluntary Sector Quarterly* 44, no. 3 (2015): 539–63.

2 Ann Goggins Gregory and Don Howard, "The Nonprofit Starvation Cycle," *Stanford Social Innovation Review*, Fall 2009, 49–53.

3 Taylor S. McPheeters, "The Slow Death of the Nonprofit Sector and How to Stop It in Three Steps," *Marriott Student Review* 3, no. 4 (2020): Article 32.

4 Hala Altamimi and Qiaozhen Liu, "The Nonprofit Starvation Cycle: Impact of Underfed Overhead on Program," *Academy of Management Proceedings* 2019, no.1 (Summer 2019).

5 Leslie MacKrell, Andrew Belton, Mark Gottfredson, and Jake Fisher, "Cutting Costs to Increase Impact," *Stanford Social Innovation Review*, Spring 2017, 34–39.

LAW 26:
Don't spend—invest.

> *No group in the entire population is comprised of so many rank individualists as is that group categorized as "the aging and the aged." As we grow older, we not only accumulate years, but we also acquire all the effects, good or bad, of all the events of a lifetime.*
>
> **Ollie A. Randall (1890–1984)**

For Ollie Randall, the idea of the elderly being a useless group weighing down the rest of the population was utterly unthinkable.

As a child living in a small sod house in western Kansas, she was raised in a multigenerational household; she had wonderful, happy memories of caring for older family members. Those memories and values inspired Randall to pursue a career as a welfare administrator and social worker.

After graduating from Brown University, Randall took a position in New York as the assistant to the director of the Association for Improving the Condition of the Poor (AICP). After ten years, she took over as the executive director of Ward Manor, an AICP home for the aged. In this role, Randall observed that the elderly were grouped with other "needy" populations, which meant their specific needs weren't being addressed.

Randall strongly believed that older people needed companionship, time with family, a reasonable income, and access to healthy food. They needed help combatting feelings of uselessness, financial insecurity, and social isolation. Yet they weren't getting this help from any existing resource Randall could find; instead, they were labeled, shunned, or given treatment without heartfelt care. It became clear to Randall that older Americans needed someone to serve as their advocate.

Randall decided to make it her mission to raise national awareness for the issues the elderly face. She began to develop key relationships nationwide with leaders in the field of aging, and, in 1950, she cofounded the National Council on Aging (NCOA). It was the first charitable organization to work toward securing benefits, jobs, health, and independent living for older citizens.

NCOA honed in on the issues that older Americans face and began addressing them one by one. Together, Randall and her team initiated the National Institute of Senior Centers to provide better living environments for the elderly. Their National Adult Day Services Association offered daytime care for older citizens. The now well-known Meals on Wheels program delivered nutritious food to people who couldn't get out to shop, and the Falls Free Initiative addressed the growing problem of falls among the elderly.

By focusing on and putting time and care into a relatively small number of well-planned strategic investments, NCOA has been able to provide older Americans with an unprecedented level of physical and psychological care.

How did Ollie Randall and NCOA shape the public perspective on caring for the elderly?

By recognizing that *amateurs think in terms of spending, and professionals think in terms of investment.*

Focus, Focus, Focus

The distinction between spending and investing may seem merely semantic—in both cases, after all, money goes out and something of value comes in. So why split hairs?

As so often is the case with leadership, it's all about the underlying mindset. *Spending money* is a mindset focused on the here and now. We spend to satisfy a present need. *Investing money*, however, shifts the mindset to future growth. Every dollar *spent* fills a present need, whereas every dollar *invested* is thoughtfully placed to persist, grow, and multiply.

As nonprofit leaders, we invest in—not spend on—equipment, programs, ideas, and relationships, the use of which will compound in value over time.[1] Through careful and selective placement of investments and learning from what works, your impact will appreciate accordingly.

Whenever the subject of investment comes up, the word "diversification" is likely to emerge. Diversifying makes total sense in one's personal wealth strategy. After all, the more variety you have in your financial portfolio, the more opportunities you have for one or more high-performing investments. In contrast, the key for effective nonprofit investment is better captured by the word *focus*.

As a nonprofit leader, it's easy to be tempted to broaden your organization's reach. After all, the thinking goes, if you were to step just a bit outside of your mission and take on one more separate-but-related project, you could have even more impact. Tempting as this impulse may be, it is misguided. While growth and innovation are good, losing focus is not. Straying from your mission muddies your story and confuses your staff and your supporters.

Pursuing multiple goals, workstreams, and initiatives typically leads to underwhelming results across all of them.[2] An example of this phenomenon is nonprofits that tend to make their decisions based on donor interest, turning what should be fact-based discussions into debates over preference or politics.[3]

Organizations whose investments are too broadly diversified also restrict innovation. In large nonprofits, new ideas get caught in departmental silos and are unable to translate into impact. Even in smaller nonprofits, individual agendas can have staff and volunteers running around chasing the latest shiny object. The best way to avoid this issue is to *narrow your focus*.

Hone in on one thing, do it well, and very deliberately expand the scope as resources, talent, and beneficiary demand allow.

Wanting to serve your community in a broader capacity is a noble goal, but trying to be all things to all people results in disappointing everyone and crushing team morale. Rather than providing additional services to your beneficiaries, consider partnering with another agency so you can provide support while still remaining focused on your mission.

As successful for-profit organizations have long known, focus can be the differentiator that sets you apart from the crowd. A targeted scope focuses innovation and removes doubt from donors who are delighted to understand exactly what they are funding.

From Budget to Investment Plan

Every nonprofit should understand its impact aspiration, the financial resources required to achieve that aspiration, and how the organization expects to obtain these resources. This understanding is reflected in the nonprofit's annual budget, an essential document that guides how the staff and board manage the organization financially and programmatically throughout the year.

Essentially, a budget is a plan that outlines how a nonprofit will obtain and spend money to reach specific goals on certain timelines.[4] But there's a lot in a name. Harkening back to the distinction between spending and investing, there is power to using the name of this plan to shift mindsets in the organization. This is why I recommend to my clients that they rename their annual "budget" an annual "investment plan." Renaming the document sends a signal to staff, board, volunteers, and donors that your nonprofit is doing more than spending—it's *investing*.

Bear in mind the following guiding principles when creating your nonprofit's investment plan:

- **Clearly identify programmatic objectives.** You must know what you're trying to achieve and ensure that you're working toward goals that align with your mission and strategic plan.
- **Determine what financial resources are needed.** Understand what it will take financially to carry out your programs, and know what funds are available to meet those objectives. Err on the side of conservatism.
- **Involve both staff and board in the process.** Nonprofit governance suffers from an unclear understanding of the division of labor between executive directors and board members.[5] Communication improves accuracy of information and solidifies commitment to the plan.
- **Document everything.** Take notes on formulas and assumptions so you have something to reference as you manage your organization's finances throughout the year.
- **Customize the process.** Every investment plan is different, so the steps you take to build yours will (and should) be unique to your needs and circumstances.

Proper investment planning takes time. Start working on your investment plan at least three months prior to the fiscal year's end to ensure your board has sufficient time to provide their input and ultimately approve your proposed plan before the new year begins. To ensure a smooth planning process, follow this ten-step checklist for developing your nonprofit's investment plan:

1. *Identify timeline.*

    Set a target date for board approval, then work backward. Create checkpoints for each step and review, and allow time for discussion. Aim to have the timeline approved before the start of the new fiscal year.

2. *Agree on goals.*

   Prioritize your program delivery goals and set your organizational financial goals. Take this opportunity to clarify annual goals from your strategic plan.

3. *Know your current status.*

   Review your current income and expenses compared to your investment plan. Forecast to the end of the year and analyze any variances.

4. *Agree on your approach.*

   Assign roles and responsibilities. Agree on who is offering input, who is drafting what, and who has the authority to make final decisions.

5. *Develop draft investment plan.*

   Determine the expenses needed to achieve your programmatic, organizational, and strategic objectives.

6. *Develop draft income plan.*

   Use your current fundraising and revenue activities to project income from legacy activities. Then project income based on new activities you plan to implement.

7. *Review draft investment plan.*

   Syndicate the draft plan far and wide to verify that the plan meets the organization's impact objectives. Adjust along the way to match realistic projections.

8. *Approve plan.*

   Present your plan to the necessary committees and ultimately the full board for final approval.

9. *Document decisions.*

   Create a consolidated spreadsheet and notate all assumptions.

10. *Implement plan.*

   Assign financial management responsibilities and incorporate the plan into your accounting system. Monitor your plan and make adjustments as needed.

Involving all stakeholders in drafting next year's investment plan ensures you enter the new year as a cohesive team. It also builds trust and confidence among your staff, board, and donors that you're responsibly managing your sacred resources to maximize impact.

Summary

Ollie Randall was raised with an appreciation and respect for the elderly. She learned entering adulthood, however, that not everyone shared this view. While serving as the executive director of a home for the aged, Randall realized that the needs of older Americans weren't being met. They desperately needed an advocate. Randall helped found the National Council on Aging (NCOA), the first charitable organization of its kind to work toward improving the quality of life of senior citizens. A series of small strategic investments has enabled the NCOA to address numerous physical and psychological issues for the elderly that had previously gone unresolved. Randall's example shows that investing trumps spending. When organizations selectively invest in a focused portfolio of one to three programs, they can make a much more significant impact. By reframing your budget as an "investment plan," you establish the mindset that you're not simply spending money on near-term needs. Instead, you're investing in programs, ideas, and people that will appreciate into long-term, world-changing impact.

The key to the twenty-sixth law of nonprofit impact—*don't spend, invest*—is shifting mindsets from near-term needs to long-term impact.

Recommended Further Reading

BATTS, MICHAEL E. *Nonprofit Financial Oversight: The Concise and Complete Guide for Boards and Finance Committees.* Scotts Valley, CA: CreateSpace, 2017.

GRACE, KAY SPRINKEL. *Beyond Fundraising: New Strategies for Nonprofit Innovation and Investment.* Hoboken, NJ: Wiley, 2005.

WODTKE, CHRISTINA. *Radical Focus: Achieving Your Most Important Goals with Objectives and Key Results.* Palo Alto, CA: Cucina Media LLC, 2021.

---

1 Moonhee Cho and Giselle A. Auger, "Extrovert and Engaged? Exploring the Connection Between Personality and Involvement of Stakeholders and the Perceived Relationship Investment of Nonprofit Organizations," *Public Relations Review* 43, no. 4 (2017): 729–37.

2 Dilip Soman and Min Zhao, "The Fewer the Better: Number of Goals and Savings Behavior," *Journal of Marketing Research* 45, no. 6 (2011): 944–57.

3 Dave Algoso, "Doing Less, Better," *Stanford Social Innovation Review*, July 31, 2015.

4 Murray Dropkin, Jim Halpin, and Bill La Touche, *The Budget-Building Book for Nonprofits: A Step-by-Step Guide for Managers* (San Francisco: Jossey-Bass, 2007), 1.

5 Jerry D. Marx and Christie Davis, "Nonprofit Governance: Improving Performance in Troubled Economic Times," *Administration in Social Work* 36, no. 1 (2012): 40–52.

LAW 27:

Activate one donor per day.

> *What you do for yourself is fleeting and dies with you. What you do for others has unending benefit and is eternal.*
>
> Jerold Panas (1928–2018)

Jerold Panas believed that life is a wheel—the more you give, the more you get back.

That's why he devoted his life to helping others.

A leading force in philanthropy, and one who did more than he said, Panas founded a financial development firm that helped more than 3,900 clients and was instrumental in raising more than $11 billion for hospitals, faith-based institutions, educational facilities, and social service organizations.

Panas noticed a common issue among nonprofits: they struggled with major gift fundraising. Panas decided to create a solution to help nonprofit leaders and educate organizations on this crucial topic.

In 1991, with teacher and consultant William Sturtevant, Panas founded the Institute for Charitable Giving. The organization presented seminars and workshops, teaching useful and practical applications for increasing successful donor response. Panas served as a consultant and coach whose advice and guidance has impacted thousands of people and touched charitable organizations worldwide.

Although Panas was an expert in philanthropy (he had been consulting and advising high-level nonprofit leaders well before starting his firm), it wasn't his knowledge alone that earned him his reputation and successful decades-long career. Panas was a master communicator and expert interviewer. He took a genuine interest in people, asking questions about their lives to get to know and understand them better.

He valued these connections, and created opportunities to follow up on previous conversations. For example, after a discussion at a dinner party, he would send someone a book or an article that pertained to their talk. When he heard that a friend was trying to win a bid on a job opportunity, he sent an unsolicited letter of recommendation on their behalf. He always put others' needs first and sought ways to serve individuals and organizations alike.

How did Panas's penchant for communication help him build a fifty-year career that inspired and reminded other nonprofit leaders that they could change the world?

Panas recognized that *activating daily donors means talking (and following up) with as many people as possible.*

Prospecting

Prospecting is one of the most important tasks—and one of the greatest challenges—of working in the nonprofit sector. In order for most nonprofits to survive, they need to find individual donors who are willing to give and keep giving. Retaining donors is an issue for numerous reasons, from poor communication and cultivation strategies to changing donor priorities and an increasingly oversaturated mail and email atmosphere.[1]

Nonprofits often overlook untapped resources when prospecting. Begin with your in-house network. Your staff and board members all have contacts who would be glad to support your cause. Provide your team with the tools, resources, and training they'll need to prospect on the organization's behalf.

Closely related to your in-house network, volunteers are often viewed as only generous with their time. The truth is they're often generous with their money and contacts when asked.[2] After all, they already believe in the work you're doing and have a passion for your cause—why not ask (in a timely, thoughtful way, of course) if they want to invest financially in your work?

High school and college students are another rarely tapped resource for funds. Nonprofit leaders assume these young people don't have the money to contribute, but this is shortsighted. Prospecting isn't just about reaching people who can give thousands of dollars immediately. It's about cultivating relationships that will fund the work over the long term. Catch young people early and develop their awareness of how they can help, and you'll eventually have lifelong givers in substantial numbers.[3]

Another area to look to improve donor success is online giving. Although these online donors tend to give less than those offline, even a small contribution can help feed a hungry organization and spread the word about its work. By nurturing these relationships and staying top-of-mind through direct messages, you can secure ongoing funds for your organization.

It doesn't take thousands of major donors to fund your work. In fact, most healthy nonprofits raise 60% of revenue from the top 10% of donors.[4] At its most basic, a successful annual funding strategy boils down to finding a few new individual donors and seeking ways to retain and incrementally upgrade the giving of existing individual donors. This is only possible by meeting as many people as possible, cultivating relationships, and making the Ask.

Asking

As Panas was fond of reminding his students, there comes a point once you've identified your prospects, understand who they are, and built a relationship that it's time to make the Ask. Every Asking experience will be different. Each person you visit (mark that word, it was an important one in Panas's fundraising lexicon) will be in a different financial position and will have unique motivations and stressors. But, as Panas was also fond of emphasizing, it matters less *how* you ask than *that* you ask.[5]

Still, Panas acknowledges there are some guiding principles that can help fundraisers successfully make the Ask. He recommends nonprofit leaders follow these Seventeen Golden Rules for Asking for a Gift:[6]

1. *Know all you can about your organization.*

   You must be crystal clear in your mission, vision, programs, and impact.

2. *Make certain you're completely committed to the worthiness of your cause and the significance of your project.*

   If you don't believe in what you're doing, how can you expect others to care enough to contribute to your mission?

3. *Learn all you can about the prospect you're visiting.*

   The more you know about them, the better prepared you will be to develop a meaningful relationship that can result in financial support.

4. *Ask for a specific amount.*

   Have an educated understanding of exactly how much the prospect is willing and able to give and ask for that amount.

5. *Carefully consider the way you should express the amount of your request.*

   Build your confidence by saying the specific amount out loud several times before you visit with your prospect.

6. *Now you're ready to secure the appointment.*

   Getting the meeting is harder than getting the gift. If you get the visit, you're 85% of the way to securing the donation.

7. *Practice, practice, practice.*

   Write out what you plan to say and rehearse the presentation out loud. The more you practice, the more confident you'll be, and the smoother your presentation will go.

8. *Write out in advance all the reasons your prospect may put you off.*

   Consider your ask from every angle and prepare responses to potential objections.

9. *When you make the visit, go in pairs.*

   A colleague, board member, or significant donor is a magic partnership. They can share their own experience and help answer questions.

10. *Call on your most probable donors first.*

    This can start you off with immediate success and help build your confidence.

11. *Establish rapport in your early moments with the prospect.*

    While the short-term goal is to receive a contribution, the long-term goal is to build a relationship with someone who will continue to give to your organization.

12. *It's essential that you probe for concerns.*

    Ask questions to find ways to alleviate any hesitations with your prospect. You should listen 75% of the time and talk 25%.

13. *Convey the benefit to the donor.*

    Even kindhearted people want to know what's in it for them. It has to be a win-win for the institution and the donor.

14. *Remember: it's not about money and it's not about your organization.*

    Everything you do during the Ask is about the prospect and connecting them to a worthwhile cause.

15. *When you're finally ready to ask for the gift, use careful wording.*

    The phrase, "I would like you to consider a gift of..." is powerful without being pushy.

16. *Don't let objections rattle you.*

    Objections give you an opportunity to gain more insight into the mindset of the prospect. Probe for concerns and provide answers to their questions.

17. *Don't leave a meeting without getting a commitment to something.*

    Whether it's the gift itself or a date for a follow-up visit, get a firm answer from your prospect.

Following these golden rules will embolden you to look for the right Asking moment, help you establish a relationship with your prospect, and increase your chances of securing the gift. Taken together, the above principles on prospecting and asking give rise to a meta-principle (mine, not that of Jerry Panas): make every effort to work toward making an Ask every single day. This is not to say that you should immediately ask everyone you meet to become a major donor. Rather, you should be talking to so many people, building relationships, and consistently cultivating prospective donors that someone is reaching the status of "Ask-ready" on a daily basis.

How about it? Are you up to the "Ask every day" challenge?

Summary

Jerold Panas built a fifty-year philanthropic career by becoming an expert in fundraising and a master communicator. He not only built initial connections with people, but maintained them by following up on a professional and personal level. His passion for helping nonprofits led him to found the Institute for Charitable Giving, an organization that creates seminars and workshops to educate nonprofit leaders on how to effectively raise funds. As a result, Panas has impacted thousands of people, helped raise billions of dollars in donations, and fueled charitable organizations worldwide. Panas realized that fundraising is all about building relationships. By continually and thoughtfully prospecting with a heart for giving first, nonprofit leaders can find new donors and incrementally upgrade existing donors.

The keys to the twenty-seventh law of nonprofit impact—*activate one donor every day*—are prospecting and asking.

Recommended Further Reading

FAY, NATHAN. *Precision Prospect Development.* Charlotte, NC: Precision Philanthropy, 2018.

FILLA, JENNIFER J., *and Helen E.* Brown. *Prospect Research for Fundraisers: The Essential Handbook.* Hoboken, NJ: Wiley, 2013.

PANAS, JEROLD. *Mega Gifts: Who Gives Them, Who Gets Them.* Medfield, MA: Emerson and Church Publishers, 2005.

———. *Wit, Wisdom & Moxie: A Fundraiser's Compendium of Wrinkles, Strategies, and Admonitions That Really Work.* Lanham, MD: Taylor Trade Publishing, 2003.

---

1 Heather Yandow, "Benchmarking Individual Donors," *Stanford Social Innovation Review*, October 7, 2016.

2 René Bekkers, "Giving Time and/or Money: Trade-Off or Spill-Over?" *University of Groningen Default Journal* (2002).

3 Leslie Berger, "Untapped Donors," *Stanford Social Innovation Review* 3, no. 4 (Winter 2005): 14.

4 Heather Yandow, "Building Your Individual Donor Base," *Stanford Social Innovation Review*, October 15, 2014.

5 Jerold Panas, *Asking: A 59-Minute Guide to Everything Board Members, Volunteers, and Staff Must Know to Secure the Gift* (Medfield, MA: Emerson and Church Publishers, 2013), 11.

6 Panas, *Asking*, 84–87.

LAW 28:

Sell things.

> *You can't help a man by doubting him. When he tells us he wants to work, we assume that he does. When you give a man a job, you are not dealing with a pauper. He is not an applicant for charity. He wants to give something for what he receives.*
>
> *Reverend Edgar J. Helms (1863–1942)*

Reverend Edgar J. Helms learned from a young age the value of pursuing a better life.

Born in the mid-1800s in a small lumber camp in upstate New York, Helms watched his parents emerge from poverty to build a better a life. When Helms was still young, his parents bought a covered wagon and traveled west, settling on a one-hundred-acre farm in Iowa where Helms and his three siblings were raised.

Seeing his parents buy land and improve life for their family, Helms decided to leave the small town he grew up in for a greater cause. He studied at Cornell College, where he graduated with a bachelor's degree in philosophy, earning the highest grades ever received by a Cornell student.

After graduation, Helms felt called to the church. He left Iowa for Boston University, where he earned a bachelor's degree in sacred theology. Helms wanted to travel to India for missionary work, but, in 1902, he learned he'd been assigned to a Boston settlement house for poor immigrants.

To Helms' shock, the Boston settlement house was located in one of the worst slums in America. He was horrified by the residents' living conditions, which he expected to find in a third-world country, not a preeminent US city.

Not only did these immigrant residents find themselves in a new country without jobs, but they were surrounded by lice-infested tenements and desperate for food, clothing, and shelter. Helms could see these people didn't need a handout; they needed a hand up.

And that's when he had a revolutionary idea.

Helms slung a burlap sack over his shoulder and went door-to-door through Boston's wealthiest neighborhoods seeking donations. Instead of money or food, Helms asked for damaged or discarded items like clothing and household goods that the affluent could no longer use. He took them back to the immigrants at his settlement house and offered residents $4 a day to repair the items. Then, they would sell the refurbished items to their community.

Helms's strategy— paying the poor for their labor refurbishing donated goods and then selling those goods for profit—was completely unconventional. The workers Helms hired were eager to learn a trade, gain new skills, and earn their own income. They didn't want charity. They simply wanted a chance.

This is how the now world-famous Goodwill Industries began. Since its inception, Helms's model has helped people with disabilities and disadvantages earn a living. During the Great Depression, it connected people with basic services. After World War II, it provided training and jobs to soldiers returning home. When digital technology entered the American workplace, it trained people on computers. During times of recession, it has been instrumental in connecting people to jobs.

How was Helms's innovative idea for a new way of helping people able to have such a far-reaching impact?

He understood that *every nonprofit can and should do less begging for bucks and more making for markets.*

Sales for Charitable Purpose

When most people consider income generation for nonprofit organizations, they immediately think of contributions from charitable donors. But the idea that nonprofits get all their revenue from donations is a misconception.

Few people realize that nearly half of the total revenue for public charities comes from fees for services and goods.[1] Organizations rely on a mix of income sources, diversifying their revenue stream with funding from money-raising events, foundations, corporate gifts, and government grants. This cross-subsidization enables nonprofits to grow, become more sustainable, and mitigate risk.[2]

The majority of private entities are for-profit companies. Their priority is to make a profit that is either distributed to owners and shareholders or reinvested back into the business. Nonprofits, on the other hand, exist to fulfill a mission. However, they still can and do sell related goods or services to help raise funds for advancing their mission.

For years I've taken the controversial stance that every—yes, every—nonprofit can and should sell something. Whether in leadership meetings or webinars or conferences, one of my favorite questions to ask is whether a participant can name a type of nonprofit that has nothing to sell.[3] To this day, I have yet to be stumped—every nonprofit can adapt its mission into something salable. Whether you're a music therapy nonprofit charging a discounted rate for music lessons, an at-risk youth program helping local businesses staff open positions, or a church running a preschool in its facilities during the workweek, your nonprofit can supplement donations with sales of products or services while still maintaining its status as a nonprofit.

The income of most nonprofit organizations is tax-exempt under Internal Revenue Code Section 501(c)(3). To qualify for this status, an organization must exist for one or more exclusively charitable purposes. These purposes range from religious and scientific to educational and humanitarian. In order to retain this tax-exempt status, the activity that generates your income must be directly connected to your nonprofit's mission. This is determined by a series of guidelines, including but not limited to:

- Extent and size of the activity
- Continuity and frequency of the activity
- Circumstances around each case
- Nonprofit's tax-exempt purpose

If your financial gains come from activities unrelated to your mission (for instance, charging an occupant rent for use of your facility), then that revenue must be taxed as business income. While you're certainly not prohibited from selling goods and services to bring in money, you must adhere to the regulations surrounding charitable purpose in order to claim that revenue as tax exempt.

The Internal Revenue Service monitors these matters carefully; they provide a publication that outlines the aspects of earned and unearned income.[4] If your earned income is deemed inappropriate or misaligned with your charitable purpose, you could face large taxes or penalties, and even run the risk of losing your tax-exempt status.

Managing earned-income ventures takes research, strategy, and effort. In the end, however, the work required to become a sales-funded organization is worth the effort. The sale of goods and services keeps nonprofits from relying solely on fundraising, helps them attract and retain staff, builds their reputation, and contributes to their overall self-sufficiency.[5]

Examples of Nonprofit Selling

Since Helms developed his groundbreaking philanthropic model with Goodwill Industries, other nonprofits have followed suit. Of all nonprofit organizations, YMCA holds the distinction of being the nonprofit with the highest annual sales revenue.[6] By charging a membership fee for community members to use their amenities, the nonprofit pays its staff, provides programs for the community, and maintains its facilities. Some YMCA locations even offer job training, leadership skills training, and homeless shelters.

Big Brothers Big Sisters of America accepts donated clothing, furniture, and household goods, and sells them to fund their mentoring services. These funds allow them to pay for the recruitment, enrollment, and support of the volunteers who create meaningful mentoring relationships with children to ensure they reach their full potential.

The most recognizable example of a nonprofit who has mastered the art of selling goods is the Girl Scouts of the United States of America. In 1917, girls and their mothers baked cookies in their home kitchens and sold them at the high school cafeteria to help finance troop activities. The idea gained popularity when a Girl Scout director posted a cookie recipe in *The American Girl* magazine, outlining the cost of ingredients and the potential profits they could bring. This inspired girls nationwide to bake cookies and sell them door to door.

Soon they were selling these cookies in city gas- and electric-company windows, and eventually setting up tables in front of suburban shopping malls. The annual system has become a nationally recognized fundraiser that brings in $800 million a year, and it helps young girls develop essential marketing and business skills.

Nonprofit selling isn't taboo; you probably encounter dozens of examples of nonprofit selling every day. The resale shop on the corner who sells clothing to raise money for victims of domestic violence. The children's choir who sells singing telegrams during the holidays to help pay for competition fees. The animal shelter who charges an adoption fee to pay for the care of its animals. They succeed because they provide a product or service that people need. They educate people about their services through advertising or word of mouth. Many of them have an e-commerce shop where people can easily discover their goods or services online. Most importantly, these organizations go to great lengths to show their customers that every dollar spent helps the nonprofit advance their mission.

What products or services can your nonprofit take to market to advance your mission?

Summary

Reverend Edgar J. Helms was horrified by the living conditions of the immigrants in Boston's settlement houses in the early 1900s. These newly arrived Bostonians had no jobs, no skills, and no money to improve their situation. Realizing these people needed a hand up and not a handout, Helms sought donations of discarded items from nearby wealthy neighborhoods. He paid immigrants $4 a day to repair them, and then sold these refurbished goods to the community. This idea of nonprofit selling was revolutionary. Since then, many charitable organizations have followed suit. By meeting the requirements outlined by the Internal Revenue Service, a nonprofit can and should sell products or services and still maintain its nonprofit status. As long as the sale is directly related to the organization's charitable purpose, its tax-exempt status remains secure. Nonprofits like the YMCA, Big Brothers Big Sisters, and the Girl Scouts have successfully mastered the art of nonprofit selling.

The key to the twenty-eighth law of nonprofit impact—*sell things*—is finding a salable product or service related to your nonprofit's charitable purpose.

Recommended Further Reading

CAREY, SHELLEY JOHNSON. *Thin Mint Memories: Scouting for Empowerment Through the Girl Scout Cookie Program.* Woodbridge: Clear Message Media, 2016.

FISHMAN, STEPHEN. *Every Nonprofit's Tax Guide: How to Keep Your Tax-Exempt Status & Avoid IRS Problems.* Berkeley, CA: NOLO, 2019.

HELMS, EDGAR J. *Pioneering in Modern City Missions.* London: Forgotten Books, 2018.

1 Estelle James, "Commercialism and the Mission of Nonprofits," in *In Search of the Nonprofit Sector*, ed. Peter Frumkin and Jonathan B. Imber, 73–84 (New York: Routledge, 2004).

2 Brice McKeever, *The Nonprofit Sector in Brief 2015: Public Charities, Giving, and Volunteering*, Urban Institute, 2015.

3 Asim Ansari, S. Siddarth, and Charles B. Weinberg, "Pricing a Bundle of Products or Services: The Case of Nonprofits," *Journal of Marketing Research* 33, no. 1 (1996): 86–93.

4 IRS, "Publication 17 (2020), Your Federal Income Tax," 2021, https://www.irs.gov.

5 Baorong Guo, "Charity for Profit? Exploring Factors Associated with the Commercialization of Human Service Nonprofits," *Nonprofit and Voluntary Sector Quarterly* 35, no. 1 (2006): 123–38.

6 Burton A. Weisbrod, "The Pitfalls of Profits," *Stanford Social Innovation Review* 2, no. 1 (2004): 40.

LAW 29:

Keep it legal.

> *My goal is that someday every low-income and working-class family can choose the learning environment that is best for their children, just like families with money already do.*
>
> **John F. Kirtley**

As a successful venture capital entrepreneur in New York, education reform was the furthest thing from John F. Kirtley's mind.

Yet when he learned about The Patron's Program, a philanthropic project created by fellow Wall Street financier Peter Flanigan, Kirtley felt a desire to investigate. The Patron's Program encouraged business leaders to offer their skills, knowledge, and donations to support Catholic schools in the city's low-income areas. Curious to learn more, Kirtley enrolled as a participant and was assigned to a private K-8 school in a South Bronx neighborhood. He'd believed that private education was expensive, so he was surprised to discover that this school had nearly three hundred students who qualified for the free or reduced-price lunch program. Kirtley wondered why parents of these students were working two jobs and foregoing television service to pay an annual tuition of $3,200 per child. After all, there was a tuition-free public school nearby. Parents, he learned, believed that their children could receive a better education from these private schools and prioritized accordingly.

From this experience, Kirtley saw the importance of parental choice in education.

This revelation inspired Kirtley to chart a path for education reform. In 1998, he started a nonprofit that distributed scholarships to needy students. Now named Step Up for Students, the organization initially offered 700 partial scholarships ($1,500 maximum) to help low-income families enroll their children in private schools. With hardly any advertising, Step Up received a startling 12,000 applications. That's when Kirtley knew they were on to something.

Around this time, Jeb Bush won the Florida gubernatorial election on a platform of school choice for children of failing public schools. Kirtley and Step Up helped to get Bush's education program passed, and in 1999, the country's first statewide voucher program was established.

Under this program, the state would provide families with some or all of the funds that would have been used to educate their child in public school. The families could then use that money to enroll their children in the private school of their choice.

Thrilled by the prospect of so many children receiving vouchers, Kirtley was disheartened when every school that had previously been considered "failing" was suddenly deemed "passing." Either the schools had improved drastically, or grades weren't reported accurately. Either way, Kirtley felt thousands of children were being robbed of a life-changing opportunity.

Kirtley began working with lawmakers to pass the Florida Tax Credit Scholarship program. The law would provide state tax credits for contributions to nonprofit scholarship organizations. Those organizations could then award scholarships to eligible children of low-income families. The law was passed and took effect in January 2002.

Since then, the Florida state legislature has increased the fundraising cap and added new potential tax sources for credits. Today, more than 30% of students who are funded by taxpayers attend educational institutions other than their zoned public schools. As for Kirtley, he left his financial career to focus on school choice full-time. As a result, Step Up has awarded more than one million scholarships to students from low-income families.

How did a finance executive from Wall Street become the driving force behind one of the largest educational reforms of our time?

He understood that *laws aren't enemies; they're allies.*

Basics of Nonprofit Legality

One of the financial benefits to working in the nonprofit sector is that many charitable organizations qualify as tax exempt. As such, these nonprofits don't have to pay taxes to the government on the funds they're able to raise and can therefore apply every cent they receive toward their mission.

To qualify for this status, nonprofits must comply with stringent federal and state laws. If a nonprofit fails to meet certain requirements, the government could revoke their tax-exempt status, which typically leads to the nonprofit's closure.[1]

There are two types of nonprofit organizations that can qualify for tax exemptions: *nonprofit corporations* and *unincorporated nonprofits*.[2] Nonprofit corporations exist for a purpose other than profit. In fact, all profits go back into the organization. As long as nonprofit corporations meet certain standards and regulations, they can receive tax-exempt status at the federal and state levels.

Unincorporated nonprofits are formed when two or more people work together toward a common goal. If that goal is to make a profit, then a partnership has formed. If the goal is to provide a public service, then no legal paperwork needs to be filed and the nonprofit is unincorporated. These are often formed for short-term purposes on an as-needed basis, such as a lemonade stand to raise money for the local animal shelter or a community fundraiser to help a friend offset hospital bills.

Regardless of which type of nonprofit you lead, your organization must meet the appropriate legal qualifications to maintain its operation as a tax-exempt entity. Here are some basics:

- **Laws vary from state to state.** Not only must nonprofits follow the laws of the state in which they operate, they must also abide by the laws of other states when seeking contributions from long-distance donors. Know your specific state nonprofit laws.
- **The board of directors has the final say.** When making decisions for a nonprofit organization, the only authorities who can override the board are the Attorney General and a state court of law.
- **Every nonprofit must have charter documents and bylaws.** These articles state the name and location of the nonprofit as well as the names and addresses of founding members. They document the purpose of the organization and declare how assets should be distributed in the event the nonprofit dissolves. Attorneys should review the wording to ensure the organization qualifies for tax exemption.
- **Determine whether your organization is a public charity or a nonprofit entity.** Public charities receive their funding from large donors and investment income and are subject to stricter rules. Nonprofit entities get their funds from fundraising, donors, grants, and government contracts.
- **The government prohibits nonprofits from engaging in certain activities.** You may not do anything to impact a politician's chances during an election or dedicate a significant part of your activities or resources to lobbying.

As far as the IRS is concerned, your nonprofit organization is rule-bound. There are activities you can and cannot perform. As long as you follow the local, state, and federal laws for your type of nonprofit, your organization will retain its tax-exempt status.

Putting the Law to Work

The goal of most nonprofits is social change in communities. Sometimes this change can be accomplished through programs and local efforts. Other times, it requires the help of public leaders in positions of influence.[3]

A common misconception of nonprofit organizations is that the government prohibits them from any and all lobbying. But if that's true, then how were Kirtley and Step Up for Students able to get the Florida Tax Credit Scholarship program passed?

First, the law states that a nonprofit cannot dedicate a *significant* part of its activities to lobbying. If an expenditure test reveals that an organization's lobbying spending doesn't surpass a specific amount (usually based on the nonprofit's size), then the organization is within its lobbying limits. If it exceeds its limits, it can lose its tax-exempt status and will have to pay taxes on all of the income gained in that period.

Second, there are very strict requirements for nonprofit activities to be considered lobbying. For instance, lobbying occurs when an organization either communicates directly with a legislator to express a view about a specific legislation (direct lobbying) or urges the public to contact a legislator for this purpose (grassroots lobbying).[4] The truth is, most government officials, from the Executive Branch to local school boards, aren't considered legislators, so discussions with them are not considered lobbying.

Additionally, influencing administrative rules, policies, executive orders, and regulations is not considered lobbying. The vast majority of governmental organizations are simply interpreting and implementing laws that legislatures have already passed. These activities are considered *advocacy*. Since advocacy isn't the same thing as lobbying, 501(c)(3) organizations can engage in a wide range of activities to influence decisions without exceeding lobbying limits.

Between the IRS and state and federal disclosure laws, nonprofit organizations must be careful in how they go about creating change. If one or more employees spends more than 20% of their time lobbying at the federal level, the Lobbying Disclosure Act requires them to register. They'll then have to submit quarterly reports to Congress that outline time and money spent on lobbying.

Many nonprofits lobby for the good of society and their organization in multiple policy domains, directly and indirectly, and at several levels of government.[5] Lobbying is possible, and it can be highly beneficial to your organization's mission, but it requires careful tracking of the time and money spent for this purpose.[6]

The work you're doing is too important to go away—so keep it legal.

Summary

When John F. Kirtley realized he wasn't making headway in his efforts to provide vouchers that would enable low-income parents to choose their children's schools, he sought help from a higher level. Working with lawmakers and politicians, he was able to get the Florida Tax Credit Scholarship program passed. This was a huge step for education reform, as thousands of students were able to seek a higher quality of learning that was otherwise cost prohibitive for their families. While there are financial benefits like tax-exempt status available to nonprofits, organizations must meet standards and regulations to ensure they qualify. That's why it's important for nonprofit leaders to have an understanding of basic nonprofit legality. This knowledge can position you to advance your mission through lobbying and administrative advocacy limited to a level that permits retention of tax-exempt status. Government officials and lawmakers can help you create the change you seek, but only if you abide by the required rules and regulations.

The keys to the twenty-ninth law of nonprofit impact—*keep it legal*—are knowing and abiding by the laws of the land.

Recommended Further Reading

AVNER, MARCIA, JOSH WISE, JEFF NARABROOK, JANNIE FOX, AND SUSIE BROWN. *The Lobbying and Advocacy Handbook for Nonprofit Organizations, Second Edition: Shaping Public Policy at the State and Local Level.* Nashville, TN: Fieldstone Alliance, 2013.

DUBOFF, LEONARD D., *and Amanda Bryan. The Law (in Plain English) for Nonprofit Organizations.* New York: Allworth Press, 2019.

HESSENIUS, BARRY. *Hardball Lobbying for Nonprofits: Real Advocacy for Nonprofits in the New Century.* London: Palgrave Macmillan, 2007.

---

1 Bruce R. Hopkins, *Starting and Managing a Nonprofit Organization* (Hoboken, NJ: John Wiley and Sons, 2017).

2 Harry G. Henn and Michael George Pfeifer, "Nonprofit Groups: Factors Influencing Choice of Form," *Wake Forest Law Review* 11, no. 2 (1975): 181.

3 David F. Suárez and Hokyu Hwang, "Civic Engagement and Nonprofit Lobbying in California, 1998-2003," *Nonprofit and Voluntary Sector Quarterly* 37, no. 1 (2007): 93–112.

4 J. S. Vernick, "Lobbying and Advocacy for the Public's Health: What Are the Limits for Nonprofit Organizations?," *American Journal of Public Health* 89, no. 9 (1999): 1425–29.

5 Christopher R. Prentice and Jeffrey L. Brudney, "Nonprofit Lobbying Strategy: Challenging or Championing the Conventional Wisdom?" *International Journal of Voluntary and Nonprofit Organizations* 28, no. 3 (2017): 935–57.

6 *A Nonprofit's Guide to Lobbying and Political Activity* (Washington, DC: DC Bar Pro Bono Center, 2016), 3.

LAW 30:

Dream bigger.

> *We have but one life. We get nothing out of that life except by putting something into it. To relieve suffering, to help the unfortunate, to do kind acts and deeds is, after all, the one sure way to secure happiness or to achieve real success. Your life and mine shall be valued not by what we take...but by what we give.*
>
> **Edgar F. Allen (1876–1937)**

A personal tragedy in 1907 forever changed the course of Edgar F. Allen's life—and, ultimately, the lives of millions of others.

Allen, a successful businessman, was living with his family in the small town of Elyria, Ohio, when his eighteen-year-old son, Homer, was involved in a serious streetcar accident. The town's makeshift hospital didn't have the resources to provide the care Homer needed, and he did not survive.

Allen, wanting to spare other parents from the horrible loss and pain he had endured, sold his business and devoted his life to raising money to build a real hospital in Elyria. Just one year later, in 1908, the Elyria Memorial Hospital opened, and it impacted Allen's life in ways he could have never expected. While volunteering at the hospital, Allen met Jimmy, an eight-year-old orphan seeking treatment to straighten his crooked legs. Realizing the need for a facility for kids like Jimmy, Allen raised funds to open the country's first hospital for physically disabled children.

Seeing the hospital's positive impact on patients and their families, Allen remained devoted to this cause. In 1919, he and fellow Ohio Rotary Club members established the Ohio Society for Crippled Children (OSCC). They lobbied their state legislature to provide funding for the care of children with physical disabilities. Legislation supporting their initiative was passed; in 1920, Ohio hospitals could open centers for children with disabilities.

When the Great Depression hit and private contributions and government funding came to a halt, the OSCC developed a campaign selling stamps, or seals, to thank donors for their support. In the middle of these toughest of times, their campaign raised an incredible $47,000, more than twice the organization's annual budget. This financial success enabled the nonprofit to expand its mission to include adults with disabilities, and it became the Society for Crippled Children and Adults (SCCA).

The SCCA believed there should be more federal laws to benefit people with disabilities. It helped to pass the Social Security Act in 1935, providing facilities and services for children with physical challenges. Soon after, the SCCA's seal campaign featured a lily, a representation of spring and the Christian resurrection. In the 1960s, the SCCA adopted this as their official symbol and changed its name to the National Easterseal Society.

In 1972, the Easterseals held a telethon to raise funds and awareness for their cause. The event brought in $800,000 and served as a platform to educate viewers and politicians alike. It opened the door to legislators who could help the disabled find affordable healthcare, secure jobs, and receive education. During the next several years, great strides were made, including the Rehabilitation Act of 1973 and the Americans with Disabilities Act of 1990.

Over time, the Easterseals expanded their services to help people with varying disabilities lead fuller, more independent lives. Today, their offerings range from adult day care centers and early childhood intervention programs to physical therapy and technological tools for the disabled.

How did Allen create an organization that began by assisting disabled children and went on to help over 1.5 million people overcome a multitude of physical and mental challenges?

He understood that *the only things limiting a nonprofit are talent, time, and imagination.*

The Power of Boldness

Not all dreams are created equal. To be sure, nearly all nonprofits start with good intentions to address serious social ills. However, many have naïve ideas about the complexity and magnitude of the issues they aim to solve.[1] That's why organizations often work around the edges of an issue without successfully eradicating the root of the problem. What makes a dream big and bold isn't necessarily its geographic, financial, or demographic scale. Rather, *big dreams target the root causes of big problems.*

Put another way, the efforts of many nonprofits focus on the symptoms rather than the disease. As a result, they tend to create programs that provide only near-term relief instead of creating significant and lasting change. Such efforts serve only—if meaningfully—to relieve the symptoms, yet are not bold enough to make a transformative impact.

There are numerous reasons why nonprofit leaders focus on symptoms over root causes. We live in a society that places value on immediate results rather than long-term investments. The pressure of financial responsibility, both to our organization and to the public, can result in a fear of failure that causes us to choose an easier, more budget-friendly agenda, as opposed to a deeper solution that addresses underlying problems. To get to the heart of the issues we face, we need bold strategies that resist persistent demands for immediate results.

The first step is to rethink the way we approach our missions. Instead of anesthetizing people to the pain of a problem, our goal should be to *solve* the problem itself. Once we declare this bold aim as our mission, we can begin to take the steps necessary to deliver impact that gets to the root of society's ills.

The truth is, if transformational change isn't the goal, nonprofits fall short of serving their beneficiaries. Instead of focusing on the transactions involved in the delivery of direct services, we should exert the influence necessary to solve problems at their core. This will ensure significant and lasting change for everyone affected by an issue.

Setting a bold goal that you have a chance to achieve not only requires a shift in mindset, but also a shift in strategy. Consider doing fact-based research to identify the source of your community's problems. Once you've pinpointed the issue at hand, you can begin to solve for ways your organization can eradicate the root causes.

Expand your network and consider alliances with diverse partners, from corporate executives to legislative leaders.[2] Their contacts and financial support could be the key to tackling the root of your targeted problem. A reorientation to root causes may also require bold changes to your nonprofit's internal systems. Long-sacred and popular programs designed to bring only relief may need to be reimagined in order to address the root issues causing beneficiaries' suffering.

When you shift your mission from short-term results to long-term solutions, desired results may take longer to achieve. Be transparent with your stakeholders. When they see your progress, even if it's slow, they'll be more likely to stand by you through this longer journey to impact. Although this process may look different for various organizations, thinking big and setting bold goals not only unlocks new paths to impact—it yields greater results.

FAST Goals

Goal-setting or management by objectives has been a common practice in the workplace since the early 1950s. According to the typical pattern, managers review employee performance throughout the year against a rubric of measurable goals and reward them accordingly. The problem with this system is that, by setting individual goals that are linked to incentives, managers can actually restrict the full-team coordination and alignment required for a nonprofit to execute its strategy, thus driving the organization in the wrong direction.[3]

Moreover, when an employee must meet 100% of their objectives to receive a bonus, they're likely to set more easily attainable goals. As nonprofit leaders, we aren't aiming to achieve conservative goals. Enter the FAST framework, a way for nonprofit leaders to inspire team cohesion and ambitious goal-setting:[4]

- **Frequently discussed**—*Goals should be under constant review. This helps maintain focus on what's most important and guide key decisions. If efforts aren't working, you can make adjustments that yield better results.*
- **Ambitious in scope**—*Bold goals should aim high, but not be so unrealistic they're deemed impossible. This encourages workers to find innovative ways to meet their objectives and keeps them engaged in the organization's success.*
- **Specific**—*When goals can be measured against specific metrics, staff members have a clear understanding of expectations. This can help boost overall performance organization-wide.*
- **Transparent for all to see**—*It's helpful for employees to see how their efforts support the organization's goals. Transparency holds people accountable and reveals efforts that are not aligned with the nonprofit's strategy.*

As you use this approach to set big goals that address the root of a problem, here are some helpful questions to ask yourself:

- Are we on track to reach our goal?
- Do we anticipate any unforeseen changes that could require course correction?
- How can we exceed our own expectations?
- Is our goal actually addressing the root cause of the problem?

FAST goal-setting provides a solid foundation for building a high-performing nonprofit organization. By creating opportunities for impact and providing a way to counsel underperformers, the FAST framework is a helpful tool for setting bold goals that lead to lasting social change.

Summary

After his son's death due to lack of necessary medical care, Edgar F. Allen sold his business and raised money to build a hospital in his small town. While volunteering there, Allen met a young orphan seeking treatment and realized the need for a hospital that specialized in children with physical disabilities. Allen raised the money to build such a facility, then devoted his life to raising funds and awareness for people with physical disabilities. He founded the Ohio Society for Crippled Children, now known as the Easterseals. This nonprofit lobbied on behalf of people with physical disabilities and contributed to the passing of such laws as the Social Security Act of 1935, the Rehabilitation Act of 1973, and the Americans with Disabilities Act of 1990. Allen understood the power of boldness, realizing that big dreams worthy of nonprofit attention need to target the root causes of societal problems. By setting FAST goals (frequently discussed, ambitious, specific, and transparent), organizations can dream big enough to drive lasting impact.

The key to the thirtieth law of nonprofit impact—*dream bigger*—is targeting the root cause of the problems you're trying to address.

Recommended Further Reading

MEURISSE, THIBAUT. *Goal Setting: The Ultimate Guide to Achieving Goals That Truly Excite You.* Scotts Valley, CA: CreateSpace, 2015.

MEYER, JEFF. *Fear Not, Dream Big & Execute: Tools to Spark Your Dream and Ignite Your Follow-Through.* New Providence: Bowker Identifier Services, 2018.

SHALLENBERGER, ROBERT R. *Start with the Vision: Six Steps to Effectively Plan, Create Solutions, and Take Action.* Manchester: Star Leadership LLC, 2020.

---

1 Amy Celep, Darell Hammond, and Bill Shore, "When Good is Not Good Enough," Stanford Social Innovation Review, Fall 2013, 40-47.

2 Amy Celep, Bill Shore, and James Siegal, "Bolder Goals, Bigger Breakthroughs," Stanford Social Innovation Review, May 1, 2019.

3 Martin Reeves and Jack Fuller, "When SMART Goals are Not So Smart," *MIT Sloan Management Review* 59, no. 4 (2018): 1-5.

4 Donald Sull and Charles Sull, "With Goals, FAST Beats SMART," *MIT Sloan Management Review*, June 5, 2018

*LAWS OF
ENGAGEMENT*

LAW 31:

Start and learn.

> *Out of the tragedy of losing my son and watching the joy he was given in his last days, it all came together. This is what I was supposed to do, to help make other kids' dreams come true and to be able to give those memories to other families. That became a mission for me.*
>
> **Linda Pauling (1948–)**

When Linda Pauling's four-and-a-half-year-old son Christopher was diagnosed with acute leukemia, she asked the doctors a simple question: "Okay, how do we get rid of it?"

She was shocked when they told her that her little boy had, at most, three more years to live. That night, Pauling promised Christopher that he would live a lifetime in those three years.

Christopher's lifelong dream was to be a law enforcement officer like their family friend, US Customs Agent Tom Austin. In April 1980, Christopher was growing sicker and Pauling sensed they were running out of time. She made a phone call to Austin that set in motion a world-changing course of events.

Austin faced the Customs Department's bureaucratic red tape, but he wasn't deterred. One evening, while kneeling in the desert weeds during a late-night stakeout, Austin looked over at his fellow officer, Department of Public Safety Officer Ron Cox, and asked him for help. Austin told Cox about Christopher's wish, and Cox agreed to contact the head of DPS to see what could be done.

He was granted permission to do whatever they could to make Christopher's wish come true. Through a series of phone calls, the community came together to help realize a sick little boy's dream.

On April 29, 1980, a Ranger helicopter flew Christopher from his hospital to the empty DPS parking lot. There, he was given a tour of the facilities and had an opportunity to "drive" a police car. The following day, the boy was presented with an official DPS uniform in his size, something that employees had worked throughout the night to prepare. Christopher was also given a badge and a holster set, and he was sworn in as Arizona's first and only honorary DPS officer.

The following morning, Christopher woke up not feeling well. He was admitted to the hospital, still holding on to all of his police officer gear. The next day, May 3, 1980, Christopher lost his battle with leukemia. He was given the funeral ceremony of a fallen officer.

Frank Shankwitz and Scott Stahl, two DPS officers who attended Christopher's funeral, began talking with others in the force about creating a wish-granting organization. That summer, Linda Pauling and a group of officers, friends, and family members came together to talk about ideas for creating such an organization. That was the first meeting of the Make-A-Wish organization. Since then, the nonprofit has granted the wishes of more than 315,000 children with critical illnesses.

When trying to fulfill the dreams of her only child, Linda Pauling didn't set out to create a global movement of wish-granting. She simply made a phone call to ask for a favor that would make the final days of her son's life special.

What words of advice might this loving mother have for someone wanting to make an impact?

Don't overthink future planning. It's better to begin and overlearn from the past.

Inside the Mind of a Chronic Overthinker

The entire how-to-communicate industry exists because of chronic overthinkers like me. I'm that person who watches YouTube videos on how to behave in a job interview, act during social gatherings, or ask for a donation. In my early days as a nonprofit leader, I would stress for hours over every word of an email to a list of twelve people (only three or four of whom would open it). And of course, after sending it, I would feverishly refresh the reports page in my Mailchimp account to see how recipients responded. Maybe you can relate?

The good news is a simple lesson can save you the needless time and worry of being a chronic communication overthinker: *instead of worry-and-send, resolve to send-and-learn*. In other words, accept the truth that you're going to blow it and just send the damn email. Make the first phone call giving yourself full permission for it to be terrible. Stumble and bumble your way through the first presentation. The time to strain isn't before, but *after*.

Why? Study after study shows that trial and error (and, most important of all, *learning*) beats genius every time.[1]

Trial and Error for the Win

So, what does this mean for nonprofit communications and engagement?

Concerning your initial brand identity, consultants and designers would love nothing more than to charge you thousands of dollars to generate your logo, colors, fonts, templates, and other visual assets. Linda Pauling started Make-a-Wish without any of these. The takeaway? Just begin. A simple brand kit generated from a $200 contest on 99designs.com will work just fine. If your nonprofit mission, vision, and values are compelling enough, a simple brand identity package will give you everything you need to engage professionally with your audiences.

Nonprofit leaders also get tied up in knots about their websites. Contrary to what many vendors will tell you, it doesn't take a $10,000 months-long project to get going with a viable web presence. Consider posting a simple website using one of the high-quality, affordable build-and-host online tools like Leadpages or Unbounce. With no technical knowledge required, you'll be up and running with a visually interesting, mobile-responsive website in less than a full day's work. After you've established your web presence, look for small tweaks you can make each week to maximize engagement with clear calls to action.

Email is another channel that can benefit from a trial-and-error approach. Nonprofits that make effective use of email know not to try to accomplish too much using this channel. For example, email is not the place to ask for gifts or recruit volunteers. For that, meet in person or, in a pinch, pick up the phone. Email works best as a tool for keeping your impact top-of-mind while sending some little nugget of value that educates, entertains, or encourages the receiver. Mailchimp and ConvertKit are two popular and intuitive tools that my clients and I have enjoyed.

Don't overthink it—sign up and simply begin. Start with a list of ten email addresses of people who love and support your mission; build the list over time through website popups and manual entry; send concise, helpful, and personalized emails to your list on a daily, bi-weekly, or weekly basis; monitor open rates (typically 20–30%) and click rates (typically 2–4%) to determine which emails resonate most; and prune the list of addresses from time to time so that emails are only going to people who care. Above all, just press SEND.

Trial and error is just as applicable to social media communications. As of this writing, the major platforms are Facebook, Instagram, LinkedIn, Twitter, Pinterest, and TikTok. As screen time in the developed world continues to increase, nonprofits and their leaders feel increasing pressure to be on every social media platform and engage every day. A far more manageable long-term strategy is to pick one platform where your audience is engaging and learn to master it before getting started on another platform. For example, if your current and prospective donors spend most of their social media time on Instagram, it may make the most sense to have a nominal presence on the other platforms and focus your daily engagement efforts cultivating relationships exclusively on Instagram. By focusing your efforts, you'll learn and grow far more quickly.

One channel that may at first appear to be less amenable to trial and error is video streaming. After all, high-quality audio and visual equipment can easily run into the thousands of dollars, not to mention the costs of editing software and the time required to make great content. For nonprofits with limited funding and time, this would appear to be a "trial" they can't afford.

The good news for many nonprofits is that recent trends toward authenticity—stripped-down videos that are low on production quality but high on candor and utility—means that good content is producible for little to no money and very little time. In many cases a nonprofit leader need only take out their phone, point the camera at something of interest to prospective donors, and press record. If you post weekly and make each video just a bit better than the last, over time you're sure to grow a following that will supply your organization with new donors and volunteers.

Many more examples abound. The implication for your nonprofit's engagement with the outside world is just to *get started*. The perfect strategy doesn't exist. Get a logo and learn. Publish the website and learn. Press send and learn. Hit record and learn. Be open to trial and error as your strategy for continuous improvement.[2] Every day you spend "preparing" is a day you could have spent learning while giving the world the glimpse into your work they needed to spur them to action alongside you.

Summary

Through a phone call to a family friend, Linda Pauling was able to fulfill a lifelong dream for her terminally ill son, Christopher. After his passing, Christopher's story inspired Pauling and others to establish a wish-granting organization. Since then, the Make-A-Wish Foundation has granted the wishes of more than 315,000 children with critical illnesses. In fulfilling her son's wish, Pauling didn't overthink her communication strategy. She simply made a phone call and figured out the details along the way. When it comes to communication strategy, nonprofit leaders can learn a lot from Pauling's method: rather than worry-and-send, resolve to send-and-learn. Through a little bit of courage and some trial-and-error learning, we can make the most of the precious little time we have to spread the news about our work. Trial and error can improve a nonprofit's brand identity, web presence, email outreach, social media communications, and video strategies.

The keys to the thirty-first law of nonprofit impact—*start and learn*—are accepting that the beginning will be terrible, beginning anyway, and improving a little every day.

Recommended Further Reading

BERGENDAHL-PAULING, LINDA. *Little Bubble Gum Trooper: A Mother's True Story of How the Make-A-Wish Foundation Began.* Forestport: Red Rose PR LLC, 2000.

DIMITRIJEV, SIMA, AND MARYANN KARINCH. *Trial, Error, and Success: 10 Insights into Realistic Knowledge, Thinking, and Emotional Intelligence.* Estes Park, CO: Armin Lear Press, 2021.

MCCOY, JULIA. *So You Think You Can Write? The Definitive Guide to Successful Online Writing.* Scotts Valley, CA: CreateSpace, 2016.

NOLEN-HOEKSEMA, SUSAN. *Women Who Think Too Much: How to Break Free of Overthinking and Reclaim Your Life.* New York: Holt and Company, 2004.

SMITH, GWENDOLINE. *The Book of Overthinking: How to Stop the Cycle of Worry.* London: Atlantic Books, 2021.

---

1 Jim Manzi, *Uncontrolled: The Surprising Payoff of Trial-and-Error for Business, Politics, and Society* (New York: Basic Books, 2012).

2 H. Peyton Young, "Learning by Trial and Error," *Games and Economic Behavior* 65, no. 2 (2009): 626–43; Claus Rerup and Martha S. Feldman, "Routines as a Source of Change in Organizational Schemata: The Role of Trial-and-Error Learning," *Academy of Management Journal* 54, no. 3 (2011): 577–610.

LAW 32:

Aim small.

> *For whatever reason, we feel that we need more training, more education, more skills assessments, more time, or more money. We don't. We are the answers to others' prayers.*
>
> **Dr. Gary Morsch (1952–)**

The early 1990s were a distressing time for Russian citizens.

The new decade brought the end of the post–World War II rivalry between the United States and the Soviet Union. The end of the Cold War caused a major financial crisis for Russia and resulted in a recession worse than America's Great Depression. Many Russian citizens were in dire need of medical care, yet unable to receive the medications and treatment they required.

The Russian recession also came on the heels of the Chernobyl nuclear disaster, which contaminated the country and was still exposing citizens to high volumes of radiation. People were experiencing illnesses, life-threatening cancers, and other diseases related to the meltdown.

There was no question that Russia's people needed help.

Several American medical professionals came together to offer their services to the Russian people, in particular Kansas City family physician Dr. Gary Morsch. When he and his colleagues arrived in the former Soviet Union to assess the state of patient care, they found a healthcare system on the verge of collapse.

Morsch didn't understand it—Russia had plenty of talented physicians and several high-quality medical facilities, so why was the state of healthcare so appalling? As it turned out, pharmacies were experiencing a shortage of medicine and supplies, leaving doctors helpless and unable to provide life-saving care. For Morsch, this was unacceptable.

He returned home and immediately sought help from his local Rotary Club. Morsch asked them to provide the supplies and medication that Moscow hospitals needed to function. Before long, Morsch and his Rotary Club had set up collection drives all over Kansas City. Major pharmaceutical companies donated essential products. The US government noticed Morsch's efforts and offered their largest cargo plane to deliver the medical aid to Russia.

In all, America delivered seventy-five tons of donated aid to thirty-two hospitals and nine orphanages throughout the Moscow area. Patients were finally able to receive the care they needed. Because of the kindness and generosity of hundreds of volunteers and corporate partners, the United States provided the largest private humanitarian airlift in American history; this gift became known as the Heart to Heart Airlift.

Originally envisioned as a one-time effort, the Heart to Heart Airlift created tremendous momentum. Morsch and others saw the need to bring aid to other places around the world, and Heart to Heart International (HHI) was established in 1992. Since then, HHI has delivered medical aid to countries hit by natural disasters, delivered goods to refugees, provided training to medical teams in other countries, and even helped Mother Teresa in her missionary work.

How did Dr. Morsch manage to inspire hundreds of volunteers and create a nonprofit organization that has provided humanitarian service in more than 130 countries, shipped over $2 billion in aid, and logged 1.1 million volunteer hours?

He realized that, *when it comes to engagement, it's better to dominate something new and small than disrupt something old and big.*

Domination Beats Disruption

Although you may not instantly recognize his name, you certainly know the work of Peter Thiel. An entrepreneur and investor, Thiel is a cofounder of PayPal and an early investor in companies like LinkedIn and SpaceX. He's also the author of *Zero to One: Notes on Startups, or How to Build the Future* (2014). His book is an exercise in thinking, questioning, and rethinking received wisdom to create the future.

One of Thiel's central arguments in *Zero to One* is that organizations looking to do something big need to figure out a way to be around for a long time. Organizations get so caught up in the idea of *growth* that they tend to overlook the need to *endure*. The truly enduring for-profit companies are those that establish monopolies in durable markets. But this idea is not limited to for-profits; nonprofits that aim to be around for a long time can use Thiel's rationale also.

According to Thiel, a long-running organization exemplifies four properties:[1]

Property 1: Significantly superior proprietary tech—*much better and no one can reproduce it. (Think Google Search.)*

Property 2: Network effects—*increased numbers of participants increase its value. (Think LinkedIn.)*

Property 3: Economies of scale—*a few employees can serve millions of people. (Think software development.)*

Property 4: Deeply integrated branding—*the promise is embedded in into the service or product. (Think Apple MacBook Pro.)*

Thiel spends considerable time spelling out the early stages of long-enduring ventures. He stresses the need to begin by serving a very small target market, a group of particular people concentrated together and served by few or no competitors.[2] Rather than disrupt a large market, it is far better to serve an obscure niche and gain a foothold. By doing so, you're free to learn and grow unchallenged while beginning to accrue the early network effects of expansion.[3] Then, once you're big enough to keep the market, you can expand into slightly broader markets that are closely related to the one you're dominating. Your nonprofit can follow the same principles to start small and build on an accumulation of early, unchallenged wins.

This core progression has been part of the founding narrative of some of the most successful organizations of recent times. When Amazon was first established, it only sold books—and primarily only hard-to-find textbooks. Now the company sells more than twelve million products on its site. eBay began in 1995 by targeting obsessive collectors. Just four years later, the company was an internet legend worth more than Sears, JCPenney, and Kmart combined.[4]

Choose your nonprofit's first small market carefully and expand with deliberate intention. Resist the temptation to "look big" by claiming to serve too big a market too early. The text on your website is easy to change from "Eastern Smallville" to "Northern Hemisphere" once you reach a certain level of impact. But until then, the fatal mistake of *claiming* you serve the entire Northern Hemisphere will prevent you from having those early wins in Eastern Smallville.

Avatar Your Prospects

One important implication of this micro-domination philosophy is the need to very narrowly define your prospective audience, variously called a *dream customer*, *donor persona*, or *ideal donor avatar* (IDA). An IDA is a hypothetical member of your target audience with a detailed profile. Your IDA has traits, wants, needs, and pain points you've identified through market research into a set of characteristics that may include the following:

- **Demographics**—*Statistical data that relates to a population and particular groups within it (e.g., name, gender, age, location, family background, current family).*

- **Geographics**—Compartmentalization of a market based on geographic location (e.g., cities/towns/neighborhoods, home size, urban/suburban/rural).
- **Psychographics**—Study of a population based on their interests, activities, and opinions (e.g., personality, values, beliefs, preferences).
- **Employment**—Targeting a market by their career path (e.g., industry, company size, job role, satisfaction with position).
- **Tribal affiliations**—Identifying a subgroup based on their community attachments (e.g., sports teams, interest clubs, faith communities, other nonprofits).
- **Challenges/hurts/needs**—Finding common ground among people who share specific experiences (e.g., past scars or current frustrations from home/work/community).
- **Decision-making habits**—Categorizing people based on what influences their decisions (e.g., solution sources, decision criteria, trusted advisors).
- **Communication habits**—Determining how people prefer to share and receive information (e.g., technology used, outreach preferences, tone preferences).

Typically, your ideal donor is someone who has a passion for your mission, a history of giving, and the means to contribute to causes like yours. Creating an IDA can help narrow the focus for your target audience and find the donor, corporate sponsor, or grant-making organization that is most likely to support you. This saves you from wasting time and resources trying to locate and solicit prospects who don't have money to contribute, aren't interested in your mission, or are already committed to other organizations.

The insight provided by an IDA also helps you know where to find your audience and how to effectively reach them. You can focus your marketing and outreach through meaningful messaging that drives traffic to your website, elicits more email responses, and entices people to donate more to your cause. When a message resonates with someone, they're more likely to act on it, so every piece of content you distribute should narrowly target your IDA.[5]

The information you gather from creating an IDA also allows you to provide invaluable resources to your fundraising team. Volunteers, board members, and staff members can use the IDA you provide them to keep an eye out for potential prospects in their everyday lives and determine how best to cultivate them.

The alignment between your organizational identity, your IDA, and your engagement efforts will ultimately determine whether or not your organization can scale its impact.[6] Knowing your ideal donor—what they want, where they spend their time, and how best to reach them—can make all the difference in the world-changing impact of your nonprofit.

Summary

In the wake of the Cold War, when Dr. Gary Morsch discovered that Russian hospitals and pharmacies were out of medicine and supplies, he asked his local Rotary Club for help. Before he knew it, fundraisers were taking place all over the city. Major pharmaceutical companies donated supplies and medications, and the US government provided their largest cargo plane to deliver the collected aid to Russia. From that small beginning serving a specific, one-time need, Heart to Heart International was born, and has since provided humanitarian service in more than 130 countries and shipped over $2 billion in aid. Entrepreneur and author Peter Thiel provides a helpful theoretical framework for what Morsch and his allies discovered. By first dominating something new and small rather than disrupting something old and big, you can stack the odds in your favor that your organization will endure. One method of doing this is narrowly defining your prospective audience by creating an ideal donor avatar (IDA). An IDA helps you better understand your audience and reach them with meaningful content that resonates, leading to more engaged donors for your organization.

The key to the thirty-second law of nonprofit impact—*aim small*—is winning uncontested impact with a small starter group of beneficiaries.

Recommended Further Reading

MORSCH, GARY, AND DEAN NELSON. *The Power of Serving Others: You Can Start Where You Are.* San Francisco: Barrett-Koehler, 2006.

REVELLA, ADELE. *Buyer Personas: How to Gain Insight into your Customer's Expectations, Align Your Marketing Strategies, and Win More Business.* Hoboken, NJ: Wiley, 2015.

VAN DER HOPE, ERIC V. *Mastering Niche Marketing: A Definitive Guide to Profiting from Ideas in a Competitive Market.* Culver City, CA: Globalnet Publishing, 2008.

---

1 Peter Thiel, *Zero to One: Notes on Startups, or How to Build the Future* (Redfern, NSW: Currency Press, 2014).

2 Thiel, *Zero to One*, 42.

3 Tevfik Dalgic and Maarten Leeuw, "Niche Marketing Revisited: Concept, Applications and Some European Cases," *European Journal of Marketing* 28, no. 4 (1994): 3–55.

4 Adam Cohen, *The Perfect Store: Inside eBay* (New York: Back Bay Books, 2003), 5.

5 Rosu Mircea-Alexandru, "Creating and Measuring the Impact of a Content Strategy," *CES Working Papers* 13, no. 1 (2021): 128–52.

6 Alexei Heinze, Gordon Fletcher, Tahir Rashid, and Ana Cruz, "Understanding Your Buyer Persona," in *Digital and Social Media Marketing: A Results-Driven Approach* (New York: Routledge, 2016), 69.

LAW 33:

Use email to inform.

> *No one keeps UNICEF going but the idea itself.*
>
> Maurice Pate (1894-1965)

Maurice Pate knew all too well the seriousness of childhood illness and mortality.

A Nebraska native and the oldest of seven children, he witnessed three of his infant siblings die from polio, diphtheria, and other diseases. The helplessness he felt left an indelible mark. Perhaps that's why, at the onset of World War I, Pate decided that, instead of joining the armed forces, he would join Herbert Hoover's Belgium Relief Commission to alleviate the suffering of children.

While organizing food supplies to Belgium and France during the war, Pate and Hoover formed a deep friendship. At the war's end, Pate worked to organize and direct the American Relief Administration, which helped to feed more than one million Polish children.

This mission complete, Pate remained in Poland to conduct financial and sales work for a New Jersey oil company. In 1935, he and his Polish wife moved to America so Pate could take a position as an investment banker and businessman. Just four years later, World War II erupted, and Pate was called upon once again to contribute to relief efforts.

Hoover relied on Pate to lead the Commission for Polish Relief, which supplied food and clothing to hundreds of thousands of Polish refugees.

They worked closely with the American Red Cross, and Pate eventually joined that organization as director of relief supplies. There, he helped coordinate aid efforts for prisoners of war in Asia and Europe.

While conducting food surveys with Hoover in 1947, Pate witnessed a particular need for relief efforts for children. European children were suffering from disease and famine after World War II, and survival rates of children in developing countries were plummeting.

Pate and Hoover resolved to form the United Nations International Children's Emergency Fund (UNICEF), an organization intended to combat the threats posed to children of ex-enemy countries, regardless of politics or race. UNICEF has had a far-reaching impact; in addition to working to eradicate whooping cough, tuberculosis, and malaria, the organization implemented programs to improve maternal and child health by applying low-cost, preventive health measures. Pate continued to work with UNICEF until his death in 1965. His philanthropic efforts continue to impact children across the world.

UNICEF has adapted with changing technology; today the organization takes full advantage of the latest techniques in email marketing to reach prospects and donors with tailored messages. Emails enable the organization to easily inspire and engage supporters, as well as thank donors for their contributions. Through vivid photographs and videos, UNICEF tells the stories of the brave children they serve. Above all, UNICEF uses email to highlight the difference that donors have made in the lives of children worldwide.

Inspired by the leadership of Maurice Pate, how has UNICEF managed to help more than 250 million children worldwide?

The organization understands that *nonprofits that learn to harness the power of email have significantly more impact.*

Email Is Here to Stay

Every few years, someone makes a pile of money forecasting the "death of email," warning of the imminent downfall of the now-ubiquitous form of communication. These predictions, of course, invariably turn out to be wrong. It's been twenty-five years and counting since email went mainstream. Today, email is so deeply embedded in the digital-cultural landscape that it's nearly impossible to imagine a world without it.

Although chat and direct messaging are also common in everyday interactions, email has become the world's first and only truly universal instant communication tool.[1] People of all ages have email accounts that work the same way in every country across the globe. Accordingly, the vast majority of people above a certain age have grown accustomed to being contacted that way.

As with most modern things we've grown accustomed to, it's easy to forget what a technological miracle email represents. Using only an address of ten or so characters, people can send a note to many recipients at once, forward messages to others, include clickable links and downloadable attachments, easily search for past notes, and organize concurrent discussions with hundreds of contacts.[2] Email has moved beyond being simply a means of communicating in the here and now; it's become the central, comprehensive archive of our interpersonal lives.[3]

In short, email still works.

In a professional context, email outreach is carried out through *campaigns.* An email campaign is simply sending an email to a select group of people for a specific reason. The key to a successful campaign is to *deliver the right message to the right people at the right time.* Sending out untargeted messages for unclear reasons isn't a good use of resources. Conversely, sending the right number and kind of emails is vital for long-term impact.[4]

Professional email tools such as Mailchimp provide a rich array of analytics for each campaign. Be sure to check open rates, click rates, and even which recipients opened your email the most times. This information can provide crucial insights to help you understand what your audience liked (for example, a higher number of clicks on an article or content piece), what they didn't like (high unsubscribes, a lack of clicks), and which subscribers are the most and least passionate about the emails you're sending (number of opens, their individual open rate across all campaigns).

An example of email analytics, typically built into the tool(s) you use to manage and send email. This is from Mailchimp. The account owner has set up tags and analytics around what constitutes someone buying from this email, and shows an incredible 15 orders, for a $450,000 order volume.

People are overloaded with emails every day. Improve your response rates by targeting specific emails to subgroups of people or *segments*. Sending an email that resonates with a specific audience segment will increase engagement, boost interest, and elicit more responses.

Growing Your List

There are a few things in nonprofit life worth obsessing about. Staying on the up-and-up legally is one (see Law 29). Growing and pruning your email list is another. Here are what I've found to be the essentials of email list management:

- **Focus.** Email is one of the main reasons to develop your ideal donor avatars (IDAs), as discussed in Law 32. Everything about your emails needs to be exclusively targeted to your IDAs, from the subject line to the content. A good subject line to seasoned executive directors might read, "Busy (and Tired!) Nonprofit Leaders Need This"
- **Purity.** It's far better to have a pure list of superfans than a mixed bag of folks who you hope will learn to love you. Be ruthless. Find and remove cold subscribers often.
- **Value.** The most tried-and-true method of collecting email addresses is to offer something for which your IDAs would gladly exchange their email address: a topically relevant e-book, cheat sheet, guide, or something else that gives some real value without giving up the farm. If you have a book, you could offer the first chapter for free in exchange for an email address.
- **Immediacy.** Show up in their inbox with a warm welcome immediately after they sign up to let them know you appreciate their support and contact information. Go a step further: An initial subscription can trigger an automated welcome sequence of multiple emails sent over ten days that encourages the subscriber to engage further. These can convert very well and build long-term trust.

Remember, email lists degrade over time. People change or abandon their email inboxes, reader preferences change, and users opt out of communications. Segment your audience into like-minded subgroups, then develop targeted strategies to address each subgroup's unique characteristics and needs.[5] Email lists are well worth a nonprofit leader's obsessive attention—continually purge, segment, and grow your list to maximize the impact of your outreach.

Using Your List

Email is a great way to inform but a terrible way to influence. Keep a modest objective for your email efforts. If you can keep a growing (but pure!) audience informed with a timely, high-value, bite-sized nugget and the chance to respond to one simple call to action, your email's job is done. Some best practices for using your email list include:

- **Consistency—Show up with a frequency you can repeat forever.** If that's just once per week, stick to it.
- **Mobility—Graphically styled newsletters are dated.** Today's emails need to look on a smartphone as if they were sent by an individual person from a smartphone. Keep it text-based and simple.
- **Brevity—Can single sentences be paragraphs? Technically, no.** But don't tell that to a good email. Think scannable and snackable content.
- **Informality—Letters wear dress shoes, text messages wear flip-flops.** Depending on your IDA, of course, emails fall somewhere in between. Sneakers?
- **Subject line—A good subject line gestures toward the content of your email in a way that stokes intrigue.** "This is why your subject lines aren't working." "These nonprofits know the deal." "Don't make this fundraising mistake."
- **Auto signature—A good auto signature can do a lot of amazing marketing work for you.** At the time of this book's publishing, HubSpot offers a great (and free) auto signature generator that I've used to create excellent signatures for all of my email accounts.

Remember, email lists aren't just for selling your organization. In addition to telling your constituents' story, this invaluable tool is a great way to connect with audiences on a deeper level. Provide updates about your nonprofit's successes. Show donors how their sacred gifts are impacting the lives of the people you serve. Take advantage of this opportunity to connect with your audience and build lasting relationships that earn their loyalty. Once you've won a subscriber's attention and provided them with valuable information, you've earned the right to reach out to them to meet in person, cultivate the relationship, and ultimately make the Ask.

Summary

While conducting food surveys with Herbert Hoover in 1947, Maurice Pate realized a particular need for relief efforts for children who faced disease and famine. Pate and Hoover formed the United Nations International Children's Emergency Fund (UNICEF), an organization intended to combat the threats posed to children of ex-enemy countries, regardless of politics or race. Since its inception, UNICEF has helped more than 250 million children worldwide. UNICEF continues to thrive today due in part to targeted email campaigns that celebrate impact, thank donors, and cultivate prospective donors. Because of its deep roots in every aspect of the digital landscape, email is here to stay. Growing and maintaining an updated email list is imperative to a nonprofit's email outreach. Following a few essentials of list management and email effectiveness can ensure you're using your list to its fullest potential.

The key to the thirty-third law of nonprofit impact—*use email to inform*—is sending the right messages to the right people at the right time.

Recommended Further Reading

HASELWOOD, JEREMY. *The Digital Fundraising Blueprint: How to Raise More Money Online for Your Nonprofit.* Independently published, 2018.

SHATTUCK, STEVEN. *Robots Make Bad Fundraisers: How Nonprofits Can Maintain the Heart in the Digital Age.* Lexington, NC: Bold & Bright Media, 2020.

TORBERT, ADAM. *Email List Building: Beginner's Guide to Building an Email List of Dedicated and Loyal Fans Without Spending a Lot of Money.* Independently published, 2020.

---

1 Maureen James and Liz Rykert, *From Workplace to Workspace: Using Email Lists to Work Together* (Ottawa: IDRC Books, 1998), v.

2 Mari Hartemo, "Email Marketing in the Era of the Empowered Consumer," *Journal of Research in Interactive Marketing* 10, no. 3 (2016): 212–30.

3 Lipika Dey, H. Sameera Bharadwaja, G. Meera, and Gautam Shroff, "Email Analytics for Activity Management and Insight Discovery *2013 IEEE/WIC/ACM International Joint Conferences on Web Intelligence (WI) and Intelligent Agent Technologies* 1 (2013): 557–64.

4 Xi (Alan) Zhang, V. Kumar, and Koray Cosguner, "Dynamically Managing a Profitable Email Marketing Program," *Journal of Marketing Research* 54, no. 6 (2017): 851–66.

5 Sarah E. Boslaugh, Matthew W. Kreuter, Robert A. Nicholson, and Kimberly Naleid, "Comparing Demographic, Health Status, and Psychological Strategies of Audience Segmentation to Promote Physical Activity," *Health Education Research* 20, no. 4 (2005): 430–38.

LAW 34:

Use in-person visits to influence.

> "[My teammates] would come off the practice field all sweaty, and Kim would just jump in their arms and give them a big hug and kiss. When they found out that she was sick, they all felt it."
>
> **Fred Hill (1943–)**

Surprisingly, Fred Hill's biggest challenge wasn't on the NFL football field.

It was 1969, Hill's fourth year as a tight end for the Philadelphia Eagles, when he heard the news that his three-year-old daughter Kim was diagnosed with leukemia. Dedicated to helping their little girl fight this terrible disease, Hill and his wife, Fran, spent countless nights curled up on uncomfortable hospital benches in crowded waiting rooms while little Kim received the medical treatment she needed.

Dr. Audrey Evans, the head of pediatric oncology at Children's Hospital of Philadelphia, noticed their struggle. She shared an idea with the Hills: a temporary home where families could reside comfortably while their children were in the hospital. Fred and Fran were immediately on board. The Hills enlisted Fred's teammates to help back the project, and very soon, they realized they needed more funds.

The Eagles' general manager, Jim Murray, turned out to be their greatest ally. Murray reached out to local McDonald's advertising executive Don

Tuckerman, who then contacted McDonald's Regional Manager Ed Rensi. Together, they developed a promotion for a St. Patrick's Day "Shamrock Shake," whose proceeds helped purchase an old seven-bedroom house near the hospital. The first-ever Ronald McDonald House was renovated to offer all the comforts of home, including laundry machines and a full kitchen.

Most importantly, it was accessible to families regardless of income, helping offset some of the financial burden that comes with battling prolonged illness.

Today there are 364 Ronald McDonald Houses in 43 countries and regions that serve nearly 8,000 people daily. Thanks to the Hills' efforts, families of seriously ill children can live comfortably and affordably just a brief walk from where their children are being treated.

How did Fred and Fran Hill help to create a world-renowned nonprofit that provides comfort, relief, and support to thousands of families every day?

They understood that *when it comes to nonprofit impact, there's no substitute for conveying your passion for the cause in an in-person visit.*

The Power of Face-to-Face Passion

Though it's hard to admit as a lifelong Dallas Cowboys fan, I've got to tip my hat to the Philadelphia Eagles for showing the nonprofit sector what it takes to create large-scale change.

When telling the story, it's easy to miss all of the in-person visits that were necessary in the early 1970s to make it possible for today's 8,000+ families to be near their sick kids every single night around the world. But nonprofit leaders who want to replicate this scale of impact can't afford to ignore the essential role that these in-person moments of truth played in the growth of Ronald McDonald House Charities.

It began with the in-person visit with brave little Kim, who told her mother Fran that she didn't feel well. Fred was initially out of town with his team; it was Fran who broke the news to him that Kim had been hospitalized. In person, the couple agonized over the right course of action. They agreed it was crucial to be near Kim as she fought her battle with leukemia, which meant they spent nearly every night for the next three years on hospital cots and in waiting rooms. Fran eventually convinced Fred to ask his Philadelphia Eagles teammates for support.

Next, Fred met in person with his fellow football players. They knew and adored his sweet little daughter and were devastated to hear she was ill. They saw the anguish on Fred's face as he explained the severity of her condition, and what it meant to him and his family. Seeing his pain and his passion, they quickly agreed to assist in any way they could. The team knew they would need help with fundraising, and suggested Fred meet with their general manager, Jim Murray.

Murray met with Fred in person and offered his support to the Hills. Fred explained Dr. Evans's idea for temporary housing for families of sick children. The two began brainstorming ways they could raise the money needed to purchase a house.

Murray visited in person with Dr. Evans to learn more about her dream and understand what kind of financial support she needed. During these visits, Murray could see firsthand the passion Dr. Evans had about the importance of proximity, involvement, education, and support for families of hospitalized children.[1] This encounter inspired Murray to seek help from his own contacts.

Through his in-person visits with Don Tuckerman and Ed Rensi of McDonald's, Murray learned about the "Shamrock Shake" promotion the advertising team was already working on. The men adapted that existing idea into a fundraiser to purchase the house that would eventually become the first Ronald McDonald House.

But the in-person visits didn't end there.

Once the McDonald's team and the Eagles agreed on the proceeds from the shake sales, Rensi met in person with his store managers in his region to explain how the program would work. Then, the store managers trained their employees in person on how to sell the program to customers. And finally, the store cashiers and servers had tens of thousands of in-person visits with the customers who purchased the shakes and, ultimately, contributed to a greater cause.

An in-person visit is a powerful method of communication. When you can see another person face-to-face, information flows through multiple channels at once. Facial expressions, tone of voice, and body language all subconsciously convey and mirror emotion. They create a connection grounded in mutual receiving.[2] The person you're visiting can see and feel your emphasis of key points and truly sense the passion behind your message.

Written communications do not have these characteristics, which is why it's so easy to misinterpret an email or text message. With face-to-face communication, the intent behind a message is easier to determine. In-person interactions are information-rich, and can even provide helpful glimpses of an individual's underlying values. When we can socialize and interact with other people in person, we help lay the foundation for a trusting relationship.

One of the greatest benefits of in-person interactions is that they establish engaging, real, collaborative environments in an efficient way. In communications via computer, words get lost in translation and sharing information takes more time.[3] When people can share ideas in person and brainstorm together to develop creative solutions, they experience far more interpersonal influence.[4] The teamwork it took to turn the "Shamrock Shake" promotion into a leukemia fundraiser only became a reality through the collaborative in-person efforts of Murray, Tuckerman, Rensi, and hundreds of McDonald's frontline workers.

Don't Overthink It

I am an extreme introvert. My natural tendency is to overthink and over-architect every in-person interaction. Over many years, however, I've learned that far greater outcomes occur when I simply throw myself into as many face-to-face visits as possible and let the chips fall where they may. Don't ask me how it works to generate countless opportunities, but it does!

In today's world, there are countless ways to get in front of people and share your passion. If you're just getting started, consider attending recurring networking groups, like Business Network International, Rotary Club, Chambers of Commerce, and local business associations. Not only can you connect with people in person and convey your passion for your projects, but these regularly scheduled meetings enable you to build deep relationships with people who can ultimately become ambassadors for your ideas.

While virtual meetings are convenient, in-person conferences afford a multitude of opportunities. You can gather with like-minded people and discuss challenges, brainstorm solutions, and share the contacts in each other's networks.

When meeting in-person, bear two things in mind. First, find a way to ask the person you're visiting with *"Who are two people you know who you think I should get to know?"* If Murray hadn't known the McDonald's advertising executive, it's unlikely that Ronald McDonald House Charities would have come into existence. Everyone you meet has a network, and those networks are sure to contain some individuals who can help you create solutions the world needs. Find out who those people are, meet with them face-to-face, and ask them the two-people question.

Second, the most important part of face-to-face communication is to *be present*. As you interact with people, let the sacredness of the moment in: you're taking up a precious segment of this person's life by being in front of them. *Really* be there. *Really* see them. *Really* find a way to give them something before the end of that same day.

For some (me included), meeting with new people in person can be a bit scary—on account of my introversion, I'd much prefer digital or phone communication.[5] Sometimes even now I'll catch myself rehearsing a conversation ahead of time and preparing responses to hypothetical questions. But at the end of the day, I remind myself that people are moved far more by the passion behind an idea, not an over-polished presentation. Take it from the introvert of introverts—don't overthink it.

Summary

When Philadelphia Eagles tight end Fred Hill learned his daughter's oncologist wanted to create temporary housing for families of sick children, he sprang into action. Having spent countless nights on uncomfortable hospital benches while his daughter was treated for leukemia, Hill believed there had to be a better solution for families like his. He met with his teammates and general manager, who then met with a McDonald's ad executive and regional manager. They developed a plan to raise funds through a promotion that would help purchase the first Ronald McDonald House. Today, the organization has helped nearly 8,000 families worldwide. The true story of Ronald McDonald House Charities illustrates the critical importance of in-person visits for nonprofit impact. When the stakes are as high and the needs as great as they are in nonprofit work, there is no substitute for in-person facial expressions, tone of voice, and body language to convey one's passion for the cause. By asking each person you meet with to refer two more people and by being present in your in-person conversations, you develop relationships and discover opportunities for world-changing impact that could have never been scripted.

The key to the thirty-fourth law of nonprofit impact—*use in-person visits to influence*—is having as many face-to-face interactions as possible.

Recommended Further Reading

GRAZER, BRIAN. *Face-to-Face: The Art of Human Connection.* New York: Simon & Schuster, 2019.

LEAL III, BENTO C. *4 Essential Keys to Effective Communication in Love, Life, Work—Anywhere!* Scotts Valley, CA: CreateSpace, 2017.

NEWMAN, AMY, AND SCOT OBER. *Business Communication: In Person, In Print, Online.* Boston: Cengage Learning, 2016.

1 Linda Franck and Nicole Rubin, "The Role of Ronald McDonald House Charities in Keeping Families Close," *Pediatric Nursing* 43, no. 4 (2017): 202–5.

2 Lennart Fredriksson, "Modes of Relating in a Caring Conversation: A Research Synthesis on Presence, Touch and Listening," *Journal of Advanced Nursing* 30, no. 5 (2001): 1167–76.

3 Bonita L. Daly, "The Influence of Face-to-Face Versus Computer-Mediated Communication Channels on Collective Induction," *Accounting, Management and Information Technologies* 3, no. 1 (1993): 1–22.

4 Kazuhiro Otsuka, Junji Yamato, Yoshinao Takemae, and Hiroshi Murase, "Quantifying Interpersonal Influence in Face-to-Face Conversations Based on Visual Attention Patterns," *Extended Abstracts on Human Factors in Computing Systems* (2006): 1175–80.

5 David C. Mohr, Juned Siddique, Joyce Ho, Jenna Duffecy, Ling Jin, and J. Konadu Fokuo, "Interest in Behavioral and Psychological Treatments Delivered Face-to-Face, By Telephone, and By Internet," *Annals of Behavioral Medicine* 40, no. 1 (2010): 89–98.

LAW 35:

Be social on social media.

> "I read this newspaper account of this new organization in London that had been formed for young men who had pledged their lives to Jesus Christ and needed a wholesome alternative to life on the street. I thought this would fit my young men just fine."
>
> **Thomas Valentine Sullivan (1800–59)**

Retired Boston whaling captain Thomas Valentine Sullivan was deeply concerned.

In the 1850s, big cities held numerous temptations for young sailors on shore leave. A sailor himself, Sullivan knew that a young man could find himself in a lot of trouble if he wasn't careful. He spent his retirement serving as a lay missionary for the Baptist Church, and he wanted to show local sailors that there were more wholesome ways to enjoy life.

He organized groups to distribute pamphlets sharing the message of God's love in Jesus Christ. As impactful as this was, Sullivan wanted to do more. He dreamed of creating a home-away-from-home where young men could find friendship with people who shared their values and were committed to a life of meaning and purpose.

While reading the newspaper, Sullivan learned about a London-based organization called the Young Men's Christian Association (YMCA). Formed by twenty-two-year-old George Williams, the YMCA was developed in response to the run-down tenement housing and dangerous influences of industrialized London. The organization aimed to unite young men who would live by Christian faith and fellowship. Sullivan was intrigued by this organization and traveled to London to see the YMCA firsthand. He found the answers he was looking for in a program that was well-organized, effective, and growing rapidly.

Sullivan returned to Boston inspired. He gathered Christian leaders in his area and shared the stories he'd seen and heard on his visit. Sullivan inspired the group to establish America's first YMCA in Boston on December 20, 1851.[1]

Today, the YMCA is open to men and women of all ages and backgrounds. The organization is dedicated to building healthy, confident, connected children and families, and reaches an incredible eleven million community members every year in the US.

How did a retired sea captain help establish America's first YMCA and launch a movement that has delivered lasting personal and social change in almost every American community?

He realized *the value of storytelling for impact*. And 170 years later, we can add that *there has never been a better time to be a storyteller for impact than the era of social media*.

Still Social Almost Two Hundred Years Later

The original mission statement of the YMCA was "to unite those young men, who regarding Jesus Christ as their God and Savior, according to the Holy Scriptures, desire to be his disciples in their faith and in their life, and to associate their efforts for the extension of His Kingdom amongst our young men."[2] Sullivan brought this England-born mission to America by organizing groups in Boston to distribute pamphlets about the new US chapter.

One-hundred-seventy years later, the YMCA is doing the very same thing over social media—it equips its team members to be *digital storytellers*. For the YMCA, storytelling is not just a part of recruitment and promotional efforts. It is a crucial way for members to process trauma and assess the causes of and possible solutions to community problems.

Digital storytelling is especially appropriate for marginalized groups.[3] It can be an important, therapeutic part of the healing process, particularly for young people. One specific example is the YMCA's Story Squad, a digital program whereby teens can share their experiences with others via social media. This narrative therapy fosters critical thinking, self-reflection, and artistic expression. The program also helps teens develop important written and verbal communication skills that can help them build a brighter future.

Digital storytelling is powerful, as it helps to relay stories in a very personal way. Watching videos that feature human faces and voices while scrolling through Instagram, we get a window into someone's life. According to a common lament, social media is a place where people only broadcast the highlights of their lives. While there are certainly many accounts like this, there are plenty that traffic in authenticity as well. People often disclose the anguish and turmoil they've experienced. For nonprofits, this provides an invaluable window into a person's plight. We can relate more closely to what someone has gone through and marshal the resources necessary to help them. As a society, we are only just beginning to understand how the cumulative influence of this social-media-inspired assistance forms new cultural norms and contributes to gradual social change.[4]

Your Merry Band of Digital Storytellers

Most nonprofits treat their social media accounts like one-way bulletin boards. But a forward-thinking few have learned to approach social media in essentially the same way that Thomas Sullivan approached his pamphlet campaign: get people who have stories to tell out there having as many two-way conversations as possible. The important difference is that Sullivan's 170-year-old strategy now plays out on digital platforms accessible to tens of millions.

If the YMCA example teaches us anything, it's that social media isn't a one-person job. While it may be the responsibility of an individual role or department, the true benefits of social media don't materialize unless all stakeholders are intentionally mobilized. As author Lauren Major explains in a recent article, "the YMCA not only trains their staff on how to use social media, but their strategy ensures that staff members understand the impact of their engagement and how to monitor their social media efforts."[5] The YMCA understands the value of social media and has taken steps to ensure their team members are prepared to maximize it to its full potential. Here's how they empower their staff for effective digital storytelling:

- **Equip and Train**—They make resources easily accessible and provide tailored training to stakeholders which allows them to work with the platforms, skills, and tools they already use and like.
- **Measure and Discuss**—They provide regular data on reach/impressions (how well they're connecting with people through social media platforms) and engagement/comments (what kind of response they're getting from posts). They also measure which posts/topics/series perform best.
- **Anticipate and Monitor**—They give guidance on how-to-handle and what-if scenarios via simple flow charts. A social media content hierarchy identifies who will respond to what types of posts and how, ensuring that the organization's messaging is clear, consistent, and appropriate.

Digital storytelling brings a timeless form into the digital age.[6] At no other time in history have people been able to create, edit, and share on a simultaneously personal and global scale. However, because social media is such a widely used tool, it's becoming increasingly difficult to break through the noise, capture people's attention, and engage them in meaningful ways.

Nonprofit organizations must understand how to use the power of narrative and networks to generate social impact. In developing content for digital platforms, content creators should remember:

- **Storytelling is personal.** Know your ideal donor avatar (IDA) (see Law 32). Speak to them as though it's a one-on-one conversation. This will help you craft meaningful content that educates, entertains, and encourages the donors, volunteers, and prospects who care about your cause most.
- **Effective storytelling requires creative writers.** The best performing posts on social media tend to be insight-rich stories shared in a relatable and creative way. Social media writing isn't a doctoral thesis—it's the creative use of text, punctuation, and emojis to connect with people in fifteen seconds or less.[7]
- **Stories must motivate.** Your stories must portray how a growing number of joyful protagonists (your donors and volunteers) are fighting a formidable villain. Who wouldn't want to join a story like that?
- **Use the digital tools that work best for you.** It can be difficult to determine which platforms and software to use. Begin with one and learn as you go. Over time, as you expand onto other platforms, the content you create on your "home base" platform can be repurposed across many others.[8]

With thorough training, attention to metrics, and consistent creativity, your digital storytelling team can increase your following and amplify your nonprofit's world-changing impact.

Summary

Upon returning from his visit to the London YMCA, Baptist missionary and retired sea captain Thomas Valentine Sullivan shared with his friends in Boston the stories he had seen and heard. These accounts inspired them to come together and form the first YMCA in America. Even after 170 years, the YMCA still relies on compelling stories to engage communities, only now through digital storytelling. The creative use of social media can help your nonprofit make deep connections, enabling all those who play a role in your mission to celebrate the impact you're having through their unique vantage point. By equipping and training, measuring and discussing, and anticipating and monitoring, digital storytellers can craft creative, meaningful messages that resonate with audience members and spread contagious enthusiasm for your nonprofit's impact.

The key to the thirty-fifth law of nonprofit impact—*be social on social media*—is unleashing a team of people who love your cause and enjoy social media engagement.

Recommended Further Reading

BIESENBACH, ROB. *Unleash the Power of Storytelling: Win Hearts, Change Minds, Get Results.* Chicago: Eastlawn Media, 2018.

CAMPBELL, JULIA. *Storytelling in the Digital Age: A Guide for Nonprofits.* Nashville, TN: CharityChannel Press, 2017.

CLARKE, CHERYL A. *Storytelling for Grantseekers: The Guide to Creative Nonprofit Fundraising.* Hoboken, NJ: Wiley, 2001.

---

1 Northeastern University, "Boston Welcomes America's First YMCA," accessed August 9, 2021, https://dsgsites.neu.edu/ymca-exhibit/beginnings-a-ymca-in-boston/boston-welcomes-americas-first-ymca.

2 World YMCA, "Paris Basis 1855," accessed August 9, 2021, https://www.ymca.int/about-us/ymca-history/paris-basis-1855/.

3 Adele de Jager, Andrea Fogarty, Anna Tewson, Caroline Lenette, and Katherine M. Boydell, "Digital Storytelling in Research: A Systematic Review," *The Qualitative Report* 22, no. 10 (2017): 2548–82.

4 Sonja Vivienne, "Digital Storytelling as Everyday Activism: Queer Identity, Voice and Networked Publics," PhD diss., (Queensland University of Technology, 2013).

5 Lauren Major, "How YMCA Chicago Transforms Staff into Digital Rock Stars," Socialbrite, July 17, 2012, https://www.socialbrite.org/2012/07/17/how-ymca-chicago-transforms-staff-into-digital-content-rock-stars.

6 John Hartley and Kelly McWilliam, eds., *Story Circle: Digital Storytelling Around the World* (Hoboken, NJ: Wiley-Blackwell, 2009).

7 Ruth Sylvester and Wendy-lou Greenidge, "Digital Storytelling: Extending the Potential for Struggling Writers," *The Reading Teacher* 63, no. 4 (2009): 284–95.

8 Rebecca Pera and Giampaolo Viglia, "Exploring How Video Digital Storytelling Builds Relationship Experiences," *Psychology & Marketing* 33, no. 12 (2016): 1142–50.

LAW 36:

They are the heroes.

> *"Youth is a frightening age. So many problems; so little wisdom to solve them."*
>
> **Walter Hoving (1897–1989)**

If there was one thing World War I servicemen seriously needed, it was off-duty support.

Military camps, both stateside and abroad, were sorely lacking in wholesome extracurricular activities. Excessive drinking and venereal disease were undercutting combat readiness as servicemen suffered constantly from hangovers and illness. They were a danger to themselves and were jeopardizing the entire war effort. At that time, however, little was done to curtail the abuses.

Twenty-three years later, a second World War was taking shape. The US government began to position its military to support Britain and its allies, and waves of young men spread across the country to train for the imminent conflict.

Already seeing a potential repeat of the earlier trends of irreverent camp life, Army Chief of Staff General George C. Marshall was ready to take proactive steps to ensure that this war's servicemen wouldn't fall victim to unseemly temptations.

To create this support, General Marshall reached out to civilians and social agencies like the YMCA and the Salvation Army, and gained the support of

President Franklin D. Roosevelt. They pressed local leaders to acknowledge the problem and act to address the vices that posed a serious threat to the war effort.[1] In 1941, the United Service Organizations for National Defense (USO) was formed, providing nongovernmental support that focused on welfare and religious services for military members.

Walter Hoving, president of the Salvation Army Association of New York, was one of the original ten USO directors and served as its first president. Under his leadership, the USO created clubs that served as places for soldiers to relax and unwind. Volunteer support helped the USO hold chaperoned dances where soldiers could socialize with women. Instead of drinking alcohol, men could enjoy time together over coffee, sodas, sandwiches, and donuts. At USO centers and lounges, soldiers could play board games, ping pong, and cards. Eventually, the organization began bringing celebrity entertainment to perform for the troops.

Although the USO certainly improved the troops' physical condition, the boost in morale it provided was even more important. Through the USO's efforts, soldiers felt closer to home and could sense that the nation stood with them in their fight for freedom.

How did Hoving and the USO enable more than a million civilian men and women to improve the physical and emotional conditions of American soldiers during WWII?

They internalized the philosophy that *it's not about you; it's about them*.

A Personal Remembrance of the USO

2003 was an unforgettable year in my life.

At twenty-two years old, I was deployed with the 4th Infantry Division as a part of the 2003 invasion of Saddam Hussein's Iraq. After seven months of temperatures over 120 degrees, endless work hours, and constant battlefield tension, there was a bright spot in sight. My commander let me know I was on my way home for two weeks of mid-tour leave. I was beyond ecstatic.

However, as I boarded the twenty-hour flight scheduled to land at a small airport in Maine to refuel before continuing to my home in Fort Carson, Colorado, I had no idea what to expect.

I had heard horror stories of combat veterans returning from Vietnam to the bitter scorn and harsh judgment of the American public. Reports from that time suggested that it began in the airport with a soldier's first steps back on American soil. So, as excited as I was when the wheels touched down in Maine, I was also wary of what I might encounter at the end of the jet bridge.

The memory of that moment still brings tears to my eyes, even these many years later. My first glimpse of a stateside civilian was an elderly USO volunteer. He wore a rumpled mesh hat, barely visible under what looked like twenty pounds of patriotic pins. In one shaking hand he held a little American flag, and in the other he held a plastic bag packed to the brim with candy and hygiene products. His blue eyes sparkled with pride as he thrust the bag in my direction. "Welcome home, son!"

Perhaps more than any other, this memory embodies everything I want to convey about the tremendous impact potential of nonprofits. More specifically, it captures the not-about-me ethos of the most effective nonprofit organizations. The grizzled veteran who welcomed me had nothing to gain from our ten-second encounter, not even the remembrance of his name. He was content simply to serve a weary young man who was serving America.

This is indicative of the core selflessness of the USO. From the first moments of its founding, the USO has never been about its founders or board or executive team. Rather, these individuals choose to elevate the heroism of the USO's beneficiaries and the volunteers who serve them.

The result is a juggernaut of volunteer energy that needs almost no top-down direction. Within months of its founding in the early 1940s, the USO had over a million volunteers operating at the local level with very little direction from any sort of headquarters. Passionate volunteers did everything from carpentry to plumbing to organizing dances to serving ice cream.

In 1946, the USO director of Honolulu's Victory Club said in a report, "Five stories high, it has accommodated as many as 447,000 attendees in a single month." The club's signature delicacy, the banana split, required "a ton of bananas and 250 gallons of ice cream every day."[2] Cheerful volunteers not expecting the slightest inkling of recognition ensured that this colossal daily operation went off without a hitch.

Of course, I had no idea about this legacy when I stepped off the plane in Maine. Nor do most forlorn soldiers when they return home. But as a beneficiary looking back on the experience, I am—and forever will be—grateful for the USO.

Be Careful What You Celebrate

As nonprofit leaders, the world is watching intently to see who we choose to exalt as heroes. Candidates abound: original founders, current executive directors, board members, deep-pocketed funders, celebrities who post about our cause, and countless others. As tempting as these options for veneration may be (and they *will* be alluring at times), the best nonprofit leaders resist this urge. Who, then, *should* we celebrate?

The hero of your nonprofit is ANYONE who contributes to or benefits from the nonprofit's work in any way, no matter how small. The $5 donor is infinitely more heroic than someone who gives nothing, and just as heroic as someone who gives $10 or $100. The constituent who reaches out to your nonprofit and benefits even the slightest bit is infinitely more heroic than the prospective beneficiary who doesn't ask for help.

I recognize how odd this sounds. Though it may seem intuitive to treat major donors and miracle stories as your nonprofit's superheroes, taking this approach will eventually destroy your nonprofit. Think hard on this: the moment we begin to distinguish heroism by size of gift or extent of life change is the moment we begin to shrink our pool of supporters and beneficiaries. Eventually a nonprofit is left chasing only the biggest of gifts and only the most spectacular of results. How to prevent this? *Everyone* helping or being helped are the heroes, without exception.

Donor trust and commitment depend upon the perceived impact on beneficiaries and the ways that impact is communicated back to donors (see Law 18).[3] The YMCA sends handwritten, personal thank-you notes to each donor. Leaders provides templates and resources that staff members can use as inspiration for their correspondence. This idea applies to volunteers as well—studies show that volunteer recognition reduces volunteer turnover.[4] Each year, the Salvation Army sends out a thank-you letter to each and every volunteer no matter whether they stuffed a single envelope or donated hundreds of hours of time.

Honoring your contributors isn't just the right thing to do; recognition increases charitable behavior.[5] Moreover, an offer of recognition has greater power to increase contributions when a larger proportion of donors are recognized.[6] By honoring all donors, large and small, you have far more potential for increasing your annual revenue.

Remember also to celebrate your beneficiaries. The brave survivors who call the National Domestic Violence Hotline do so despite serious risks to their safety. The addict who steps into a clinic for a better life is fighting every bodily impulse to use again. The young woman from a troubled family who seeks help getting accepted to college is fighting through tremendous fear and insecurity. In every case, their courage deserves to be honored. Your public efforts to convey praise for these beneficiaries can raise awareness about societal problems, and may be the catalyst needed to inspire other beneficiaries to seek help. No matter how small their involvement, all volunteers, contributors, and beneficiaries deserve to be celebrated as heroes.

Summary

During WWI, servicemen were suffering from the debilitating effects of poor choices in camp. What began as the behavior of a rowdy few eventually grew into an alarming threat to the readiness of the entire war effort. Years later, in preparation for WWII, General George C. Marshall worked to ensure that soldiers would be better supported with more wholesome options to relax and unwind. Civilians and social agencies joined forces and the USO was formed. Under the leadership of Walter Hoving, the USO was instrumental in driving down rates of alcoholism and disease among servicemen, and providing a much-needed boost of morale. A volunteer-driven organization, the USO values everyone who participates in and benefits from its efforts. The most effective nonprofit leaders understand that the hero of their organization is *anyone* who contributes to or benefits from the nonprofit's work in any way, no matter how small.

The key to the thirty-sixth law of nonprofit impact—*they are the heroes*—is celebrating the efforts, large and small, of all of your volunteers, donors, and beneficiaries.

Recommended Further Reading

BOLTON, MARTHA, WITH LINDA HOPE. *Dear Bob: Bob Hope's Wartime Correspondence with the G.I.s of World War II*. Jackson: University Press of Mississippi, 2021.

STEVENSON, SCOTT C. *128 Recognition Ideas for Donors, Volunteers and Members*. San Francisco: Jossey-Bass, 2013.

WILSON, THOMAS C. *Winning Gifts (Make Your Donors Feel Like Winners)*. Hoboken, NJ: Wiley, 2008.

---

1 Gretchen Knapp, "Experimental Social Policymaking During World War II: The United Service Organizations (USO) and American War-Community Services (AWCS)," *Journal of Policy History* 12, no. 3 (2000): 321–38.

2 Paul X. Rutz, "Here's How the First USO Centers Were Created," USO, February 24, 2020, https://www.uso.org/stories/150-here-s-how-the-first-uso-centers-were-created.

3 Sanja K. Hudson, "Improving Volunteer Engagement in Nonprofit Healthcare Organizations," *Open Journal of Business and Management* 9, no. 3 (2021): 1367–408.

4 Adrian Sargeant, John B. Ford, and Douglas C. West, "Perceptual Determinants of Nonprofit Giving Behavior," *Journal of Business Research* 59, no. 2 (2006): 155–65.

5 Karen Page Winterich, Vikas Mittal, and Karl Aquino, "When Does Recognition Increase Charitable Behavior? Toward a Moral Identity-Based Model," *Journal of Marketing* 77, no. 3 (2013): 121–34.

6 Jordan W. Richmond, "Giving on the Margin: The Power of Donor Recognition," PhD diss., (Bowdoin College, 2016).

LAWS OF OPERATING

LAW 37:

Map your value streams.

> "Every man is a valuable member of society, who, by his observations, researches, and experiments, procures knowledge for men."
>
> James Smithson (1754–1829)

In 1835, $500,000 was a lot of money for a British scientist to bequeath to the United States government.

This unlikely story began in 1754, when James Smithson was born illegitimately to the first Duke of Northumberland. Growing up deprived of his father's name or status, Smithson was intent on building a reputation for himself. He attended Pembroke College at Oxford University, where he developed a passion for natural sciences and chemistry. His research was so impressive that, within just a year of graduating, he was admitted as a Fellow of the renowned Royal Society of London.

While London was his home, Smithson enjoyed traveling the world to explore and study. Smithson was scrupulously meticulous in his research; he valued the importance of detailed work, regardless of how minor the investigation, and believed in publishing even the most minimal advances. His scientific writings and reports helped him become a well-regarded mineralogist and chemist.

In 1826, after a lifetime of slowly accumulating wealth, Smithson drew up a will naming his nephew the sole benefactor of his estate. If his nephew died, the estate would be bequeathed to any of his children. If there were no heirs, the entire estate would transfer to the government of the United States of America for the development of the Smithsonian Institution, a museum to support the broad pursuit of knowledge.

As Smithson had no affiliation with the United States, his bequest raised more than a few eyebrows.[1] It seemed a moot point, however, considering his nephew was in his early twenties when Smithson died in 1829. But, just six years later, the young man died of unknown causes, leaving no heirs to claim the late scientist's fortune.

That's how America received more than $500,000 to establish what today remains one of the most iconic destinations in America's capital city.

But the road to construction was no simple matter; when originally notified of the donation, members the American government couldn't agree on how to handle the situation. While some felt the gift was in the spirit of the age, others believed it was beneath the dignity of the country to accept such a gift. Finally, three years later, Congress sent an envoy to London to bring back the money.

Two years crawled by at the Court of Chancery, as various parties debated the will's validity and demanded promises that the US would build the institution per Smithson's request. Finally, in May 1838, the court awarded the estate to America. Everything was converted into currency and delivered to the US Mint. Nearly a decade later, Congress finally realized Smithson's dream.

Today, the Smithsonian Institution is the world's largest museum complex and a renowned center for research. Smithson not only helped to perpetuate the increase and diffusion of knowledge; he proved that private individuals can voluntarily establish beneficial partnerships with the US government that yield long-term impact for society.

How has the Smithsonian Institution managed to develop and succeed over time, continuing to serve as one of the most impactful centers for knowledge and research?

By embracing the idea that *all successful organizations, nonprofits included, operate according to repeatable systems.*

Value Stream Mapping: Current State

When he penned his will, Smithson could hardly have envisioned the network of nineteen world-class museums, galleries, gardens, and a national zoo that now bear his name. But the founding gift is only a small part of the story. The organization's tremendous impact is a result of repeatable yearly, monthly, weekly, and hourly *systems* that host upwards of twenty million visitors a year. Such systems are a testament to the meticulous nature of their benefactor and serve as a worthy model for all nonprofit organizations.

A system is an organized, consistent, repeatable method that helps ensure an organization is fulfilling its overall mission. In your nonprofit context, this could mean your intake system for a new beneficiary, your budget planning system for the next fiscal year, or your golf tournament system for executing your big annual fundraiser. Roughly put, anything your nonprofit does repeatedly counts as a system.

For decades, for-profit organizations have used a technique known as a Value Stream Map (VSM) to determine their systems' current states and design optimized systems' future states. A VSM is one of the best tools to map a process and identify the "critical path," the most essential steps to achieve the desired outcome.[2] The VSM process creates an itemized visualization of every step in your system and how long each step takes. By seeing the full picture of your processes, you can decide with your team what changes will yield the most impact. A VSM helps organizations measure, understand, and improve the flow and interaction of tasks to keep costs, services, and quality as competitive and productive as possible.[3]

Five simple principles will help you apply a VSM to assess the current state of any of your systems:

1. *Specify the system's value from the standpoint of the end "customer."*

   The customer may be a beneficiary, a donor, a volunteer, or even the community as a whole. Identify the customer of each specific system and what *they* would consider a valuable outcome of the system (e.g., in a nonprofit's monthly donation system, value from the donor's standpoint could be knowing that their donation was received, appreciated, and converted into impact).

2. *List every stage of the current process, and be brutally honest.*

   Every stage means *every stage* that you observe happening in the process. No step is too small to address, even if it's as simple as "email sits in inbox." Include even stages that are optional, occasional, or infrequent. The current-state VSM is meant to be reported as-is. Necessary improvements will come later, but first you must be willing to reveal the ugly side of your systems. Adopt a policy of honesty through amnesty—nobody gets in trouble during the building of a current-state VSM.

3. *List the time or time range that each stage takes.*

   The duration could be seconds, minutes, days, weeks, or months depending on the system. For instance, you might notate that "email sits in inbox, 2–48 hours." If creating your current-state VSM in a spreadsheet, consider incorporating three columns to record the minimum, normal, and maximum time duration.

4. *Make sure the stages represent both activities and information transfer.*

   Activities could be, "The staff member on-duty opens and inspects the facility, 10–15 minutes." Information transfer could be, "On-duty staff member sends an 'all clear' email to executive director, 5 minutes." Details surrounding activities and information transfer are equally important to building a clear picture of the current state.

5. Build a VSM using real life observation.

This point cannot be emphasized enough—the entirety of your organization's systems improvement depends on it. To build an accurate current-state VSM, *you must see each stage happen for yourself*. It's imperative that you witness each stage of a system play out. Only by observing can you notice the things that get left out of verbal walkthroughs or explanations (e.g., 25% the time, your nonprofit's 1990s era copier jams up and the repair can take up to a day).

By following these five principles, you can gain the insight necessary to have a problem-solving session that will significantly improve the system's future state.

Value Stream Mapping: Future State

The hard work of understanding a system's current state lays the groundwork to figure out ways to improve what's working well and fix (or eliminate) what's not. The desired end result of your improvements is called the *future state* of a system. Improvements need not be comprehensive or all at once, nor does the future state need to be anything close to perfect. The best nonprofit organizations continuously define slightly better future states and make improvements to their systems on a rolling basis.

The future state of your systems depends on questions (1) *about* your systems *(Are these the systems we need in order to accomplish our nonprofit's mission?)* and (2) *within* your systems *(How do we minimize things the customer doesn't truly value?)*.

Concerning the second of these two questions, the ultimate goal of every system is to provide value for the customer. However, distinguishing between value-adding and non-value-adding activities can be difficult.[4] Thankfully there is a long track record of expertise in combatting what operations experts refer to as *waste*, the chief enemy of impact that manifests in eight forms:[5]

1. **Defects**—Mistakes that require additional time, resources, or money to fix. (Example: expired food at a food pantry.)
2. **Overproduction**—Producing too much too early that the customer doesn't really want. (Example: printing 500 annual reports but only mailing 150 to potential donors.)
3. **Waiting**—Whenever the flow of value significantly slows or stops. (Example: a delayed start time due to late attendees.)
4. **Talent**—Failing to recognize or utilize people's talents, skills, or special knowledge. (Example: a volunteer with a graphic design degree isn't asked to help with social media posts.)
5. **Transportation**—Transporting value-giving things from one place to another. (Example: an email is copied to additional people who didn't need to see it.)
6. **Inventory**—Money spent, time involved in handling, and space/storage requirements for a surplus of materials. (Example: fifty volunteers signed up last month but haven't been contacted.)
7. **Motion**—A single person or work group doing unnecessary movements to accomplish a task. (Example: a beneficiary has to take three buses across town to receive service.)
8. **Overprocessing**—Unnecessary production or communication which adds no additional value to a product or service. (Example: an online training lasts an hour when a half-hour lesson would suffice.)

A future-state VSM is the result of taking your current-state VSM and eliminating as many of the eight wastes as possible.[6] If you've done a diligent job of spelling out all of the steps and their durations—especially those you would rather not admit are there—then you can expect significant improvements. Together with your team, sit down and stare at the current-state VSM looking for waste. The more you can build a waste-identification and

-elimination into your nonprofit's culture, the more you'll see your nonprofit's impact increase over time.

Summary

When British scientist James Smithson bequeathed his estate to America, he intended to contribute to the pursuit of knowledge through the construction of the Smithsonian Institution. It's unlikely he could have imagined at that time that the Smithsonian would one day become the world's largest museum complex welcoming upwards of twenty million visitors a year. The Smithsonian Institution has thrived largely as a result of repeatable systems that make large numbers of daily visitors possible. A tool called a Value Stream Map (VSM) allows organizations of all sizes to assess the current state of their systems by listing each step and the time that each step takes. A VSM also helps nonprofit leaders reimagine a future state for their systems. Teams can solve for ways to remove eight different kinds of waste from the current-state VSM to yield a future-state VSM that makes better use of the organization's resources.

The keys to the thirty-seventh law of nonprofit impact—*map your value streams*—are finding and removing waste from current-state systems to continuously improve future-state systems.

Recommended Further Reading

MARTIN, KAREN, AND MIKE OSTERLING. *Value Stream Mapping: How to Visualize Work and Align Leadership for Organizational Transformation.* New York: McGraw-Hill Education, 2018.

NASH, MARK A. *Mapping the Total Value Stream: A Comprehensive Guide for Production and Transactional Processes.* New York: Productivity Press, 2008.

ROTHER, MIKE, AND JOHN SHOOK. *Learning to See: Value Stream Mapping to Add Value and Eliminate MUDA.* Boston: Lean Enterprise Institute, 1999.

1 George Brown Goode, *The Smithsonian Institution, 1846-1896: The History of its First Half Century* (London: Forgotten Books, 2017), 22.

2 M. Braglia, G. Carmignani, and F. Zammori, "A New Value Stream Mapping Approach for Complex Production Systems," *International Journal of Production Research* 44, no. 18-19 (2011): 3929-52.

3 Beau Keyte and Drew A. Locher, *The Complete Lean Enterprise: Value Stream Mapping for Administrative and Office Processes* (New York: Productivity Press, 2004), 1.

4 Muhittin Sagnak, Erhan Ada, Yigit Kazancoglu, and Atul Mishra, "Integration of Lean Approach with Energy Efficiency: Application in Kitchenware Manufacturing Company," *International Journal of Mathematic, Engineering and Management Sciences* 5, no. 6 (2020): 1128-39.

5 Kai Magenheimer, Gunther Reinhart, and Cornelius S. L. Schutte, "Lean Management in Indirect Business Areas: Modeling, Analysis, and Evaluation of Waste," *Production Engineering* 8, no. 1-2 (2014): 143-52.

6 Ibon Serrano Lasa, Carlos Ochoa Laburu, and Rodolfo de Castro Vila, "An Evaluation of the Value Stream Mapping Tool," *Business Process Management Journal* 14, no. 1 (2008): 39-52.

LAW 38:

Establish improve-and-lock systems.

> "Nature often gives hints to her profoundest secrets, and it is possible that she has given us a hint which, if we will but follow, may lead us on to the solution of this difficult problem."
>
> **Dr. William B. Coley (1862–1936)**

At only twenty-nine, Helen Coley Nauts was devastated by the death of her father.

To honor her father, Dr. William B. Coley, and cope with her grief, Nauts resolved to write his biography. The late Dr. Coley had been a bone surgeon and cancer researcher who practiced in New York between 1890 and 1936. While sorting through his papers, his grieving daughter made a remarkable realization.

In the early 1890s, Dr. Coley noticed that numerous cancer patients experienced remission in their tumors whenever these individuals contracted acute bacterial infections. Certain that there was a correlation between the two, Dr. Coley made a bold move. In a patient with an inoperable malignant tumor, he injected live bacteria to bring about a virulent infection. His theory was that the infection would stimulate the body's natural immune defenses and eliminate the tumors. Sure enough, the patient recovered fully and lived a long and happy life.

This confirmation encouraged Dr. Coley to develop a safe and effective bacteria mixture for treating patients with cancer. Although his discoveries were on the cusp of greatness, his efforts were overshadowed by the introduction of the X-ray, radium treatment, and chemotherapy.

Nauts knew her father's work was significant and needed to be revisited. A young housewife and mother with no medical training, Nauts realized she needed a better understanding of pathology, bacteriology, and radiology. Every day for nearly twenty years, she visited the New York Academy of Medicine's library to analyze thousands of papers and textbooks on cancer diagnosis and treatment.

Finally, after documenting 896 cases of microscopically confirmed cancers treated with Dr. Coley's mixed bacterial toxins, Nauts published her findings. The data not only showed the benefits of her father's treatment; it was so exact and compelling that it is still referenced by researchers today for clues about cancer.

At the time, the field of biological sciences was experiencing significant medical advancements. Immunology, however, was a neglected topic of study. Nauts's groundbreaking work piqued the medical community's interest in learning more about the link between the immune system and cancer. As a result, Nauts created an organization to elevate the profile of cancer immunology and support the establishment of immunotherapy as a weapon against cancer.

Nauts secured a $2,000 grant from Nelson Rockefeller and, with a good friend, founded the Cancer Research Institute (CRI) in 1953. In the institution's first twenty years, cancer immunology science grew exponentially. Some of the world's most prestigious immunologists and oncologists were recruited to the CRI Scientific Advisory Council. Since then, the organization has developed vaccines, provided funding for extensive cancer research, and coordinated research efforts across international borders.

How did one man's theory about using bacteria as a cure lead to an organization that continues to develop cutting-edge cancer treatments more than a century later?

CRI realized that *standardization and continuous improvement are concepts that can and should work together.*

Lean

Despite having no medical background, Nauts sought the information and education she needed to pick up where her father left off. Her example, along with countless others, demonstrates that the world-changing potential of a nonprofit lies in the mindsets of its leaders. By shifting oneself and one's organization from impact-limiting to impact-enhancing mindsets, we open up new frontiers of what is possible—even the curing of cancer.

This idea is in no way limited to nonprofits; some of the most influential innovations of the last century occurred as a result of for-profit leaders refusing to succumb to limiting beliefs. A notable example is the case of Japanese industrial engineer and businessman Taiichi Ohno. In the late 1940s, Ohno was working for Toyota, a Japanese automobile manufacturer. As the growing complexity of vehicles was pushing Henry Ford's assembly-line manufacturing method to its limits, Toyota needed a way to manufacture cars with far fewer delays. Under Ohno's leadership, Toyota shifted its focus to *continuous improvement* (in Japanese, *kaizen*), and adopted an approach that was later popularized in the business world as *Lean Management*. Lean sought to eliminate waste and value the contributions of employees to drive continuous improvement.[1]

Lean is a powerful operating philosophy whose benefits can be enjoyed by all organizations, nonprofits included. There are fourteen principles at the heart of Lean Management:[2]

1. **Base your management decisions on long-term philosophy, even at the expense of short-term financial goals.** *(Example: Forgo a large government grant that doesn't adhere to your mission.)*

2. **Create continuous, "just in time" process flows to bring problems to the surface.** *(Example: A homeless shelter receives food in the morning for that evening's meal.)*
3. **Use pull systems to avoid overproduction.** *(Example: A homeless shelter orders food based on real-time occupancy.)*
4. **Level out the workload.** *(Example: Each shelter worker has the same amount of work to accomplish.)*
5. **Build a culture of "stopping to fix problems" to get quality right and eliminate rework.** *(Example: Staff at a daycare notice a safety issue and stay late that same day to fix the problem.)*
6. **Standardized tasks are the foundation for continuous improvement and employee empowerment.** *(Example: A home-building nonprofit standardizes everything from nail hammering to house assembly.)*
7. **Use visual controls so no problems are hidden and opportunities are exposed to all.** *(Example: A construction nonprofit posts a large work schedule board at each construction site that workers can see at all times.)*
8. **Use only reliable and thoroughly tested technology that serves your people and processes.** *(Example: A grant-making foundation uses a paper grant application and adjusts it until it's ready, and only then turns it into an app.)*
9. **Grow leaders who thoroughly understand the work, live the philosophy, and teach it to others.** *(Example: A long-serving volunteer is promoted to train new volunteers in standardized methods.)*
10. **Develop exceptional people and teams who follow your company's philosophy.** *(Example: An executive director mentors her successor, a talented leader who has served at the nonprofit for twelve years.)*
11. **Respect your extended network of partners and suppliers by challenging them and helping them improve.** *(Example: A veterans' organization works with a local hospital to help improve their care of returning combat veterans.)*

12. **See the situation for yourself to thoroughly understand it.** *(Example: An after-school care center executive sits in on a different classroom each week.)*
13. **Make decisions slowly by consensus, thoroughly considering all options, and then implement rapidly.** *(Example: A nationwide nonprofit holds problem-solving sessions with its regional chapters over the course of six months.)*
14. **Become a learning organization through relentless reflection and continuous improvement.** *(Example: At each staff meeting, the group reads through all of the submissions to their "big ideas" box.)*

Despite the simplicity and intuitive appeal of Lean Management principles, most organizations haven't realized their full potential for lack of putting all fourteen into practice. Nonprofit organizations have much to gain by infusing their operating culture with these principles.

Standardization and Continuous Improvement

For many organizations, "standardization" and "continuous improvement" seem like a contradiction in terms. Standardization is often associated with rigid regulations that limit creativity, resulting in processes that are strictly adhered to regardless of their effectiveness.

Obviously, this intransigent way-we've-always-done-it mindset precludes further improvement. However, there are dangers on the other extreme as well. Adaptation without standardization can lead to everyone doing things their own way, which ultimately leads to inefficiency or even chaos within an organization.

To avoid these issues, organizations must establish a *culture of continuous improvement* that instills a sense of respect for the standard processes in place, while also allowing them to be improved. *Improve-and-lock systems* operate the way their name implies; in a Lean context, a system remains standardized across the organization until there is consensus around a way to materially improve it. Once the system is improved, the organization once again locks it in as the new standard until another better way comes along.

In actuality, standardization is a powerful yet underutilized tool. Standards promote consistency, and consistency is one of the major foundations of good quality.[3] By documenting the current best practices, standardized work establishes a baseline for continuous improvement. As the standard improves, the new standard becomes the benchmark, and so on. Improving standardization reduces the variations of systems and improves quality.[4]

By determining the best work sequence for each process, a nonprofit can create current standards and set parameters for continuous improvement. To establish a standard, an organization must:

- *Observe and record variations to find the most efficient work sequence.*
- *Practice the sequence up to ten times. If staff and volunteers can repeat it precisely and consistently, it's a viable sequence.*
- *Document the standard to help employees repeat the optimum work sequence.*

Standardization isn't an obstacle in the way of improvement. Rather, it is the essential foundation for a continuously improving organization that operates by improve-and-lock systems.

Summary

Helen Coley Nauts realized her late father, a cancer surgeon, had made a radical medical discovery connecting immunology to cancer treatment. She took it upon herself to learn all she could about cancer diagnosis and treatment. Eventually, she was able to publish her findings with such authority that she rekindled the medical industry's interest in cancer immunology. Nauts founded the Cancer Research Institute (CRI) in 1953, which has been instrumental in cancer research and treatment. The success of CRI and nonprofits like it has depended on a healthy interplay between standardization and continuous improvement. For-profit organizations have led the way in developing an operating philosophy that makes the most of this interplay. An exemplar in this regard is automobile manufacturer Toyota, who developed what is now known as Lean Management. Lean is a collection of principles whereby a group works together to expose and eliminate waste from its processes. Nonprofits also can apply Lean by creating standardized systems that help to lay the foundation for quality and consistency. Then, through consensus around waste elimination, the nonprofit's systems can continue to improve, raising the levels of efficiency, quality, and productivity.

The key to the thirty-eighth law of nonprofit impact—*establish improve-and-lock systems*—is to document and train to the standard system, while always encouraging collaborative problem-solving toward a better standard.

Recommended Further Reading

EL-HOMSI, ANWAR, AND JEFF SLUTSKY. *Corporate Sigma: Optimizing the Health of Your Company with Systems Thinking*. New York: Productivity Press, 2009.

MANN, DAVID. *Kaizen: Creating a Lean Culture: Tools to Sustain Lean Conversions*. New York: Productivity Press, 2014.

ROTHER, MIKE. *Toyota Kata: Managing People for Improvement, Adaptiveness, and Superior Results*. New York: McGraw-Hill Education, 2009.

---

1 Thomas L. Jackson, *Implementing a Lean Management System* (New York: Productivity Press, 1996), 3.

2 Jeffrey K. Liker, *The Toyota Way: 14 Management Principles from the World's Greatest Manufacturer* (New York: McGraw-Hill Education, 2020), 69–250.

3 Robert W. Hall, "Continuous Improvement Through Standardization," *AME Target* (Summer 1986): 3–6.

4 Miroslava Mĺkva, Vanessa Prajová, Boris Yakimovich, Alexander Korshunov, and Ivan Tyurin, "Standardization: One of the Tools of Continuous Improvement," *Procedia Engineering* 149 (2016): 329–32.

LAW 39:

Measure what matters.

> "I started the conservation society because there needed to be somebody or some group that was concerned with what was happening."
>
> Richard Pough (1904–2003)

His mother's fear led young Richard Pough to a life-changing observation.

In 1912, during the Pough family's annual summer vacation to Block Island, a terrible flu pandemic broke out back home in Brooklyn.

The illness was fatal for many children, so Pough's mother, a botanist and public health specialist, kept the family on the island for the duration of the year. While walking home after school that winter, Pough was captivated by the migrating birds he saw soaring above him. He set a goal to see how many he could identify using bird guides. This experience instilled in Pough a love for bird-watching that would become a lifelong passion.

Pough graduated from Massachusetts Institute of Technology and took over a chain of bankrupt camera stores he hoped to revitalize. This inspired him to pursue a new hobby of photography. In 1932, while visiting Hawk Mountain near Reading, Pennsylvania, Pough discovered hundreds of dead hawks that had been shot by farmers who were protecting their crops and livestock.

Pough photographed the carnage, and the pictures were so impactful that he convinced a New York socialite to purchase 1,400 acres for the Hawk Mountain Sanctuary. It was one of the first refuges for birds of prey, and the beginning of Pough's lifelong career as a conservationist.

The National Audubon Society deployed Pough as a "roving warden" to document rare birds. He would take careful notes about his observations, measuring and tracking the impact of various factors on the land and animals around him. He advocated for legislation to end the practice of using the feathers of endangered species in fashion and fishing, and was instrumental in the fight against the pest repellant DDT, warning about its adverse effects on plants and animals.

Pough's attention to detail and thorough documentation eventually landed him a position as the curator of conservation at New York's Museum of Natural History. While there, he continued to write bird guides for Audubon.

In 1950, Pough collaborated with several biologists and ecologists to found the Nature Conservancy, one of the world's largest environmental conservation groups. Pough served as its first president and secured private funds that enabled him to devote the rest of his life to preserving lands of conservation value. He established dozens of additional organizations to continue this work, receiving land and funds to preserve habitats all over the country.

Today, the Nature Conservancy is a global environmental nonprofit working to build a world where people and nature can live in harmony. Through its grassroots efforts, the Nature Conservancy has grown to become one of the world's most impactful environmental organizations; it currently protects eleven million acres of ecologically important land in the United States, and more than sixty million acres overseas, from dual threats of climate change and biodiversity loss.

How did Pough help establish the Nature Conservancy and cultivate it into an organization that protects land and animals across more than seventy countries and territories?

He realized that *the best nonprofits measure things in order to facilitate full-team continuous improvement discussions.*

Impact Measurement

The Nature Conservancy's mission is to preserve the diversity of plants and animals by protecting the habitats of rare species around the world. In its day-to-day work, the organization could measure any number of things to assess its progress. For example, it could measure total revenue or volunteer hours. These metrics, however, wouldn't necessarily tell the Conservancy's leaders much about the organization's mission accomplishment. After all, their goal isn't to raise money or keep volunteers busy, but to preserve the diversity of life. What the Conservancy needed was not a way to measure *inputs*, but a way to measure *impact*.

The Conservancy realized that species were continuing to decline, and it was happening on their protected land. This discovery caused the organization to look for new ways to measure the real impact they were having. The Conservancy adopted five stages of impact measurement:[1]

1. **Theory of Change.** *This is the foundation for what your organization does and why. It should answer the following:*

   - *What impact do you hope to achieve?*
   - *What is the mechanism by which you achieve that impact?*
   - *How will you know when you've achieved it?*

2. **Key Performance Indicators (KPIs).** *Choose five to seven clear metrics for your team, department, or organization. Each layer of an organizational hierarchy can have its own KPIs, but they should be cascaded so that lower level KPIs feed up to higher level ones.*
3. **Data Collection and Analysis.** *For each of the KPIs, collect data to determine a current state. Look for indications revealing strengths and opportunities.*
4. **Quasi-Experimental Design.** *Use control groups to gain an understanding of how well your organization is impacting beneficiaries.*

5. **Randomized Controlled Trial.** Although differences may exist between individuals in different conditions, randomly distributing those differences will not impact the results of your trial.

Only after a nonprofit observes and records the outcomes of its work can it release its fixation on inputs and instead begin to fully understand its impact. Gaining this insight can help an organization determine what areas need to be improved, and whether its efforts are making any difference toward its mission.

Efforts toward impact measurement can, of course, be taken to extremes. Along the way to becoming an impact-measuring organization, stay healthy by avoiding the five performance measurement traps:[2]

1. **Micromanagement Trap**—Overanalyzing which causes people to lose motivation and forget the worthy cause underlying the metrics.
2. **Hedge Trap**—Measuring secondary performance indicators to hedge against the risk of a negative evaluation holds you back from focusing on what matters most.
3. **At-Least-It's-Measurable Trap**—Easily measurable items are often less important than harder-to-measure items.
4. **Full-Control Trap**—Reluctance to focus on just five to seven performance metrics instead of twenty or fifty.
5. **Complexity-Cannot-Be-Measured-Objectively Trap**—Reluctance to new work or a shift in methodology hinder tracking and discussion of meaningful metrics.[3]

Understandably, well-intended organizations can fall into these pitfalls. Nonprofit leaders serve their organizations best when they avoid the two extremes of not measuring what matters and making measurement the mission.

Display and Discuss

As nonprofit leaders, we must realize that measurement is not an end—it is simply a means by which real humans can make decisions that improve nonprofit outcomes. Therefore, we shouldn't ask, *"Are we measuring the right thing?"* but rather, *"Are we having conversations that help us improve?"*

Rather than debating the suitability of a metric, *redirect attention to the suitability of the performance dialogues about those metrics.* All too often, those conversations aren't happening at all. Teams that are committed to continuous improvement should have the following dialogues on a regular basis:

1. **Impromptu Kaizen.** *Solve a specific problem that has been identified on the front lines of the organization.*
   - **Step 1:** *Visit the site of the problem and watch the issue happen.*
   - **Step 2:** *Map the current state and define the desired state.*
   - **Step 3:** *Brainstorm solutions and agree on changes to implement.*
   - **Step 4:** *Assign clear ownership and a timeline for implementing improvements.*
   - **Step 5:** *Monitor results and broadcast new standard work.*

2. **Start of Day/Shift Standup.** *Review previous performance and align as a team on continuous improvement priorities.*
   - **Step 1:** *Discuss progress.*
   - **Step 2:** *Discuss insights.*
   - **Step 3:** *Determine next steps.*

3. **All-Team/All-Staff Meeting.** *Gather the whole team on a weekly, bi-weekly, or monthly basis.*
   - **Step 1:** *Celebrate team wins.*
   - **Step 2:** *Review upcoming calendar.*
   - **Step 3:** *Solve one problem holding the team back.*

4. **Annual Review.** Meet with each of your direct reports for an annual, in-depth performance discussion.
    - **Step 1:** Celebrate past wins.
    - **Step 2:** Help the team member amplify their strengths.
    - **Step 3:** Help the team member mitigate their weaknesses.

Each performance dialogue follows the simple model of *Progress-Insights-Next Steps*. I learned this model early in my career and it's been a mainstay of communicating with my teams and clients ever since. These three simple points generate all the discussion needed to help an organization continuously improve and measure its impact.

Discussions are a powerful tool, but this power is only fully realized when the facts are displayed prominently where everyone can see.[4] How many annual reports have been mailed? How many days of food do we have in stock? How many occupants are in the facility? Only by displaying these KPIs prominently can team members stay on the same page regarding current-state and future progress.[5] A clear, up-to-date visual of what's happening in the organization will ensure that the performance dialogues described above will drive continuous improvement.

Summary

Richard Pough's passion for conservation and knack for documenting his observations of the plants and animals around him led to the founding of the Nature Conservancy. One of the world's most impactful and far-reaching environmental organizations, it currently protects eleven million acres of ecologically important land in the United States and more than sixty million acres overseas from dual threats of climate change and biodiversity loss. As the Conservancy and many other nonprofits have discovered, measuring mission accomplishment can be difficult. Rather than focusing on measuring inputs such as revenue or volunteer hours, an organization should measure its impact. Only the hard facts about real outcomes can tell a nonprofit if it's achieving its mission. By adhering to the five stages of impact measurement and avoiding the accompanying traps, a nonprofit can make the shift from measuring inputs to measuring impact. Through recurring performance dialogues and visual management about these measurements, nonprofits can ensure they're on a continuous improvement journey.

The key to the thirty-ninth law of nonprofit impact—*measure what matters*—is shifting focus from inputs to impact.

Recommended Further Reading

BIRCHARD, BILL. *Nature's Keepers: The Remarkable Story of How the Nature Conservancy Became the Largest Environmental Group in the World.* Hoboken, NJ: Wiley, 2005.

LEWIS, CHARLES, AND HILARY NILES. *Measuring Impact: The Art, Science and Mystery of Nonprofit News Assessment.* Washington, DC: Investigative Reporting Workshop at American University, 2013.

PARMENTER, DAVID. *Key Performance Indicators for Government and Non Profit Agencies: Implementing Winning KPIs.* Hoboken, NJ: Wiley, 2012.

---

[1] Gwendolyn Reynolds, Lisa C. Cox, Nicholas Fritz, Daniel Hadley, and Jonathan R. Zadra, "A Playbook for Designing Social Impact Measurement," *Stanford Social Innovation Review*, December 21, 2018.

[2] Robert S. Kaplan, "Strategic Performance Measurement and Management in Nonprofit Organizations," *Nonprofit Management & Leadership* 11, no. 3 (2001): 353–70.

[3] Marc J. Holley, Cheri A. Recchia, and Valerie Bockstette, "Measuring What Matters," *Stanford Social Innovation Review*, January 4, 2016.

[4] Kent Bauer, "KPIs—The Metrics That Drive Performance Management," *DM Review* 14, no. 9 (2004): 63.

[5] Koichi Murata and Hiroshi Katayama, "A Study on Construction of a Kaizen Case-Base and Its Utilisation: A Case of Visual Management in Fabrication and Assembly Shop-Floors," *International Journal of Production Research* 48, no. 24 (2010): 7265–87.

LAW 40:

Your board sets the pace.

> *"If we desire a society in which men are brothers, then we must act towards one another with brotherhood. If we can build such a society, then we would have achieved the ultimate goal of human freedom."*
>
> **Bayard Rustin (1904–2003)**

We began back in Law 1 with Martin Luther King Jr.'s 1963 *Letter from Birmingham Jail*.

The truth is, without the earlier, quieter leadership of figures such as Bayard Rustin and sixty Black ministers at Ebenezer Baptist Church on January 10, 1957, there would have been no letter. There would have been no "I Have a Dream" speech. There would have been no legendary legacy of Martin Luther King Jr.

Bayard Rustin was born in 1910 and raised by his Quaker grandparents. Rustin's grandmother was active with the National Association for the Advancement of Colored People (NAACP). While Rustin was still very young, she introduced him to prominent leaders in the Black community and sparked in him a lifelong passion for nonviolent resistance to racial injustice.

In his peaceful fight for racial equality, Rustin joined several organizations that aimed to improve race relations. In 1948, Rustin decided to devote seven weeks of his life to study the Gandhian philosophy of nonviolence in India.

Then, during the Montgomery Bus Boycott in the 1950s, a civil rights protest where African Americans refused to ride city buses, Rustin gained King's attention and became his key advisor. Rustin shared King's deep commitment to nonviolence and served as his special assistant and peace-driven strategist.

One of Rustin's proposals was the formation of the Southern Christian Leadership Conference (SCLC), uniting Black leaders in the South to coordinate local protest groups. Among these leaders were Ella Baker, a human rights activist and one of the most influential women in the civil rights movement; C. K. Steele, a preacher and one of the driving forces behind the bus boycott; Fred Shuttlesworth and Ralph Abernathy, both Baptist ministers; and Joseph Lowery, a Methodist minister.

While its initial intent was to focus on inequality in public transportation, the SCLC expanded its mission to end all forms of segregation. King took the helm at Rustin's demand. The new organization opened a small office in a former Atlanta masonic building. The SCLC was established as an organization of affiliates, mainly churches and community organizations. Governed by an elected board, the SCLC coordinated with local organizations to provide training and open citizenship schools that spread the philosophy of Christian nonviolence.

The SCLC's campaigns sent shock waves across the South, which reverberated throughout the nation and gave a decisive jolt to the federal government.[1] The SCLC led voter registration drives, the March on Washington for Jobs and Freedom, and ultimately laid the foundation for the passage of the Civil Rights Act of 1964 and the Voting Rights Act of 1965.

How did Rustin's idea of an organization to unite peaceful protesters grow into the driving force behind a world-changing civil rights movement?

The SCLC understood that *a nonprofit's board is its single most important driver of success or failure.*

Not-So-Great Board Members

Board members are entrusted to govern a nonprofit organization. The board ensures the nonprofit remains true to its mission, adheres to state and federal laws, and operates with financial responsibility.[2] However, not all board members are well-suited to these activities. In my experience, weak board members are far more common than strong ones in today's nonprofit ecosystem. What characterizes a weak board member is their absent or even negative contribution toward impact.

A number of years ago, I ran across an entertaining and astonishingly accurate article that categorized weak board members in zoological categories:

- **Turkeys**—Attend board meetings once or twice a year (the same frequency most Americans enjoy a big turkey dinner). They take up valuable spots that more committed members could fill.
- **Skunks**—Join boards for business development purposes only. They have no interest in advancing the organization's cause. You can smell these stinkers a mile away.
- **Showhorses**—Show up to take the credit for work done by others. They often stomp on the toes of those who went the extra mile behind the scenes to ensure the nonprofit's success.
- **Mockingbirds**—Attend board meetings to cackle and listen to their own voices rather than to add real value or insight. (Turkeys are bad, but at least they don't actively disrupt, as mockingbirds do.)
- **Chameleons**—Agree to do things but then disappear, never to be found when others are counting on them to deliver the promised work.
- **Monkeys**—Have a "monkey see, monkey do" attitude. When it's time to do something, they simply copy what was done previously rather than adding improvements and value.

If you find yourself with the unfortunate task of dealing with ineffective board members, you can address the situation in a way that moves the organization back in the direction of impact.[3]

Some tips for handling difficult board members:

1. **Confront the issue directly and in person.** *Immediately engage the individual in an in-person conversation for an honest, open dialogue.*
2. **Focus on the nonprofit rather than the individual.** *Set aside personal differences to focus the discussion on solutions that enable the nonprofit to achieve its mission.*
3. **Provide specific examples.** *Describe particular behaviors and give the board member a chance to share their perspective on your observations.*
4. **Utilize "I" messages.** *Mitigate defensiveness by outlining behaviors in terms of their impact on you and your work.*
5. **Listen.** *Once you've stated your objection, grant the other person a chance to talk. What seems to be a problem may simply be a misunderstanding.*

As a nonprofit leader, it's your responsibility to ensure your board works in alignment with your nonprofit and its mission. Difficult discussions are sometimes necessary to set a wayward board member on a better trajectory.

The best way to address a weak board is, of course, prevention. This is where the story of the SCLC is most instructive. Rustin and his colleagues were ruthlessly selective about the senior members of their group. And it's not hard to see why. The stakes—racial equality for all—were far too high to settle for anything less than the best people on the planet for the mission at hand.

Whenever I work with a nonprofit founder who is tempted to select board members out of expediency or affection, I try to direct them back to the SCLC's line of thinking. This approach is applicable to any nonprofit, no matter its cause. When you consider the high stakes of ending poverty, eradicating human trafficking, feeding the hungry, delivering clean water, conserving natural resources, ending animal cruelty, advocating for human rights, protecting children from abuse, educating women and girls, spreading peace, or so many other noble causes—ask yourself, do you want an Ella Baker or your Uncle Eddie governing the work?

Perhaps the most courageous thing that any nonprofit leader can do for their cause is protect their board from weak members.

World-Class Board Members

Now the good news. World-class board members generally possess the following traits:

1. **Excellent character qualities.** Great board members have an infectious passion for your mission as well as high levels of integrity, honesty, and unwavering ethics. They're trustworthy and strive to do the right thing.
2. **Commitment.** Distinctive board members gladly devote their money, time, and resources to the organization's cause. They're prepared for meetings, share ideas, and never shy away from (gently) asking the tough questions.
3. **Diversity and Inclusion.** The best board members value inclusion and monitor the many legal, demographic, and cultural trends that may impact the future. They have close ties to the beneficiary population that your nonprofit serves. They encourage self-evaluation and are instrumental in short- and long-term planning.
4. **Master networkers.** Strong board members love giving to (and growing with) an ever-expanding group of influencers. They involve their contacts in the support of the organization, and they actively enhance and nurture relationships with the community, donors, leaders, and staff.
5. **Refrain from micromanaging.** Effective board members recognize their roles as overseers and strategic planners. They help in a hands-on way as needed, but otherwise remain active in fundraising and decision-making without overstepping their mandate.

As with anyone on your team, your board needs to feel encouraged and inspired. Here are some best practices to keep them engaged and motivated, especially during trying times:

- **Clear expectations.** *A board is most effective when they know what good looks like, have signed a document laying out the nonprofit's expectations, and see their peers are living up to those clear expectations.*[4]
- **Adequate resources.** *Arming board members with material one week ahead of time allows them to brainstorm and prepare for rich, fact-based discussions.*
- **Coordination tools.** *From scheduling tools for meetings to central document storage, numerous resources exist to make duties easier and information more accessible.*
- **Recognition.** *Board service is often long-term, behind-the-scenes work that doesn't yield immediate results. Recognizing your members can give them the encouragement they need to continue. Whether it's an annual event or a handwritten thank-you note, gratitude at any level can go a long way.*
- **Mentorship.** *Ensure a steady stream of high-performing board members by having current members mentor incoming ones. Our greatest training resource for newcomers is often the people we already have on our team.*

Seek board members who exemplify the character, diversity, skills, and networks necessary to govern a world-changing organization. It doesn't take many of them. As tempting as it may be to grow your board to fifteen, twenty, thirty, or more members (all of whom are donating!), a team of five to seven is ideal for team cohesion and agile decision-making.

Summary

Bayard Rustin's Quaker upbringing instilled in him a passion for peaceful activism. As an advisor to Martin Luther King Jr. in the 1950s, Rustin encouraged the formation of the Southern Christian Leadership Conference (SCLC) to unite Black leaders in the South in their peaceful protests against social injustice. Under the governance of an elected board, the SCLC was instrumental in laying the foundation for the passage of the Civil Rights Act of 1964 and the Voting Rights Act of 1965. As the SCLC demonstrates, a strong board of directors is critical to the success of any nonprofit organization. Identifying weak members and understanding how to address their ineffectiveness is essential to becoming an engine of impact. An ounce of prevention is worth a pound of cure—work diligently to prevent any but the very best board members from getting seated on the board in the first place. Populating your board with five to seven world-class directors and providing them with ample support and motivation will equip your nonprofit for many years of world-changing impact.

The key to the fortieth law of nonprofit impact—*your board sets the pace*—is recruiting a small, diverse group of the world's very best people.

Recommended Further Reading

COVEY, JERRY. *Board Basics: A Primer for Nonprofit Board Members.* Anchorage, AK: JSC Consulting, LLC, 2011.

D'EMILIO, JOHN. *Lost Prophet: The Life and Times of Bayard Rustin.* Chicago: University of Chicago Press, 2004.

STOESZ, EDGAR. *Doing Good Even Better: How to Be an Effective Board Member of a Nonprofit Organization.* New York: Good Books, 2007.

---

1 Adam Fairclough, *To Redeem the Soul of America: The Southern Christian Leadership Conference and Martin Luther King, Jr.* (Athens: University of Georgia Press, 2001), 2.

2 Jennifer Bright Preston and William A. Brown, "Commitment and Performance of Nonprofit Board Members," *Nonprofit Management & Leadership* 15, no. 2 (2004): 221–38.

3 Arthur C. Beck, "Comfortable Confrontation," *Journal of Management in Engineering* 4, no. 4 (1988): 316–19.

4 Terry W. McAdam and David L. Gies, "Managing Expectations: What Effective Board Members Ought to Expect from Nonprofit Organizations," *Nonprofit and Voluntary Sector Quarterly* 14, no.4 (1985): 77–88

INDEX

A

Abernathy, Ralph, 299
Adrià, Ferran, 172
advisory committees, use of, 118
advocacy, as not same thing as lobbying, 221
Allen, Edgar F., 224–226
Allen, Homer, 224
Alliance for the Mentally Ill (AMI), 57
all-team/all-staff meetings, as part of dialogues about continuous improvement, 295
Amazon, 242
ambitious in scope, as A in FAST goals, 228
America's Most Wanted (TV show), 129
Andrés, José, 172–174
Annie E. Casey Foundation, 118
annual review, as part of dialogues about continuous improvement, 296
asking, for people to become donors, 203–209
at-least-it's-measurable trap, 294
Austin, Tom, 232

B

Baker, Ella, 299, 301
Bérès, Jacque, 150
Bernier, Philippe, 150
Best, Charles, 8, 135–137
Bezos, Jeff, 176

Big Brothers Big Sisters of America, 84, 214
Big Five personality framework (OCEAN), 158
board of directors
    advantages of diverse board, 117
    best practices for keeping board members engaged and motivated, 303
    not-so-great board members, 300–301
    as setting the pace, 298–304
    tips for handling difficult board members, 301–302
    world-class board members, 302
boldness, power of, 226–227
Bouton, Katie, 114–115
brand/branding
    brand identity package, 234
    deeply integrated branding of long-running organizations, 241
    importance of authenticity in, 124
    rare to find nonprofit leaders curating brand through faces of constituents, 123
Bridgespan Group, 190
budget, consider renaming annual budget as annual investment plan, 198–199
Buffet, Warren, 176
Bush, Jeb, 218
Business Network International, 258

C

Camp Shriver, 122, 123, 125
Campbell, Joseph, 166–169
Cancer Research Institute (CRI), 285–286
candid conversations, importance of, 118
Cantor, Eddie, 91
capability, laws of
    Law 9: Unleash your unique strengths, 70–76
    Law 10: Mitigate your limiting weaknesses, 77–83
    Law 11: Hire with ruthless selectivity, 84–89
    Law 12: Cultivate super-volunteers, 90–97
    Law 13: Act quickly when it's not working, 98–104
    Law 14: Win while you're sleeping, 105–112
celebration
    of all your beneficiaries, 272
    and diversity, 138–139
    of wins, 137, 138
Chambers of Commerce, 258
Chapman, Gary, 160–161
Character Lab, 64
Chertavian, Gerald, 84–86
chronic overthinkers, inside the mind of, 234
clarity
    about your world-story, 14
    foundational clarity, 13, 15
    and identity, 13–14
    and impact, 15–16
    and mission, 16–17
    situational clarity, 13, 15
Coakley, Marion, 164–166
Coley, William B., 284–285
College Summit, 189
CollegeRecruiter.com, 108
Commission for Polish Relief, 246–247
Commission on Private Philanthropy and Public Needs (a.k.a. Filer Commission), 180–181
communication. *See also* email
    being social on social media communications, 261–267
    face-to-face communication, 258
    open communication, as one of Seven Sanctuary Commitments, 133
    open communication, necessity of, 118
    open conversations, importance of, 118, 119
    send-and-learn, as better communication strategy than worry-and-send, 234
    using trial-and-error approach with social media communications, 235
community, laws of
    Law 5: Your network is everything, 42–48
    Law 6: Give to gain, 49–55
    Law 7: Assemble your dream team, 56–62
    Law 8: Run with achievers of character, 63–68
complexity-cannot-be-measured-objectively trap, 294
Conduit Communications, 84
continuous improvement
    dialogues about, 295–296
    as innovation, 286
    standardization and, 288–289
ConvertKit, 235

Cooperative Extension System, 78
core values
  defining of, 29–30
  examples of, 31
  formula for, 31
  purpose of, 29
  stating yours, 30–32
cost elimination, dangers of, 190–191
cost per unit of impact, lowering of, 191–193
credibility, as factor in Trust Equation, 52
CRI (Cancer Research Institute), 285–286
CRI Scientific Advisory Council, 285
crisis moments, as times to live your values, 152
crowdsourcing approach, benefits of, 106
curiosity
  as beginning and ending with leadership, 175
  benefits of, 174
  as real driver of learning, 174

D

data collection and analysis, as one of five stages of impact measurement, 293
DC Central Kitchen, 173
De Mello, Anthony, 166
Deaton, Laura, 34–36, 38
defining moments, 181
democracy, as one of Seven Sanctuary Commitments, 133
Diabetes Prevention Program (US National Institutes of Health), 192–193
digital storytelling, 263–265

discretionary energy, defined, 161
disruption, domination as beating, 241–242
diversity
  celebration and, 138–139
  data on, 116–117
  elevating of by celebrating wins, 137
  laws of
    Law 15: Look like your beneficiaries, 114–120
    Law 16: You get more of what you platform, 121–127
    Law 17: Acknowledge past trauma in staff and volunteers, 128–134
    Law 18: Celebrate and elevate, 135–140
  maximizing benefits of diverse workplace, 139
  organizational diversity statement and plan, 118
  strategies for increasing, 117–119
Doctors Without Borders (Médecins Sans Frontières), 150–151, 153
domination, as beating disruption, 241–242
donor persona, defining of, 242
donors
  asking volunteers to give, 205
  knowing your ideal donor, 242–244
  making the ask of, 205–206
  online giving, 205
  prospecting for, 204–205
  retention of, 204
  thank-you notes to, 137, 138, 140, 272
DonorsChoose, 8, 136–137
dream customer, defining of, 242

dream team
  characteristics of members, 59-60
  cultivation of, 58, 59-60
dreams, big dreams as targeting root causes of big problems, 226
Duckworth, Angela, 63-65
Dunbar, Robin, 65
Dunbar's Number, 65-66

E

earned income, 213
Easterseals, 225-226
eBay, 242
eccentricity
  examples of in leaders, 176
  pros and cons of, 175
efficiency, over-emphasis on as stifling culture of curiosity, 175
Elyria Memorial Hospital (Elyria, Ohio), 224
email
  analytics for, 249
  best practices for, 251
  as central, comprehensive archive of our interpersonal lives, 248
  growing your list, 249-250
  as here to stay, 248-249
  outreach with as carried out through campaigns, 248-249
  purpose of, 251
  use of to inform, 246-253
  using trial-and-error approach with, 235
  using your list, 250-251
  as world's first and only truly universal instant communication tool, 248
#emailcopywriting, 108

emotional intelligence, as one of Seven Sanctuary Commitments, 133
empowerment, as essential to continuous improvement, 175
engagement, laws of
  Law 31: Start and learn, 232-238
  Law 32: Aim small, 239-245
  Law 33: Use email to inform, 246-253
  Law 34: Use in-person visits to influence, 254-260
  Law 35: Be social on social media, 261-267
  Law 36: They are the heroes, 268-274
Environmental Defense Fund, mission statement of, 17
Erickson, T. A., 78
ESPN, 123, 124
Evans, Audrey, 254, 256
events, power of, 58

F

Facebook, 235
face-to-face communication, being present as most important part, 258
face-to-face passion, power of, 255-258
Falls Free Initiative, 196
family, use of term in talking about nonprofits, 102
FAST goals, 227-229
fatal flaws
  fixing of, 80-81
  identification of, 79-80
Filer, John H., 180
Filer Commission, 180
finance
  cost elimination, dangers of, 190-191

cost per unit of impact, lowering of, 191–193
earned income, 213
frugality, 188–194
investment, better to invest than to spend, 195–202
laws of
    Law 25: Be frugal, 188–194
    Law 26: Don't spend—invest, 195–202
    Law 27: Activate one donor per day, 203–209
    Law 28: Sell things, 210–216
    Law 29: Keep it legal, 217–223
    Law 30: Dream bigger, 224–230
revenue for public charities, percentage from fees for services and goods, 212
unearned income, 213
firing
    of low performers, 99–100
    as second most important capability-building activity that nonprofit leaders do, 100
Fiverr.com, 108
Flanigan, Peter, 217
Florida Tax Credit Scholarship program, 218
focus, as important component of investment, 196–198
4-5 Clubs, 78
Freelancer.com, 107
freelancers
    help for ambitious leaders from global team of, 106–107
    use of, 108–111, 192
    where to find, 107–108
frequently discussed, as F in FAST goals, 228

frugality, 188–194
full-control trap, 294
Fuller, Linda, 21
Fuller, Millard, 21
fundraising. *See* donors; finances

G

Game Changers campaign, 124
Gates of Fire (Pressfield), 144–145, 146
generosity
    as inspiring reciprocity, 53
    as relationship weed killer and lawn fertilizer, 51–52
gifts, Seventeen Golden Rules for Asking for a Gift, 206–208
Girl Scouts, 214
Giving in America: Toward a Stronger Voluntary Sector (Commission on Private Philanthropy and Public Needs), 180
Glassdoor, 87
goals
    FAST goals, 227–228
    setting bold goal to solve problems rather than manage symptoms, 227
goal-setting, 24–25, 227–229
Gone West, 156–157
Goodwill Industries, 211–212, 213
governance. *See* board of directors; leadership
Graham, A. B., 78
grand narrative, having one, 164–171
grand-slam moments, as times to live your values, 152
Gregory, Ann Goggins, 190
growth and change, as one of Seven Sanctuary Commitments, 133

H

Habitat for Humanity, 7-8, 22, 24
Hauser, Jerry, 98-100
healing, opportunities for within nonprofit, 130
Heart to Heart Airlift, 240
Heart to Heart International (HHI), 240
Heath, Chip, 181-182
hedge trap, 294
Helms, Edgar J., 210-212, 213
Heredia, David, 84
heroes, of nonprofits, defined, 271-272
Hero's Journey, 166-169
Hill, Fran, 254, 255, 256
Hill, Fred, 254-255, 256
Hill, Kim, 254, 255-256
hiring. *See also* people of color; recruitment
    best way to, 87-88
    cautions with "hire and fix" strategy, 86
    cultivating pipeline of referrals, 87-88
    making sure process is inclusive and equitable, 118
    obstacles in, 116
    with ruthless selectivity, 84-89
    of superstars, 100-102
    of unicorns, 86
horizon, defined, 24
Hoving, Walter, 268-269
Howard, Don, 190
Hughes, James, 156-158
The Humane Society of the United States, mission statement of, 17
The Hunt with John Walsh (TV show), 129
Hurst, Aaron, 70-72

I

"I Have a Dream" speech (King), 13
ideal donor avatar (IDA), defining of, 242-244
identity
    laws of
        Law 1: Know why you exist, 12-19
        Law 2: Define the win, 20-26
        Law 3: Know who you are when you're winning, 27-33
        Law 4: Plan a strategy to win, 34-40
    proximity and, 66-67
impact
    clarity and, 15-16
    defined, 16
    discretionary energy as important to, 161
    fundamental unit of, 22-24
    nonprofit impact, 16
    reinforcement of, 137
impact dream team, of author, 59
impact measurement, Nature Conservancy's five stages of, 293-294
Imperative, 71
improve-and-lock systems
    establishment of, 284-289
    operation of, 288-289
income generation, 212-213
Indeed, 87
influences, factors that impact the influence of people around you, 66-67
infrastructure, trend of underinvestment in, 190-191
inner work life harmony, as an intrinsic need, 138

Innocence Project (Benjamin N. Cardozo School of Law), 165–166
in-person moments, power of, 255–258
inquiry and social learning, as one of Seven Sanctuary Commitments, 133
Instagram
    as place to search for freelancers, 108
    as social media platform, 235–236
Institute for Charitable Giving, 203–204
Internal Revenue Code Section 501(c)(3), 212–213
Internal Revenue Service (IRS)
    on earned and unearned income, 213
    on nonprofit lobbying, 221
    rules regarding tax-exempt status, 220
International Farm Youth Exchange, 78
intimacy, as factor in Trust Equation, 52
investment, better to invest than to spend, 195–202
investment plan, development of, 198–201

J

Jordan, Clarence, 7, 20
Jordan, Florence, 7, 20

K

kaizen (continuous improvement), 286, 295
Keeper of The List, 59
key performance indicators (KPIs), as one of five stages of impact measurement, 293
King, Martin Luther, Jr., 7, 12–14, 15, 298
Kirtley, John F., 217–219
Kiva, mission statement of, 17
knowledge, as element of strength, 73
Koinonia Farm, 20–22, 23–24
Kopp, Wendy, 8, 27–29
Kouchner, Bernard, 149–151, 153
Koya Leadership Partners, 115
KPIs (key performance indicators), as one of five stages of impact measurement, 293

L

law, putting it to work, 220–221
leadership
    being strengths-based leader, 74–75
    as delicate interplay between self-sacrifice and command, 143
    development of, 101
    as focusing on symptoms over root causes, 226
    goal of should be to solve problem itself not manage symptoms, 226–227
    how leaders cope with trauma, 132
    importance of elevating and celebrating everyone, 139
    importance of storytelling in job description of, 166
    lack of diversity of in nonprofit sector, 116
    laws of
        Law 19: Eat last and get dirty, 142–148
        Law 20: Embody the nonprofit's values, 149–155

Law 21: Know your people, 156–163
Law 22: Have a grand narrative, 164–171
Law 23: Be interested and interesting, 172–178
Law 24: Shine in moments of truth, 179–186
leading by example, 144–146
leading with a limp, 132
most important capability-building activities that nonprofit leaders do, 100
as needing to carry heaviest load, 144
strength-based, 74–75
value of eccentricity in, 175–176
as where commitment to diversity of all kinds must come from, 117
Leadpages, 235
Lean Management, principles of, 286–288
learning
  as beating genius every time, 234
  curiosity as real driver of, 174
Letter from a Birmingham Jail (King), 12–14, 15, 298
Lifespan, 8
LinkedIn, 87, 235
Livestrong, mission statement of, 17
lobbying
  direct lobbying, 221
  grassroots lobbying, 221
  requirements for nonprofit activities to be considered, 221–222
Lobbying Disclosure Act, 221
long-running organization, four properties of, according to Thiel, 241
love languages, 160–161

Lowery, Joseph, 299
loyalty, and martyrdom, fine line as separating, 143

M

macro-win, 24, 37
Mailchimp, 235, 249
Major, Lauren, 263–264
Make-A-Wish, 233, 234
management by objectives, 227–228
The Managed Center, 99–100
March of Dimes, 91–92
"march of dimes," 8, 91
marketing. *See also* brand/branding
  guiding of by understanding of public's take on your mission, 125
  importance of highlighting real beneficiaries and volunteers in, 124
  using faces of your nonprofit in, 123–124
markets
  choosing your nonprofit's first small market carefully and expand with deliberate intention, 242
  making for as something every nonprofit can and should do more of, 211
Marshall, George C., 268–269
martyrdom, loyalty and, fine line as separating, 143
MBTI (Myers-Briggs Type Indicator), 159
McClelland, David, 65
Meals on Wheels, 196
measurement
  displaying and discussing about, 295–296
  impact measurement, 293–294

as not an end, 295
performance measurement traps, 294
Médecins Sans Frontières (Doctors Without Borders), 150–151, 153
Melman, Richard, 173
mental health resources/benefits, importance of to nonprofit workers, 131
mentoring, 64, 167, 169, 287, 303
Mickiewicz, Matt, 105–106
micro-domination philosophy, 242
micromanagement trap, 294
micro-win, 24
mindset
  fixed mindset, 73
  growth mindset, 73
Misner, Ivan, 46
mission
  clarity and, 16–17
  shifting of from short-term results to long-term solutions, 227
mission statement
  anatomy of effective one, 17
  defined, 37
  examples, 17
  purpose of, 16, 37, 118
Missionaries of Charity, 142–143
moments of truth
  examples of in nonprofit leadership, 183–184
  importance of leadership's ability to recognize and even orchestrate, 181–182
money management. *See* finance
Morsch, Gary, 239–241
Mother Theresa, 8, 142–143
motivation, boosting of, 137

Multiplier (formerly Trust for Conservation Innovation), 35–36, 38–39
Murray, Jim, 254, 257, 258
Musk, Elon, 176
Myers-Briggs Type Indicator (MBTI), 159

N

National Adult Day Services Association, 196
National Alliance for the Mentally Ill (NAMI), 8, 57, 58
National Center for Missing and Exploited Children, 8, 130
National Council on Aging (NCOA), 196
National Easterseal Society (formerly Society for Crippled Children and Adults, SCCA), 225–226
National Foundation for Infantile Paralysis (NFIP), 91
National Institute of Senior Centers, 196
Nature Conservancy, 292–293
nature trail conservation nonprofit (fictional)
  core values of, 31
  mission statement of, 23
  three-part strategy of, 38
  vision statement of, 24, 37, 38
Nauts, Helen Coley, 284, 285, 286
networking
  how it works, 258
  as your goal, 43
networks
  externally oriented networks, 44–46
  internally oriented networks, 44
  kinds of, 44–45
  your nonprofit as network, 45–46

Neufeld, Peter, 164-166
New England Center for Children (NECC), 49, 51
NFIP (National Foundation for Infantile Paralysis), 91
99designs.com, 106, 107, 234
nonprofit corporations, as able to qualify for tax exemptions, 219
nonprofit impact, defined, 16
nonprofit legality, basics of, 219-220
nonviolence, as one of Seven Sanctuary Commitments, 133

O

OCEAN (Big Five personality framework), 158
O'Connor, Basil, 91
Ohio Society for Crippled Children (OSCC), 225
Ohno, Taiichi, 286
O'Mara, Collin, 157
online giving, as activity to improve donor success, 205
open communication, as one of Seven Sanctuary Commitments, 133
open conversations, importance of, 118, 119
operating, laws of
   Law 37: Map your value streams, 276-283
   Law 38: Establish improve-and-lock systems, 284-290
   Law 39: Measure what matters, 291-297
   Law 40: Your board sets the pace, 298-304
organizational brand. See brand/branding
overthinking
   cautions with, 257-259
   inside the mind of chronic overthinkers, 234

P

Panas, Jerold, 203-204, 205-206
Partnership Housing, 21-22
Pate, Maurice, 246-248
The Patron's Program, 217
Paul (apostle), 13
Pauling, Christopher, 232-233, 234
Pauling Linda, 232-233
PeerForward (formerly College Summit), 189-190
Peña, David, Jr., 42-43
people of color
   challenges in recruiting and retaining people of color, 117
   as percentage of US population, 116
performance measurement traps, 294
Perot, Ross, 28
personal histories, importance of leader in knowing those of staff, board, and key volunteers, 159-160
personality types, classifying of, 158-159
personnel. See firing; hiring; recruitment; retention
Peter (Lifespan client), 8-9
Philadelphia Eagles, 254, 255, 256
Pinterest, 235
platform
   finding surprise and delight in your nonprofit's work to broadcast, 125-126
   giving constituents a platform, 123-124

picking of one for engaging your audience before starting on another one, 235-236
Pough, Richard, 291-293
The Power of Moments (Heath), 181-182
Pressfield, Steven, 144-145
productive passion, as characteristic of dream team members, 59-60
professional development, spending on in corporate America, 86
progress
    as fundamental need, 138
    as motivational tool, 138
Progress-Insights-Next Steps model, 296
proximity, and identity, 66-67
The Purpose Economy (Hurst), 71

Q

quantification, defined, 24
quasi-experimental design, as one of five stages of impact measurement, 293

R

Race Matters toolkit, 118
Randall, Ollie A., 195-202
randomized controlled trial, as one of five stages of impact measurement, 294
Recamier, Max, 149-151, 153
recognition
    of board of directors, 303
    as increasing charitable behavior, 272
    as key motivator, 138
    of volunteers' contributions, 93, 272

recruitment
    building networks and partnerships who facilitate effective recruitment, 118
    challenges in recruiting people of color, 116
    mega-sites for, 87
    nonprofits that make biggest impact are those that obsess over talent, 86
    of volunteers, 92, 95, 235
Redenbacher, Orville, 77
relationship weed killer and lawn fertilizer, 51-52
reliability, as factor in Trust Equation, 52
Rensi, Ed, 256, 257
retention
    challenges in retaining people of color, 117
    of donors, 204
    of volunteers, 94-95
revenue for public charities, percentage from fees for services and goods, 212
right-sizing investment, 191
Rockefeller, John D., III, 179-181
Rohn, Jim, 65
Ronald McDonald House, 256
Ronald McDonald House Charities, 255, 258
Roosevelt, Franklin Delano, 8, 90-91, 92, 269
Rotary Club, 258
Rule of Reciprocity, 52
Rustin, Bayard, 298-299, 301

S

Salk, Jonas, 91

Salvation Army, 268, 272
Sanctuary Model, 132-133
SCCA (Society for Crippled Children and Adults) (formerly Ohio Society for Crippled Children, OSCC), 225
"scenic overlook" moments, 175
Scheck, Barry, 164-165
Schramm, J. B., 188-190
SCLC (Southern Christian Leadership Conference), 15, 299, 301
self-orientation, as factor in Trust Equation, 52
selling
    for charitable purpose, 212-213
    examples of nonprofit selling, 213-214
    as something all nonprofits can and should do, 212
send-and-learn, as better communication strategy than worry-and-send, 234
Seven Sanctuary Commitments, 133
Seventeen Golden Rules for Asking for a Gift, 206-208
"Shamrock Shake" promotion, 255, 256-257
Shankwitz, Frank, 233
Shetler, Charles, 56
Shetler, Harriet, 8, 56-57
Shriver, Eunice Kennedy, 8, 121-122
Shuttlesworth, Fred, 299
SitePoint (formerly Webmaster-Resources.com), 105-106
skill, as element of strength, 73
small wins, power of, 137-138, 139
S-M-A-R-T, 24-25
Smith-Lever Act, 78
Smithson, James, 276-277
The Smithsonian Institution
    formation of, 277-278
    mission statement of, 17
social circles, optimal number of people in for strong relationships, 65-66
social media communications
    being social on, 261-267
    using trial-and-error approach with, 235
social responsibility, as one of Seven Sanctuary Commitments, 133
Society for Crippled Children and Adults (SCCA) (formerly Ohio Society for Crippled Children, OSCC), 225
Southern Christian Leadership Conference (SCLC), 15, 299, 301
Sowell, Thomas, 7, 10
Spaulding Youth Center, 49
Special Olympics, 8, 122-124
specific, as S in FAST goals, 228
spending money, mindset of as compared to investing money, 197
Stahl, Scott, 233
standardization, and continuous improvement, 288-289
start of day/shift standups, as part of dialogues about continuous improvement, 295
Steele, C. K., 299
Step Up, 218-219
Story Squad (YMCA), 263
story-listening, importance of, 160
storytelling
    as critical part of nonprofit leader's job description, 166
    power of, 123-124, 160
    Thomas Valentine Sullivan's realizing the value of, 262

YMCA as equipping its team members to be digital storytellers, 263–265
strategy statement, three-part strategy, 36–39
strengths
    being strengths-based leader, 74–75
    capitalizing on, 74–75
    case for, 72–73
    defined, 73
    discussion prompts to help identify core strengths, 74
    elements of, 73
    improving on, 72–73
    weaknesses as negating, 78
Strully, L. Vincent, Jr., 49–51, 52
Sturtevant, William, 203
subscription drift, importance of fighting, 192
Sullivan, Thomas Valentine, 261–262, 263–264
superstars, hiring of, 100–102
Sutory, Jakub, 157

T

talent
    as element of strength, 73
    nonprofits that make biggest impact are those that obsess over talent, 86
    return on investment in, 101–102
Taproot Foundation, 71
tax-exempt status of nonprofits, 212–213, 219–220, 221
TCI (Trust for Conservation Innovation), 34–35, 38
Teach for America (TFA), 8, 27–29, 31, 98–99, 101
TED, mission statement of, 17
"thank you," "exciting progress" as beating, 137–138
thank-you notes to donors, 137, 138, 140, 272
them-focused perspective, 51, 52
theory of change, as one of five stages of impact measurement, 293
Thiel, Peter, 241
third sector, origin of, 180
TikTok, 235
Tillich, Paul, 13
Toyota, 286
transformational change, as nonprofit goal, 227
transparency, importance of with stakeholders, 227
transparent for all to see, as T in FAST goals, 228
trauma
    acknowledging of in staff and volunteers, 128–129
    how leadership copes with, 132
    pervasiveness of exposure to, 130, 132
    proactive preparation to promote healing from, 131
    resilience in face of traumas nonprofit workers themselves have experienced, 130
    resiliency in face of traumas of others by nonprofit workers, 130
Tree Army, 157, 158
trial and error
    as beating genius every time, 234
    for the win, 234–235
Trust Equation, 52–53
Trust for Conservation Innovation (TCI), 34–35, 38

truth-teller, seeking help of to determine fatal flaws, 79–80
Tuckerman, Don, 254–255, 256, 257
Twitter, 235

U

Unbounce, 235
unearned income, 213
unicorns, hiring of, 86
unincorporated nonprofits
   as able to qualify for tax exemptions, 219
   formation of, 219
United Nations International Children's Emergency Fund (UNICEF), 247
United Service Organizations for National Defense (USO), 269–271
Upwork.com, 108
US National Institutes of Health, Diabetes Prevention Program, 192–193

V

Valley Alliance of Mentors for Opportunities and Scholarships (VAMOS), 42–43
Value Stream Map (VSM)
   of current state, 278–280
   of future state, 280–282
values. *See also* core values
   embodying of, 149–155
   examples of opportunities to live yours in big way, 151–152
   lived big, 151–152
   lived small, 153–154
video streaming, as inexpensive and authentic, 236
vision statement, 24–25, 37

volunteers
   asking them to invest financially as well, 205
   cultivating super-volunteers, 90–97
   fostering admiration among, 94–95
   investment in capacity of, 94
   March of Dimes as one of few nonprofits to use volunteers effectively, 92
   matching skills with assignments, 92
   measuring value of, 93–94
   recognizing contributions of, 93
   recruitment, 92, 95, 235
   retention of, 94–95
VSM (Value Stream Map)
   of current state, 278–280
   of future state, 280–282
vulnerability
   as relationship weed killer and lawn fertilizer, 51
   them-focused vulnerability, 51, 52–53

W

Walsh, Adam, 128–129
Walsh, John, 8, 128–130
Walsh, Revé, 8, 128–130
weaknesses
   fatal flaws, 79–81
   mitigating your limiting ones, 77–83
   as negating strengths, 78
   as often made worse when focused on, 72, 73
Webmaster-Resources.com, 105
websites
   focusing on creating simple website, 235

  nonprofit leaders as getting tied up
   in knots about, 234–235
  using trial-and-error approach with,
   236
Williams, George, 262
wins
  celebration of, 137, 138
  defining of, 20–26
  knowing who you are when you're
   winning, 27–33
  macro-win, 24, 37
  micro-win, 24
  planning strategy for, 34–40
  small wins, 137–138, 139
  while you're sleeping, 105–112
work martyrdom, pros and cons of,
 143–144
World Central Kitchen, 173–174
world-story
  according to King, 14
  defined, 14
  disagreements about, 16
The World-Story, 14, 16
Wounded Warrior Project, mission
 statement of, 17
#writersofinstagram, 108

Y

Year Up, 84–85
Young, Beverly, 8, 56–57
Young Men's Christian Association
 (YMCA), 193, 213, 261–264, 268, 272

Z

*Zero to One: Notes on Startups, or How
 to Build the Future* (Thiel), 241

www.ingramcontent.com/pod-product-compliance
Lightning Source LLC
Chambersburg PA
CBHW071445220526
45472CB00003B/675